THE CRUISE OF

Joseph Hilaire Pierre Belloc was born in 1870 at St. Cloud near Paris. His grandfather, after whom he was named, was a painter of some note who had married a girl of Irish descent, while his father, Louis, had married an English girl, Bessie Rayner Parkes. Although she had spent most of her life in France, when her husband died in 1872, she took her son and daughter to London and then to Slindon in Sussex. It was here that Belloc acquired his lifelong affection for the South Downs.

He was educated at Cardinal Newman's Oratory School in Edgbaston, Birmingham, and at the age of 17 was commissioned by W. T. Stead, editor of the *Pall Mall Gazette,* to write down his impressions whilst bicycling through France. Belloc then went to the United States in pursuit of Elodie Hogan, with whom he had fallen in love in London.

Following ten months' National Service in the French army, the generosity and success of his sister as a writer enabled him to go up to Balliol College, Oxford. This culminated in a triumphant career as President of the Union, establishing his reputation as a radical polemiscist. In 1896 he married Elodie Hogan in California and brought her back to live in Oxford where he earned a living as a tutor. His first poems appeared in 1896, with the publication of *Verses and Sonnets* and *The Bad Children's Book of Beasts.*

In 1899 he moved to London where he became involved in liberal politics. He established a long standing collaboration with G. K. Chesterton and had many novels published, including *Emmanuel Blunden* (1904), *Mr. Clutterbuck's Election* (1908) and *Pongo and the Bull* (1910), as well as the most famous of his travel books, *The Path to Rome* (1902), historical studies on Paris and Robespierre and the renowned *Cautionary Tales for Children* (1908).

In 1902 Belloc became a British citizen and four years later he was elected Liberal M.P. for South Salford, gaining a reputation for stinging criticism of public corruption during his five years in Parliament.

By this time he had moved to Horsham where he lived for nearly 40 years. In 1914 his whole life changed when his wife suddenly died. He threw himself into work as a propagandist for the government's war policies but was never able to overcome the misery caused by her untimely death. He wore black for the rest of his life and his melancholy was reflected in his preoccupation with Catholicism and resulted in numerous books such as *Europe and the Faith* (1920) and biographies of Wolsey (1930), Cranmer (1931) and Charles I (1933). Among these works were examples of his old virtuosity, *Belinda* (1928) and *The Cruise of the " Nona "* (1925).

In later years he continued to travel, lecture and review, but a stroke in 1942 inhibited his activities. He died in 1953 and is buried next to his wife at West Grinstead.

THE CRUISE
OF THE "NONA"

HILAIRE BELLOC

Introduction by
Jonathan Raban

CENTURY PUBLISHING

LONDON

HIPPOCRENE BOOKS INC.

NEW YORK

Introduction copyright © Jonathan Raban 1983

All rights reserved

First published in Great Britain in 1925 by
Constable & Co. Ltd

This edition published in 1983 by
Century Publishing Co. Ltd
76 Old Compton Street, London W1V 5PA

Published in the United States of America by
Hippocrene Books Inc.
171 Madison Avenue
New York, NY 10016

ISBN 0 7126 0280 1

Cover shows " Off the Coast of Devon " by David James

Printed in Great Britain by
Richard Clay (The Chaucer Press) Ltd,
Bungay, Suffolk

TO THE MEMORY OF
PHILIP KERSHAW MY BRAVE
AND CONSTANT COMPANION
UPON THE SEA : BUT NOW
HE WILL SAIL NO MORE

INTRODUCTION

No-one who now reads *The Cruise of the " Nona "* for the first time will respond to it without some sense of shock. Most people will come to it (as I did) because of its fugitive reputation as a sea-classic; an enchanting story of a voyage in a small boat down the Irish Sea and up the English Channel, a book full of idyllic solitude, of sunsets, storms, oily calms, wet sleeping-bags, tide races, tangled ropes and the rest of it. Such readers, if they skip judiciously, will manage to find what they want, but they won't be prepared for what *The Cruise of the " Nona "* actually is—an extraordinary and disturbing can of worms and glories.

For Belloc's work has mostly been expurgated by the passage of time. His career as a politician has been forgotten; his novels and history books are hardly read at all now. In literary history, he is mainly remembered, rather vaguely, as the over-energetic hindquarters of that quaint pantomime horse called Chesterbelloc. The Belloc whom everybody knows is the genial, baa-lamb author of *Cautionary Tales* and the *Bad Child's Book of Beasts*.

The Belloc of *The Cruise of the " Nona "* is a very different figure—a genuinely dangerous character. The book begins softly enough, in the language of romantic escapism, but by the time it has run its course it has laid down a seductive programme for the regeneration of England. The programme is explicitly Fascist, and the real hero of this story is Mussolini, who had come to power in Italy in 1922, three years before Belloc's *Cruise* was first published. The politics and the romance of the book are intimately, powerfully twined together. It is the weirdest imaginable blend of *Mein Kampf* and *Yachting Monthly*.

In his dedication to Maurice Baring, Belloc suggests with great charm and lucidity that his voyage should be construed as a metaphor. A man " will find at sea the full model of human life ":

The cruising of a boat here and there is very much what happens to the soul of a man in a larger way. . . . . We are granted great visions, we suffer intolerable tediums, we come to no end of the business, we are lonely out of sight of England, we make astonishing landfalls—and the whole rigmarole leads us along no whither, and yet is alive with discovery, emotion, adventure, peril and repose.

The form of the voyage, with its passages, its long reflective spells at anchor, its visits to ports, its anxious navigation, becomes the perfect vehicle for a reckoning with life at large.   En route, Belloc comes to terms both with his own personal past and with the history of England, his adopted country.   The sea supplies him with distance and perspective; it enables him to stand *aloof*—a nautical term, originally, meaning to " luff-up " into the wind, away from the shore.   The *Nona*, his engagingly untidy, leak-prone little sloop, gives him an alternative home.   The boat—sailing under no ensign—is really another sovereign state in its own right.

Afloat at sea, Belloc sees Britain as a sinking ship.   His concern with the public realm goes far beyond the usual bounds of the conscientious man of letters.   In spite of the fact that he was French-born (and was naturalised British only in 1902), he was elected M.P. for South Salford in 1906.   He stayed on in Parliament, first as a Liberal, then as an Independent member, until 1910.   He was also an historian with a distinctively European cast of mind, writing in the grand synoptic tradition of Taine and Michelet.   He loaded the *Nona* with a bulky cargo of ideas and political experience.   The boat is, in effect, the last repository of Belloc's notion of all that is best and sanest in European history and culture.

His cruise takes him far out into the most hazardous of political deep waters.   By the 1920s his disillusion with parliamentary democracy was absolute.   Watching England from a mile or two offshore, he saw a history and geography that he loved with a convert's passion, while at the same moment he saw a contemporary social order that he believed to be utterly degenerate. He characterises parliamentary government as a treacherous delegation of authority to "the slime of the Lobbies ".

> There is no form of parliamentary activity which is not deplorable, save in aristocracies.
>
> For, in aristocracies, which are of their nature, governments by a clique, a Parliament—which is a clique—can be normal and natural. In communities based on the idea of equality, and of action by the public will, they are cancers, under which such nations always sicken and may die.

Europe's tragedy, Belloc thought, lay in its return to the "vomit" of parliamentary rule at the end of World War 1, "instead of continuing the rule of soldiers as it should have done ".

Today it's very hard to swallow such facile advocacy of martial law as a moral imperative. In 1925 it wasn't so. When *The Cruise of the " Nona "* first came out, the *London Mercury* called it " the most beautiful " of Belloc's books, while the *Observer* said that Belloc " has never written better ". The reviews help to remind one that Belloc was writing in a climate far warmer than ours to the idea of final solutions.

Belloc's solution, inspected with the unearned wisdom of living in the 1980s, is one of terrible banality. Heartsick of contemporary Britain (in which corrupt and lazy politicians and charabancs of day-trippers at Clovelly are treated indifferently with the same blind rage), Belloc dreams of, and prays for, a miraculous return to a " homogeneous " society; a nation of one race and one religion. The sole spark of hope on his horizon is the mirage of Italy under Il Duce.

> What a strong critical sense Italy has shown! What intelligence in rejection of sophistry, and what virility in execution! May it last!

The word *virility* is a key one in Belloc's vocabulary. It crops up in *The Cruise of the " Nona "* over and over again, as if the real choice before the nations of Europe was between impotence and erection. It lurks significantly in the background of his exclamatory description of Mussolini:

What a contrast with the sly and shifty talk of your parliamentarian! What a sense of decision, of sincerity, of serving the nation, and of serving it towards a known end with a definite will! Meeting this man after talking to the parliamentarians in other countries was like meeting with some athletic friend of one's boyhood after an afternoon with racing touts; or it was like coming upon good wine in a Pyrenean village after compulsory draughts of marsh water in the mosses of the moors above, during some long day's travel over the range.

Belloc's hearty, open-air approach to things often led him to make judgements of infantile silliness, and infantile cruelty too. His anti-semitism (violently expressed in *The Jews*, a book designed to clear himself of the charge of being an anti-semite) sprang as much, one feels, from the conviction that Jews were pallid, cerebral people who spent too much time indoors as from any more serious perception.

None of this helps to make *The Cruise of the " Nona "* a likeable book, though it does give it real status as a rather odious historical document. The trouble is that the splendour and vitality of *The Cruise* is directly linked to its always cranky, often ugly vision of history and politics.

For the *Nona* is held up as a tiny scale model of how an idyllic society might be; it is a ship of state in miniature, and the simple virtues of life at sea are set in counterpoint against the corruption and depravity of modern England as it slides by on the beam. The boat is Belloc's great good place—a temple of virility, comradeship and self-reliance. The sea is the immutable element: while the land gets ravaged beyond recognition by the products of industrial democracy, the sea remains the same as it has always been—a mysterious and lovely wilderness.

When he deals with the sea, Belloc writes at the top of his

bent. All the most memorable stretches of *The Cruise* are full-length portraits of a particular patch of water—the Sound between Bardsey Island and the Lleyn peninsular in a high gale; the entry to Port Madoc on a still evening; the great tide-races of Portland Bill and St. Alban's Head; sailing through Spithead with its naval history still vividly printed on the surrounding landscape. These set-pieces are beautifully done. There's precious little nonsense about topping-lifts and jib-sheets and the rest of the salty talk that tends to disfigure the writing of most amateur sailors. Belloc's writing is entirely free of heroics: it is a good, plain prose, full of wonder, surprisingly humble. The page-long hymn of praise to the sea, with which the book ends, is an exact distillation of the rewards of the voyage:

> Sailing the sea, we play every part of life: control, direction, effort, fate; and there we can test ourselves and know our state. All that which concerns the sea is profound and final. The sea provides visions, darknesses, revelations. . . .

* * * *

There's an interesting comparison to be drawn between *The Cruise of the " Nona "* and that other odd conflation of politics and sailing, Erskine Childers's *The Riddle of the Sands*. For in Childers's case the politics of the book (the paranoid fear of German invasion) have dissolved away in time and left a small, purely maritime masterpiece. I doubt if anyone now is detained long by the spy-story stuff: it is, in any case, a very dim and feeble ancestor of the bureaucratic nightmares of Deighton and Le Carré. One cannot say the same of the politics of *The Cruise of the " Nona "*.

Belloc is still frighteningly topical. His loathing of " politicians " is probably more widely shared today than it was in 1925. His sense of the degeneracy of society in Britain has turned into a platitude in our own age. His particular strictures on British institutions have an unpleasantly familiar ring sixty years on. Belloc on the Press, for instance:

By the very nature of the organism, this new instrument o
power, the mob Press, must be ill-informed, unreal, and—what
is not without importance—morally vile.

If his remarks about Italian Fascism and Jewry make him sound
like a political coelacanth, Belloc's basic line on the condition-
of-England-question is bang up to date. He would be very
much at home in 1984; certainly more at home than he was in
his own time.

His cruise, too, strikes a deep latterday chord. When
Belloc took to the sea alone, he was one of a small company of
gentleman-oddballs. The motives that drove him—to escape
from England's overpopulous industrial society, to be self-
sufficient and dependent only on the forces of nature, to meditate
—were out of the ordinary. They have since become commonplace. Britain's domestic seas are crowded with *Nonas*; and
most of their helmsmen would come up with a less articulate
version of Belloc's story. Much of what in *The Cruise of the
" Nona "* is fresh first-hand discovery has now become part of the
rolling stock of cliché in the yachting press. To go to sea to
come face to face with the eternal verities, and to return to
land as a prophet of the Far Right, is now almost as conventional
a career as computer programming or chartered accountancy.
For some reason, the visions, darknesses and revelations of the
sea never apparently turn men into socialists.

So the book survives, still bright; partly for excellent
literary reasons, and partly (or so it seems to me) for bad political
ones. For every moment of enchantment in it—and there are
many—there is a corresponding spell of Mussolini-worship or
worse (" Eh, Rosenheim? Eh, Guildenstern? "). The two
aspects of *The Cruise* are inseparable: each is the inevitable
product of the other.

Belloc self-deprecatingly calls the book " a hotchpotch ", but
it is far more artistically elaborate than that. Land and sea,
society and solitude, history and the present, are intricately
balanced and woven into a pattern; and the pattern reveals a
message as unambiguous as a homily on an embroidered

sampler—forsake democracy, or be destroyed by an antlike mass-culture manipulated by tycoons and politicos.

Yet the dominant image of *The Cruise of the " Nona "* survives in spite of the crudity of the book's political intentions. Belloc, sitting alone at the tiller of the *Nona*, piloting his boat through the tricky waters of England and Wales, is cantankerously alive. One shares his adventures; quarrels furiously with him along the way; and remembers his own epitaph on himself:

> When I am dead, I hope it may be said:
> " His sins were scarlet, but his books were read."

Jonathan Raban 1983.

DEDICATION

To MAURICE BARING

My DEAR MAURICE,—
I have dedicated to you two books : one
was a book " On Nothing." This I dedicated to
you because, being on nothing, it dealt with what
is better than the fullness of life.

Another book I dedicated to you was the " Green
Overcoat," and this I dedicated to you because you
had written a play called the " Green Elephant,"
and we thereby held communion in green things.

I now dedicate you this book, because you also
have written a book upon Things That Come to
Mind, and this book may well turn into something
of the same sort. Yours was called " The Puppet
Show of Memory," and dealt with the things and
people you had seen and known. What mine will
be called I do not yet know, for I hold that a child
should be born before it is christened.

I have been led into this opinion by the action of
an acquaintance, who much disputed with his wife
what name the child should bear, it being not yet
born. To this choice they attached great issues;
for they rightly thought that a name determines a
lifetime much more than does a Horoscope, and for
this reason they consulted no Astrologer. First
they explored the grander sounds, names of dominion
and power. They considered Esmeralda, Ruhala,
Semiramis, Darumdibaba and Rimbomba, as also

Haulteclaire, following the noise of pomps and wars. Wearying of this the glamour of strangeness seized them, and they attempted Pelagia, Sonia, Mehitabel, Oona, Celimène, Mamua and Berengarde, Machuska, Gounor and Zaire ; but these seemed, upon a second reading, affected : as indeed they were. So they fell into childishness, and wallowed in gardening, reciting Pansy, Daisy, Rose, Violet, Pimpernel, and even Forget-me-Not, which led them into the Furor Hebraicus, and such terms as Miriam, Lilith, Deborah, Eve, Mizraim, Sheba, and the rest—very unsuitable ; from which they reacted to mere abstractions, such as Mercy, Peace, Charity, Grace, and what not. But these seeming insipid, they fell maundering after a donnish fashion and dared consider Æthelburga, Fristhwith, Ealswitha and other abominations, till an Angel compelled them to desist and they were driven to the solid path of the queens, and advanced Maud, Adelaide, Matilda, Elizabeth, Guinevere, Anne, and jibbed at Jezebel.

Next they ran wild and careered through Tosca, Faustine, Theodora, Athalie, Antigone, Medea, Pasiphae, and many others. Finally, they perched, she upon the name Astarte, but he upon the, to my mind, lovelier word, Cytherea. They both mean the same thing, only one was a well-modelled Greek, and the other a horrible Hittite. It was the woman who wanted Astarte, and the man who wanted Cytherea ; so the child was to be called Astarte, and she was not even allowed to have the second name of Cytherea.

All that was on Thursday, the 2nd June. On the 13th, being a Monday, in the early afternoon, the child was born, and was a boy.

There was no more discussion upon its name,

because its uncle, a rich man, was called James. So
the boy was James, and there was an end of it.

I have been led on as you see, but the essence of
this book is that it shall be a sailing through the
seas of the years, that is, a flight through the airs of
time, or, again, a leading on and a passage through
the vales of life : now culling this sour fruit, now
that poisonous herb, and now again this stinging
plant, which I had thought to be innocuous.

For whether I should write, Maurice, a book of
reminiscences or of wandering, or of extravagances,
or of opinions, or of conclusions, or of experiences,
I could not make up my mind after a cogitation of
three weeks and four days, which occupied the
whole of my remaining faculties between the town
of Blois, upon the Loire, and the town of Châlons,
upon the Marne, my journey from the one to the
other being taken this very year circuitously, in the
company of a Bear, by way of Bayonne, where the
bayonet, Rosalie, was first made ; St. John at the
foot of the Pass, where they boil crayfish in white
wine ; Roncesvalles, where Roland died, and I
nearly did ; Burguete, where they charge too much
and where the kitchen smoke goes out through
the middle of the roof ; Pamplona, the only permanent thing Pompey ever did ; Saragossa, which
never changes ; Reus, where they spin cotton ;
Tarragona, which is biding its time ; Barcelona,
which got there first ; Puycerda, and, after that,
the Gorges of the Tet.

I was by this time a long way from Blois, but I
had come to no conclusion on the name of my book,
and my mind was still like one of those conferences
to which the Parliamentarians of various countries
travel at our expense from time to time, and are
there delivered of heavy speeches without meaning,

which make one think of a corpulent elderly man
groaning across a ploughed clay field after a week's
rain in the dark of the moon. At Nîmes I had not
decided what to call the book, nor down in a valley
of the Cévennes, nor at Lyons, nor in the Jura, nor
in the Vosges, nor in Strasburg ; until at last I
came to Châlons, as I have said. And, sitting down
there to a meal in the hotel very finely called " The
House of the High Mother of God," I still remained
undecided. And I am so to this day.

I cannot make it a book of reminiscences, because
I can remember nothing for more than about two
days, and also because I will not write about my
contemporaries for fear of offending them. They
are very good fellows, they have no particular
characters or talents, they do nothing lasting, they
are a generation of saltless butter with too much
skim milk about it, there is little to say about them,
and almost anything one says gives the little fellows
offence. I would not call it " Opinions," because
I have none either, only convictions ; and if I
called it " Convictions " I might be misunderstood.
I tell you I do not know what to call this book, but
I am dedicating it to you because it has at least this
parallel with your work that it is all about things
that have passed through my mind.

Indeed, the naming of a book has always seemed
to me a thing fastidious in both senses, that is,
both a thing wearisome and a thing of picking and
choosing. I am not quite sure that books ought to be
named at all. If they were numbered, like the streets
in America, they would be very much easier to
catalogue and shelf (or shelve) and remember the
places of. Thus your next book or so might be
" Baring 32," and this " Belloc 106." And why
not ? It would in no way diminish their souls,

their connotations. Cannot a man be head over ears in love with No. 15, Parham Street, and sick of 30, Tupton Square? I can!

Numbers, I say, leave us free to give personality and emotions to things. An anniversary is but a numbered day in a month, yet it shakes a man more than any feast name.

So should it be with books. When they are named they give a false indication ; moreover, the vast crowd of books that are poured out in this our day like fugitives from a plague-stricken city is so immense that the discovery of a new title is impossible. However, it will have a title before I have done, stap me, and it is dedicated to you.

At this point I ought to end ; but, as I have already told you, it is in the very character of this book, of its essence, nature and personality, that it has only an accidental beginning, no real end, and nothing in particular between the two. It is like those rivers of the Middle West which trickle out of a marsh, and then wander aimless, without banks or shape, mere wetnesses, following the lowest land until they reach the shapeless Mississippi, and at last the flats and mud of a steaming sea.

What a book ! . . .

My mind now suggests to me (for my mind is separate from myself, and may properly be regarded as no more than an inconsequent companion) that I should do very well not to cut off the Dedication from the rest of the Opus. The putting of a dedication separately from a book has something about it of form ; and form is just what I have to avoid. I am to wander at large, setting down such things as pass before my eyes of memory, leaving out pretty well all that is of importance (reserving that for posthumous publication), and doing no more than present this, that, or the other, of ephemeral things. For there comes a time in life after which a man discovers no more, has lost through the effect of the years the multitude of what he possessed both within and without, can only repeat phrases or decisions already well worn. He is fixed, sterilised, hardened, and has nothing left to say ; that is the moment in which he is expected to set down, for the benefit of others, the full treasury of what was once his soul.

Some two to five years ago there was an outburst of books in England which I myself labelled (and, I think, justly) " The Cads' Concert." These were books in which men set down their connection with their fellows, giving each by name familiarly, purported to publish diaries which they had never kept, maligned the dead, insulted the living, and lied impudently upon both. They had a great sale, had these books, because they brought in rich, or otherwise important men and women, known already by newspapers vaguely to the readers of of such books, so that those readers had from " The Cads' Concert " a faint reflection of High Life.

It was something quite new in the history of letters, and had, I am glad to say, a very short life. I do not propose to add one more vileness to that nasty little list.

How then should I approach this task which has been set me of writing down, in the years between fifty and sixty, some poor scraps of judgment and memory ? I think I will give it the name of a Cruise ; for it is in the hours when he is alone at the helm, steering his boat along the shores, that a man broods most upon the past, and most deeply considers the nature of things. I think I will also call it by the name of my boat, the " Nona " and give the

whole book the title " The Cruise of the ' Nona,' "
for, in truth, the " Nona " has spent her years, which
are much the same as mine (we are nearly of an age,
the darling, but she a little younger, as is fitting),
threading out of harbours, taking the mud, trying
to make further harbours, failing to do so, getting in
the way of more important vessels, giving way to
them, taking the mud again, waiting to be floated off
by the tide, anchoring in the fairway, getting cursed
out of it, dragging anchor on shingle and slime,
mistaking one light for another, rounding the wrong
buoy, crashing into other people, and capsizing in
dry harbours. It seemed to me as I considered the
many adventures and misadventures of my boat,
that here was a good setting for the chance thoughts
of one human life ; since all that she has done and
all that a man does, make up a string of happenings
and thinkings, disconnected and without shape,
meaningless, and yet full : which is Life.

Indeed, the cruising of a boat here and there is
very much what happens to the soul of a man in a
larger way. We set out for places which we do
not reach, or reach too late ; and, on the way, there
befall us all manner of things which we could
never have awaited. We are granted great visions,
we suffer intolerable tediums, we come to no end
of the business, we are lonely out of sight of England,
we make astonishing landfalls—and the whole
rigmarole leads us along no whither, and yet is alive
with discovery, emotion, adventure, peril and repose.

On this account I have always thought that a
man does well to take every chance day he can at
sea in the narrow seas. I mean, a landsman like me
should do so. For he will find at sea the full model
of human life : that is, if he sails on his own and
in a little craft suitable to the little stature of one

man. If he goes to sea in a large boat, run by other men and full of comforts, he can only do so being rich, and his cruise will be the dull round of a rich man. But if he goes to sea in a small boat, dependent upon his own energy and skill, never achieving anything with that energy and skill save the perpetual repetition of calm and storm, danger undesired and somehow overcome, then he will be a poor man, and his voyage will be the parallel of the life of a poor man—discomfort, dread, strong strain, a life all moving. What parallel I shall find in the action of boats for a man of the middle sort, neither rich nor poor, I cannot tell. Perhaps the nearest would be the ravel at a fixed price upon a steamer from one port not of the passenger's choosing to another not of his choosing, but carried along, ignorant of the sea and of the handling of the vessel, and having all the while no more from the sea than a perpetual, but not very acute, discomfort, and with it a sort of slight uncertainty, which are precisely the accompaniments throughout life of your middle sort of man.

So I have given this book a name : " The Cruise of the ' Nona.' " Had I called it " The Cargo " I might be nearer my intention. At any rate, I am now off to sail the English seas again, and to pursue from thought to thought and from memory to memory such things as have occupied one human soul, and of these some will be of profit to one man and some to another, and most, I suppose, to none at all.

THE
CRUISE OF THE "NONA"

I⊤ was late in May, near midnight, the air being
very warm and still, and the sky not covered but somewhat dim, with no moon, when I took the "Nona"
out from Holyhead harbour, having on board one
companion to help me work the boat, and a local
man who could speak Welsh for me in whatever
places I might make along the coast.

The very slight breeze, which had barely moved
us through the water after we had got up the anchor,
died away long before we reached the end of the
breakwater, and it was necessary to pull her out
with the dinghy in order to fetch round the end of
the stonework and get to sea. There was at that
time of the tide a little current running towards the
Stack, which would slightly help us on our way
once we were outside, and with this we drifted a
full hour and more, aided now and then by faint
breaths of air, which rose and died again like
memories. So came we, with the turn of the night,
under the glare of the lighthouse at last, and then
put the nose of the little ship round for the point of
Carnarvonshire and the strait between the mainland
and Bardsey Island, which is called Bardsey Sound.

It was a course of about thirty-three miles, with
no chance, apparently, of covering it in all that
night, nor perhaps in all the coming day as well ;
for we had struck, as it seemed, that hot, steady,

summer weather in which one may play at a drifting match for days on end.

While it was still dark the distant mountains could barely be seen as something a little blacker than the sky. They looked astonishingly low, as mountains always do on a moonless night, when there is nothing to distinguish their details, and nothing against which to compare them, or by which to tell their distance. Already—it being now nearer two than one o'clock—a little wind had arisen, settling down, as it seemed, into somewhat east of north, and blowing over the Anglesey flats. It gave us perhaps no more than a couple of knots an hour, but it was heartening after the long calm, and as we had all sail set she pulled to it steadily enough. I was at the helm, my companion was still awake, sitting in the cock-pit and talking to me, and the hand who was to be with us till we next landed smoked beside us on deck.

The wind had freshened somewhat, we were making perhaps four or five knots, when the dawn began to show beyond Snowdon, and those great hills at once looked higher against the glimmer of grey light. Soon the whole coast was apparent, and the Yreifles with their triple peaks (clearer than I had expected ; indeed, too clear for fine weather) lay right ahead and Bardsey Island beyond them and the narrow sound in between. The wind seemed steady, as though it would hold. I reckoned that the tide would turn against us anywhere between six and seven in the morning, that it would turn back through the Sound about noon or one o'clock, and I calculated that we should be running into Cardigan Bay, past Bardsey, on the middle of the ebb, an hour or two later than that time.

But what happened was something wholly un-

expected ; it is always so at sea, and that is why it
is said that the sea brings all adventures. Indeed,
I think that as we go on piling measurements upon
measurements, and making one instrument after
another more and more perfect to extend our
knowledge of material things, the sea will always
continue to escape us. For there is a Living Spirit
who rules the sea and many attendant spirits about
him.

But on that brightening morning there was nothing to warn us. The glass was high and, if I
remember right, still rising. The sky uncovered and
clearer than it had been by night ; the wind slight,
but holding steady, and all was soldier's weather, so
that any one could have taken that little ship through
such weather where he would. It was weather, one
would say, made for the instruction of the young
in the art of sailing.

By the time it was fully light, we were making
between six and seven knots, for the wind had sharply
risen. As it was an off-shore wind, there was as
yet no sea raised, but little tumbling white caps, very
pleasant to look at, and all the movement coming
on our quarter from over the land. With the rising
of the sun it blew hard. We were yielding to it
too much ; we had taken down the topsail an hour
before, and now I thought it wise to take in a reef
as well, which we did in the headsail and the mainsail, but leaving the jib as it was, for that sail was not
a large one.

I have sailed a great deal off and on in boats of
this size (that is, somewhat more than thirty feet
over all, with eight or nine feet beam, and drawing
from five to six feet of water, cutter rigged), and I
know it is an illusion ; yet I can never get over the
idea that a reef makes no difference. Two reefs—

yes—but one reef I cannot " feel." It is an obtuseness in me ; but so it is.

However, it seemed wiser to take in a reef of some sort, and two reefs would have reduced the sail quite unnecessarily, for it was not yet blowing so hard as all that.

We slipped down the coast smartly, nearing it all the time upon our slantwise course, and as we did so, the sun being now fully risen, it blew harder and harder every minute. A sea rose, a good following sea, but higher than one would have expected so nearly off the land from a land wind ; and, as this boat has very little freeboard (it is her only defect, for she rises magnificently to the water, and bears herself better the worse the weather may be), I watched the swirl of the foam under her low counter as each wave slightly broke under the now fierce wind.

We shortened down to three reefs, but even so the helm was pulling hard, and when we changed jibs and put up the smallest we had, it griped more than I liked, straining my arm after so long a spell at the tiller. I handed it over to the man who was with us, and went forward to see that everything was clear, for it was now blowing really hard, and anything like a tangle if we got into difficulties would be dangerous. The gale rose higher and the sea with it ; but, tearing through the water as we now were under three reefs, we should soon make the Sound and get round the point of Carnarvonshire into easier water right under the lee of the land.

There was only one thing that troubled me, which was this question : should we make the Sound before the tide turned ? It was an important question, because, although I had never been in those parts before, off-shore, in a boat of my own, yet I could judge that in such a piece of water, with all the Bay pouring through a channel barely two miles wide with a deep of barely one, the tide against such a gale would raise an impossible sea. If we could just make it on the tail of the tide, on the very last of the ebb, we should have nothing to bear but a strong following sea, such as that before which we were running at the moment : for the southerly stream was still strong under us. But if the water turned before we got into the Sound, we should have a time to remember ; and so we did.

For I had done something or other to annoy the Earth Shaker, and he pursued me viciously, making the tide turn just before we reached the mouth of the Sound. In a time much shorter than I had expected, with no lull in between, the steady run of sea which had been combing behind us, towering above the counter, but regular and normal to deal with, turned into a confusion of huge tumbling pyramidical waves, leaping up, twisting, turning and boiling in such a confusion as I had never seen, not even in Alderney Race, which I had gone through many years before when I was a boy. The painter which held the dinghy to the stern parted, and that boat, a good and serviceable one, was lost. There was no question of turning in such a sea and under such a wind ; the dinghy had to be abandoned. The tide against us was so fierce that even under that gale we hardly moved ; and it was strange to see, from the leaping and struggling of the "Nona," as the foam rushed by in a millrace, how steady remained the points on the Carnarvonshire shore, and how slowly we opened the Sound. The pace was irregular. There were moments when we advanced at perhaps a knot or a knot and a half against that fierce tide. There were others when we even slipped

back. All the while the wind howled and the
sea continued to rise and to boil in a cauldron more
violent as the gale on the one hand and the tide
against it on the other grew in strength, and in the
fierceness of their struggle. In seas like this one
never knows when some great tumbling lump of
water may not break upon one's decks, for there is
no run and follow, it is all confusion ; and I remember thinking as I took the helm again in the midst
of the turmoil of something I had seen written once
of Portland Race : " The sea jumps up and glares
at you "—a sound phrase.

We had thus (in some peril, but still able to keep
a course, and, on the whole, advancing) got at last
between the point and the Island, that is, to the heart
of the Sound ; and a very few more yards would have
brought us round out of the cauldron into smooth
water and a run for some quiet anchorage right
under the protection of the coast when (since at
sea bad luck always goes gathering impetus) the jib
blew out with a noise like a gun. A few rags hung
on to its fastenings ; the rest of the canvas went away
out to sea like a great wounded bird, and then sailed
down and flopped into the seething of the water.

You may guess what that did to a boat in our
straits ! It made the helm almost impossible to
hold with the violent gripe of the mainsail, half our
head canvas being gone ; and at the same time it
stopped our way. We drifted back again into the
worst of the water, and lost in five minutes what it
had taken us more than an hour to make. The
danger was real and serious. The man that was
with us expressed his fears aloud ; my companion,
though new to the sea, took it all with great calm. As
to what happened to myself, I will record it though
it is a little detailed and personal : I will record it

for the sake of the experience, of which others may make what they will.

I looked at the Carnarvonshire coast there close at hand, the sinking lines of the mountains as they fell into the sea, and I discovered myself to be for the first time in my life entirely indifferent to my fate. It was a very odd sensation indeed, like the sensation I fancy a man must have to find he is paralysed. Once, under the influence of a drug during an illness some such indifference had pervaded me, but here it was in the broad daylight and the sun well up above the mountains, with a clear sky, in the grip of a tremendous gale and of an angry countering sea, ravening like a pack of hounds. Yet I could only look with indifference on the sea and at the land. The sensation was about as much like courage as lying in a hammock is like a hundred yards race. It had no relation to courage, nor, oddly enough, had it any relation to religion, or to a right depreciation of this detestable little world which can be so beautiful when it likes.

Such as it was, there it was. I had always particularly disliked the idea of death by drowning, and I had never believed a word of the stories which say that at the end it is a pleasant death. Indeed, as a boy I was once caught under the steps of a swimming bath and held there a little too long before I could get myself out, and pleasant it was not at all. But here in Bardsey Sound, I was indifferent, even to death by drowning. All I was really interested in was to watch what way we lost and what chance we had of getting through.

Indeed, the whole question of fear is beyond analysis, and there is only one rule, which is, that a man must try to be so much the master of himself that he shall be able to compel himself to do whatever

is needful, fear or no fear. Whether there be
merit or not in the absence of fear, which sentiment
we commonly call courage when it is allied to action,
may be, and has been, discussed without conclusion
since men were men. The absence of fear makes an
admirable show, and excites our respect in any man ;
but it is not dependent upon the will. Here was I
in very great peril indeed off Bardsey, and utterly
careless whether the boat should sink or swim ; yet
was I the same man who, in a little freshness of
breeze that arose off the Owers a year or two ago,
was as frightened as could well be—and with no
cause. And if this be true of change of mood in one
man, it must be true of the differences of mood in
different men.

I had occasion during the war, when I had been
sent to write upon the Italian front, to be swung to
the high isolated rock of a mountain peak in the Dolo-
mites by one of those dizzy wires which the Italian
engineers slung over the gulfs of the Alps for the
manning and provisioning of small high posts.
It was an experience I shall ever remember, a vivid,
hardly tolerable nightmare ; but the man I was
with, an Italian officer of great and deserved fame,
earned during that campaign, not only felt nothing,
but could not understand what my terror was. We
sat, or rather lay, in one of those shallow trays which
travel slowly along these wires over infinite deeps
of air ; and during the endless crawling through
nothingness he told me, by way of recreation, the
story of a private soldier who had been coming
down from the isolated post some weeks before. The
machinery had gone wrong, and the tray remained
suspended over the gulf, halfway across, for some
twenty minutes. When it worked again and they
hauled it in they found that the man had gone mad.

When the time came for the return journey, I very well remember asking myself whether I had the control to face that second ordeal or no. It was an obscure crisis, unknown to others, but as real and as great within as any of those which stand out in fiction or history. I would rather have gone down by the path which clung to the steep, the precipitous mountain side. This was forbidden because it was under direct Austrian fire ; I knew that I should not be allowed. So I faced the return—and it was worse than the going.

Also in my life I have known two men who have hunted lions, and each of them has told me that fear in the presence of peril from the beast was wholly capricious, and that sometimes when an exceedingly unpleasant death seemed certain, the man who had just missed his shot felt indifferent. I can believe it.

Anyhow, here I was in Bardsey Sound, with many deaths moving over the howling fury of the sea, and not one of them affecting me so much as a shadow passing over a field.

The end of that adventure was odd and unreasonable—as things will be at sea. It was perhaps because we had been buffeted and pushed into some edge of the conflict between wind and water where the tide runs slacker ; or it was perhaps because the wind had risen still higher. But, at any rate, after three separate raids forward (in the second of which we were very nearly out of our peril and into smooth water), and as many set-backs (one of which got us into the worst violence we had yet suffered) the " Nona," in a fourth attempt (it was her own, not ours—we could do nothing but keep her, as best we might, to her course), slipped out and reached an eddy beyond the tide. For a moment it was very difficult to keep her to it, she slewed round ; but then again she got her head southerly, and we found ourselves running past the great Black Rock which stands there—the Carrig Dhu—and marks the smooth water beyond the edge of the tide.

We breathed again ; and as I took her on through an easy sea, close under the land with not too much strain upon the helm (for the high shore now broke the gale), I was free to look over my right shoulder and watch, passing away behind us, further and further, the hell of white water and noise, through which we had barely come to safety.

Danger keeps men awake and makes them forget necessity, but with this relief, our fatigue came upon us. My friend and I had now been awake for some twenty-five or twenty-six hours, and it was time for sleep.

We got the poor "Nona," which had behaved so well, up into a lonely little bay where was an old abandoned mine working, but no other sign of man. The Welshman with us told us it was good holding ground ; we let go the anchor and stowed sail. I remember how I fell half asleep as I stretched the cover over the mainsail boom and yard and tied it down at the after end. The gale still blew, yet, as it seemed, more steadily and less fiercely. There was no danger of dragging. We were well under the lee of the land. I gave one look, under the violent but clear morning sky, to seaward before I went below ; and there I saw how, at a certain distance from the land, in a long line, the white water began. It was like being in a lagoon, like being protected by a bank from the sea outside ; but really it was only the effect of the lee of the land making a belt of smooth water along shore. Then we all lay down to sleep and slept till evening.

When I awoke, the hurricane—for it had been no less—had died down to a fresh gale, and it promised to fall still further before night. There were a few hours of daylight left, but I thought it hardly worth while to up anchor and run further along the coast. We were snug as it was and still fatigued after the struggle in Bardsey Sound, so I thought we would still lie there through the night and start eastward the next morning.

As I looked lazily over to Bardsey, with sunset on its streaming rocks, from the shelter of this quiet bay, I considered the islands.

Bardsey, they say, has a little community on board which governs itself and elects its own king. Whether it also pays tribute to some rich man on land, I do not know. But all the islands around Britain tend to be little kingdoms of their own : Lundy is like that, and over and over again one finds similar islands owned by one man, living either alone like a beast or companioned like a patriarch with his family and his servants and tenants all round about him ; and the truth is that man is happier in small kingdoms than in great.

Except for the pride and honour of belonging to a great kingdom, to be citizen of a small one seems to me to have all the advantages. In a great kingdom you have to pay heavy taxes. You are made falsely concerned with men whom you never see, and in doings far distant, which you do not understand ; you bear on your shoulders the burden of millions, and you must suffer a capital city, which will be a sink of crime. Your rulers will grow rich by deceit—for a very large community can always be deceived ; nothing about you will be real, and the mass of your fellow-citizens will be desperately poor. For it is the nature of large communities to

separate into strata and for the mass to grow
indigent.

But now I come to think of it, there is one
advantage in belonging to a large kingdom, which
is, that you can enjoy differences and contrasts
such as a small kingdom does not give you. Some
day, perhaps very soon, the modern organisation of
society into great communities will break down, and
then it would be amusing to come to life again and
see the little communities living their own independent lives as they did in the Dark Ages, and also
in the beginnings of Pagan history.

How pleasant it is to consider the little kingdom
of Ithaca, and Corfu alongside, and the little territory
of the Athenians.   How pleasant it is to remember
that there were four kings in Kent, grouped there
under one dread emperor at Canterbury ; and also
how there was a king with two princes, his heirs,
governing the Isle of Wight ; all Pagan when the
rest of England had already gone Catholic.   For
though you often hear it said that Sussex was the
last piece of English soil to remain Pagan (and it is,
indeed, the great boast of my county that it resisted
the Faith for one hundred years, and only capitulated
under duress and famine) it is not so.   Sussex was
not the last of England to growl in a reluctant font.
The Wight beat us by a head.   At that time our
king of Sussex and part of Hants as well, by name
Cædwalla, a Welsh name, was still Pagan ; and,
when he did get religion, he thought himself too
grand to be baptised by anybody except the Pope of
Rome.   To Rome, therefore, he went, and reached
the City, was baptised and then died out of hand
of fever—a warning to Pride.

But he had something to show for it all, since the
Pope, very much impressed that a king of Sussex

itself (and part of Hants by conquest) should have
visited him, wrote a fine epitaph for him in Latin
verse and had it engraved on a stone which he put
upon his grave in Old St. Peters. But they pulled
it up when New St. Peters was built, and to this
sacrilege I set down the very bad luck that Rome had
afterwards.

Anyhow, the truth is that not Sussex but the Isle
of Wight was the last Pagan spot in these islands,
and here we of Sussex must reluctantly yield the
palm. Yet can we in Sussex always boast that
our king was the last of the Kings in Britain to
worship the Devil twelve hundred years ago. And so
again for Bardsey.

Looking at Bardsey over an evening sea now less
tumbled and under the dying gale, I thought also
how odd it was that such Scandinavian names should
have stuck to some places more than to others.
These pirates of the eighth and ninth centuries
were not many in number. They had no culture
or traditions ; no literature ; no anything. It was
not until England had gradually civilised them and
made them Christian that they produced anything
whatsoever. How then did little bits of their
language stick on to portions of our coast ? They
say that "Dublin" is a Scandinavian name.
"Bardsey" certainly is, and so is the word "sound,"
to mean a passage of the sea, and "Skomer" is
Scandinavian, and, right high up in the estuary of the
Severn, "Flatholm" and "Steepholm" are both
surely Scandinavian. People explain it sometimes
by saying that as the attack of the pirates was always
necessarily from the sea, they would give their
names to the sea places. I could understand how
this would give them Scandinavian names in
Scandinavia, but how did *we* come to adopt such

names ? That is the puzzle. I should have thought
that the local Celtic name for Bardsey would have
held out. It has not done so, at least not in our
speech ; and there are even Scandinavian names for
inland places, such as the main hill of the Isle of Man,
and many places in the Lakes and beyond.

But the whole story of words is full of mystery,
and the attempt to reduce the process of words to a
science has always seemed to me ridiculous enough.
It is true that certain habits get formed, and you can,
from them, build up certain vague rules. For
instance, the French noun derives from the Latin,
usually—nearly always through the accusative—
and a particular Latin form will produce a corresponding French form ; but the process is not
invariable ; and though one type out of hundreds
becomes the official type of each nation, human
speech is naturally not a set of a few official languages,
but a mass of innumerable dialects, all melting one
into the other.

Watch carefully, and you will note that in the
area covered by the great official languages, most
people are bilingual. They can speak the official
language, but they also speak among themselves a
dialect of their own, usually a dialect more or less
cousin to the official language. That is certainly
true of the working people of my own county of
Sussex, and, indeed, of all rural England ; but it is
also true of the industrial districts, and, of course, it
is true of the North. You find just the same thing
through France, and Belgium, and the Valley of the
Rhine, and I am told you find the same thing in
Italy. The real spoken languages of Christendom
are to be counted by the hundred, or the thousand ;
and though they fall into great groups, yet each has
a life of its own. The official languages live a

separate life above the mass, forming the idiom of a small body of wealthy people. And even that idiom has two forms, the written and the spoken form, which are very different. It is odd how unnatural spoken English looks, for instance, when it appears in a book ; and I suppose the public are right to prefer the wholly unreal written English put into the mouths of the characters in novels.

I remember one good woman who made a very large income for many years by writing books about lords and ladies in London, which books she sold to an extensive and eager public in England, but to a much more extensive and far more eager public in the United States. In these books, which were in their time very famous, the ladies and gentlemen— the Toffs—talked in the most astonishing manner : all in linked phrases of some inches, and dependant clauses hanging on.

There was one character in one of her books which I was assured was a friend of mine : a young hereditary politician. I know the man's conversation well enough : it is of the ordinary sort, chopped sentences, grunts, continual repetitions and, in general, brief scraps : such language as you and I and everybody talks. But in the book this authoress, who knew the original well enough and lived all her life among Lords and Ladies, made the poor fellow talk in his own house like Hansard. She would make him spout great speeches at his own mother and deliver sentences of prodigious length in the midst of them.

I myself once wrote a book about politicians, called " A Change in the Cabinet." It was universally agreed in all that old world of professional politicians who were still educated men that my book, whether good or bad, was monstrously accurate to the way the people of that world talk and go on. But the book

will never be held by any large public to be accurate ;
or, at any rate, will not satisfy the desire of the large
public for a particular kind of pompous convention,
such as never was by sea or land. And on the whole
I think the large public are right. Literature
has no business to be a mirror of life. We can see
life for ourselves without literature. What literature
ought to do, I take it, is to make a type or expression
of life, which is quite a different thing from a mere
reflection, and what is more, literature is there for
fun and not for copying. Hence the greatest of
human writings have very little relation to actual
speech. The heroes of the poet Homer say things
as satisfactory as have ever been said, yet they say
them in a highly conventional and stilted way, using
a very small vocabulary and (what is really extraordinary !) talking all the time in hexameters.
Certainly no one ever did that in real life except an
old Don whom I used to know at Oxford.

This man spoke with a dactylic stammer, thus :
" Wúggă-gă, zúggă-gă, úggĕr-gă Năggă-gă, Wúg-
gă-ă, Húggĕr-gă....In my...wúgga ga...d-dúgga-g
—opinion."

He was the only living person I have ever heard
who gave the effect of speaking in ordinary life as the
persons of the poets speak. It was well worth
hearing ; but, of course, one could not understand
a word of it. Nor did he ever produce the great
effects of the ancients.

One of the most delightful things about words is
their habit of coming up out of nothing, like the
little particles of ice which float to the surface of the
Thames at the beginning of a frost, rising silently,
floating up from the bottom of the river, or like the
little oak trees that crop up everywhere like weeds
in the fields of my home. " Boy " is a word of that

kind, " girl " is another, " leg " is another, " donkey " is another, " plough," though a little earlier,
is another. No one can tell you where they came
from ; they are like our modern masters, they have
no ancestry. But, unlike our modern masters, they
remain. Some one in some clique started the
expression and it spread. One can see examples of
the process going on all round one to-day. One
sometimes even knows the man who invented a new
term and the medium through which it spread.
There are one or two Eton words of this sort, and
one or two Balliol words which are in the way of
becoming regular English ; for individual men of
large acquaintance and fertile mind started these
new words, some of which are beginning to take
root.

But of all things that words do, what pleases me
most is their habit of adventure ; the way they have
of sitting tight and doing nothing but their ordinary
job for centuries, and then shooting out and taking
quite different work and travelling about, changing
colour and shape as they go.

I am very fond of the word " cad." It is the
most useful missile in the English language. It
is very hard and knobby, and you can be certain of
your effect. And yet how brief its career ! How
singular its arrival at its present exalted state ! It
is a shortened form of " cadet," the younger son of a
great family, which came by extension to apply to the
less fortunate. It wandered about in this vague
form for about a lifetime, and then settled down into
two separate uses, applying to a particular sort of
domestic, I believe, in one of the universities, and
also to the people who used to hang on at the back
of the old horse omnibuses and take the money in
those happy days of my youth when there were no

bell punches and no uniforms, and all Charing Cross resounded to the cry of " Liverpool Street," towards which goal every omnibus cad entreated you.

" Cad " having settled down on these two honourable but ill-paid occupations, slyly got in by a side door and established itself in a totally different meaning, which it has now achieved, and which it looks like keeping. For now it means : " A male deficient in one particular small set of those many moral qualities which, when combined with the national tradition of wealth, build up what is called in England a ' gentleman.' " That is what the word " cad " means to-day, and that is what gives it its value. It is a very odd formation. The " gentleman " is the ideal of our once aristocratic and now plutocratic English state ; it is the ideal which members of the wealthier governing class must conform to or attempt to attain. That ideal (its worshippers will be surprised to hear) has not a few vices, a number of virtues, and a very great many habits or characters which are neither virtuous nor vicious—such as the accent.

Now the cad is not at all a man who lacks all these, he is only a man who lacks one particular set of the many virtues. He lacks the particular kind of reticence and the particular kind of generosity which go to the making of the character called " a gentleman." He may have a reticence of another kind, and a generosity of another kind, and still be a cad. On the whole, of the cads and gentlemen I have met, I would give the cads a shade of odds in the matter of salvation ; which is not without its importance either.

It will be interesting to watch the process of the word and see what happens to it. I do not think it will last long, for the whole civilisation to which it applies and in which it has a meaning is breaking up like mist before a rising wind. It is not a word you could translate into any other language, and the English society to which it attaches is changing in a whirl. I wonder what posterity will make of it? What will posterity make of this strange habit, suddenly arisen within fifty years (and soon to die), of regarding a particular sort of provincial wealthy man as a general ideal for all humanity, and of regarding a man lacking somewhat of that ideal's qualities as the basest of mankind?

Probably posterity will do what we all do in dealing with the past, shrug its shoulders and pass on. We, in dealing with any part of the past which we cannot understand, treat it at once as ridiculous, or only talk of the things in it which we do sympathise with. So will posterity deal with us. We cannot understand at all, for instance, the mood of a man who—like nearly everybody up to about two hundred years ago—objected to being burnt alive not on account of the pain, but because it was an indignity ; because the body was consumed. We cannot understand why he was not more concerned with the serious discomfort of being burnt alive than with the ignominy.

In the eighteenth century, men could not understand the theological discussions of the early Byzantine period. We are getting a little more sympathetic with them now, but even to-day there are a great many highly cultured men steeped in history who cannot reconstruct for themselves at all the state of mind in which the populace lost its temper over a theological point ; and the usual attitude of those who cannot understand a thing is to laugh at it. Yet wise men will notice how many intense quarrels have arisen in our own time

on what are really points of theology—though they
are masked. The two views of evidence in any
hotly disputed point, such as the new position
of Poland, are essentially differences in theology.
The long struggle between England and Ireland is
essentially a theological struggle. So at bottom
was the conflict between Prussia and Austria—in
which both have succumbed : Prussia happily for
ever ; but Austria, I hope, only for a time. The
only difference between ourselves and our fathers
in this affair is that our fathers went to the root of
the matter and discussed the essential, the opposing
doctrines, instead of quarrelling upon their products.

. . . .

That night the last of the wind fell suddenly, and
it was a still air all through the darkness, but with
the next morning there arose a moderate fresh
breeze, still from the north.

We brought up the anchor early and stood along
the coast. The wind soon fell, and at last it hardly
held us up against the slight current of the tide.
We made to skirt Penkilan Head, right across the
mouth of the bay called Port Nigel, and also Hell's
Mouth (which is no praise for Nigel), but it was
evening before we had rounded it and saw the opening
beyond, the two islands which are called St. Tudwal's ; for here (as once on Bardsey for the matter
of that) a holy man had taken up his station in the
old days when men thus hid themselves away from
the world.

It is in the youth of a society, when its emotions
are at their strongest, that men thus delight in
isolation and the single contemplation of Divine
things. We cannot understand it at all from where
we now stand, at the end of an old and decaying
society. But when Western Europe renewed its

youth in the fourth and fifth centuries and grew
epic again, after the breakdown of strict society, the
love of hermitage also grew passionately.

A young man can live by himself as long as he
will. It is later on that one needs to be supported
by the companionship of one's fellows, and to-day
most men cannot live alone.

But I did once find such a man in modern times,
full of delight in his complete isolation. He was
an Englishman by birth, but I never learnt his name.
He had built a habitation for himself on a high cliff
in Italy overlooking a plain. I came across him by
accident ; he received me kindly. But I did not
trouble him for long, for I saw that he loved to be
alone. He had no one to serve him, nor any one
even to be an occasional companion. His delight
was to watch the world in the plain below and to
commune with his own soul. But I doubt his
having had any interest in Divine things.

I looked curiously at those two islands as I passed
them. They both bear the name of the saint, and
are called the East and the West. I wondered to
myself whether the appetite for hermitage would
soon return ; for that it must return soon or late is
certain ; it is of permanent recurrence in the history
of mankind. All up and down Europe you may
mark the stage in the history of the islands, the small
islands, when they were thus hermitages or places of
seclusion for small communities of religious or for one
holy man. There is Iona, there is Holy Island,
there are the islands of Lerins, and the Farne, and
Noirmoutier and Tombelaine, and a hundred others.
The conditions seem to have been a small space,
water to drink, just enough land to support life,
and difficulty of access. So also Cuthbert found
even Lindisfarne too crowded, and went to the little

rocks far out to sea.   When it was not an island, it
was a hilltop like Monte Cassino.   When it was not
a hilltop, it was a difficult cliff, like that of my strange
friend of one hour in Italy.   But always the main
condition was security from interruption.   And here
extremes meet, for the very height of luxury and
selfishness which makes a modern man in the last
corruption of modern societies seek isolation, made
the holiest of men seek it in a better time.   Rich
men to-day are often at pains to avoid cities and even
the conversation of their kind, in order that their
expression of every appetite may be free, and that
they may have no influence about them save what is
of their own choice.   But those other holy men of our
beginnings chose the remote places in order that they
might lose their whole being in the contemplation of
God, and that they might have no temptation to
follow any appetite at all.

One might make an interesting list of the parallels
which are upon this model.   For instance, the men
of those beginnings held fast to the miraculous signs
of Divine action.   Our moderns laugh at the bare
relation of such things, but hold fast to anything,
however monstrous, which purposes to have behind
it a mysterious untested authority dressed up in
Print, violent in affirmation, ceaselessly contra-
dicting itself, empty of thought and called Science.
And so much for St. Tudwal.   I read about that
saint once, and grew quite learned on his legend (for
what is known is little, save that he lived just after
St. Martin of Tours, his exemplar), but I have
forgotten every word I read, and can tell you now
only roughly when he lived, nor anything else about
him save that he was a Welshman.

The Welsh have a curious feeling about their past.
They have been taught to detest its religion, yet

their patriotism inclines them to a sort of awe of
it. I never met a Welshman yet who ridiculed
St. David, yet very few indeed who knew either
what world St. David lived in or what mood he had
towards the universe ; and what about his Masses ?

.   .   .   .

There is no hole in the land along that coast
between the point of Carnarvonshire and Port-
madoc, except a curious little bottle harbour called
Pwllheli, with an odd entry up a sort of canal-like
entrance. For that we beat up : we came to it by
evening, but barely drifting under the lightest of
airs. A draft of tide took us in, and at the mouth
we passed a curious sight, which was a small model
of a mountain transformed by man : a solid dome of
granite, half of it already cut off like a cheese by
industry ; and men are still breaking it up and
taking it away in ships. What would be left of
the Wrekin if it crushed a few ounces to the ton ?
Eh, Rosenheim ? Eh, Guilderstern ?

As we watched that abuse of nature, a fine great
rock of granite, half murdered by man and looking
like Sunday evening's loaf, an aged mariner came
up to us in a boat of many years and chucked in his
painter to us without a word of permission, then
nodded to me to make it fast.

I did as he desired, for it is a rule in this world
always to do what you are told if there is no apparent
loss in doing it. What the old man wanted was to
be towed and to save himself the trouble of rowing.
But when we had done him this favour, and the
" Nona " was taking him up without fatigue to his
dear home, he spoke not a word, but sat there
gloomily, smoking a pipe and considering, I suppose,
the dim stories of the Ancients : the bards, and the
chieftains of Wales.

Wearied with this insolent silence I leant over the rail and asked him what we should make for and where we had best lie in Pwllheli. He pulled the pipe out of his mouth and cursed Pwllheli loudly, in English, but in English so Welsh that it reminded me of the famous story of the man who said " There will be folk in Lon-don to-day : one hundred and twenty are coming from Pwllheli." I said to him, therefore, desiring to soften his mood, " I see that you are not from Pwllheli yourself."   " Ess, put I am ! " he answered simply, and then fell to swearing again most abominably.

His grievance I found, after a little more questioning, was that a financier had persuaded the people of Pwllheli to turn it into an Earthly Paradise, with a band upon an island, and gondolas or what not, and this just after he had bought a cottage to be his very own, so that he was burdened with rates ; that was his grievance.

More of this Local Father I could not make. I think he hated all mankind as well as Pwllheli, and when we got into the broader water at the end of the entry and were moving up to the wharf in stately fashion, he gave me another surly sign to cast him off, which I did, and then, without a " good evening," he pulled for the shore. As for the " Nona," she slid alongside, and my companion and I moored, stowed, ate, slept and waited for the morning.

.   .   .   .

When morning came, and we woke late (for the fatigue of Bardsey passage was still on us, even after two days), we found under a clear but hazy sky no stir of wind.   It was well past noon and the ebb beginning, indeed, it was nearer two o'clock when there seemed to come just a breath, still from the north, that would take us down that strange entry and out to sea again. So we set sail, after casting off, and drifted rather than steered for the corridor end. As we left the stonework, I saw gathered there on the quay a group of men talking angrily and excitedly with words which I could not understand, for they were Welsh; and, as they debated, or quarrelled (but perhaps they had a common trouble, and were only doing what our papers and the French police call " demonstrating "), many more ran up, until they were quite a crowd. Whereupon one man of their number, a very intense looking, fierce fellow, jumped up on to a baulk of wood, so as to stand above them, and in a shrill, singing, passionate voice addressed them all. They fell silent, every face turned towards his, some with their mouths open, all with their eyes staring. Then, after he had spoken for a few minutes, he jumped down again and, behold, the crowd dispersed, some few knots still talking low among themselves, but the most of them remaining silent and slouching away.

Now what was it he had said in that strange tongue to achieve his result so well ?

. . . Certainly the management of men is an art ; and there are in it two factors which are nearly always set in conflict, although they ought to be harmonised. Indeed, one of them is nearly always thrust forward to the exclusion of the other : from which error in proportion civic disasters are born. These two factors in government are the direction of many and the interpretation of many. A number of men, a number too large to be appealed to individually (and the number gets too large after half a dozen or so), must be controlled and directed by him who governs, otherwise there is chaos. But it is only so controlled and directed by an interpretation of, and even a sort of subservience to, the common mind. Now control without understanding breaks a community, and sympathy without control dissolves it.

This man had succeeded, it seemed, with the mob at the wharf from which I had just sailed. His success set me thinking upon the matter of the management of men, the control of numbers : speakership, chairmanship, captaincy, and all the rest.

There is one element in the affair which is all-important, and the possession of which is a gift, like the gift of verse or " eye " in a sport. It is not to be prayed for. It is not to be acquired. It is granted by the unseen powers. This element is that which you have in the good management of a pack of hounds, or in any other kind of good generalship. It consists in a mixture of detailed and general appreciation ; for when those two faculties are combined—the faculty of seeing the individual, the faculty of seeing the whole—you have the genius of the human helmsman ; as rare a sort of genius as there is among men.

A man can only talk of the things he himself has known, and I myself have only seen one example of this inspiration in its perfection. It was (I regret to say) an experience of the House of Commons, a nasty place in which to find anything remarkable. There I saw the Speaker of my time (Mr. Lowther, as he then was) exercising the art through two Parliaments with a perfection which I had thought impossible, and which moved me, at the watching of it, as much as I am moved by great lines of Milton or Racine, or the harmonies of certain musics.

Consider what the business was ! He had before him in an ill-lit, dull, hideous, oblong room six

hundred men, dully ranged in ten or a dozen dull
rows ; half to his left, half to his right. In that dull
air of futile vulgar and unreal verbiage there could
arise, in a moment, absurdly acrid emotions. These
had to be tamed and resolved whenever they should
bubble up like gas from a marsh. It was a necessity
to the dull life of the place, if it were to crawl along
at all, that such accidents should not wholly destroy
its dull function.

This great body of men would dwindle in a
moment to a dozen or less—a dozen who only
remained for the chance of speaking, and of whom
each individual would jump up like a jack-in-the-box
the very instant the last mouther had sat down. It
would swell again to a full complement, a crowded
House, with equal rapidity.

The man managing that assembly had to remember each man by name. Those faces, which would,
for any of *us*, have become mere blobs of white
within half an hour of fatigued observation, had to
be recognised as individuals. The relations of each
with all had to be remembered ; the nature of the
matter under debate, the right of one man, through
experience of office or of personal work, to be
remembered ; the claim of another man (suffering
some unjust failure) to be recognised ; the danger
of a third who was repetitive ; of a fourth who was
mad. At the same time, the very subtle distinctions
between the lesser and the greater claim to speak,
the length of the debate, even the excessive tedium
of each speaker had to be weighed. On the top of all
that, it had to be remembered of what importance
was each discussion (in so far as you can call any of
them important—but they seem absurdly important
to the participants). On the top of all that,
again, was the general arrangement of the debate

suggested by the Whips and in possession of the Chair.

Now in all this incredibly complicated task, involving, I suppose, some hundreds of interior decisions during the day, Mr. Lowther never once failed. The House of his time was an instrument over which he had complete mastery through a complete comprehension and a rapidity of just decision which I have never seen equalled in any field of command.

We have a tendency to-day to use words too strong for the occasion, and the word genius is a very strong word; but I have no more doubt that Mr. Lowther, as I watched him day after day, displayed genius than I have a doubt that Mozart in music, or Houdon in sculpture, had genius. It was amazing, it was satisfactory, it was continuous.

There was an old squire with whom I often dined in those years, and who had great knowledge of men and things in that club, still aristocratic, which England then still was. Not long after my first election to the august Assembly, I told him with enthusiasm at his own table what my judgment was of this achievement. He answered me, wearily, "Oh ! I have heard that said of every Speaker since I can remember ! " To which I re-answered, " Yes ; but this time they are right."

Which reminds me of how a modern poet, spared to middle age in spite of the wrath of God, famous for that he could neither scan nor rhyme—let alone think or feel—once made a speech in which he carefully set out those things which had been said against Swinburne when first that meteor flamed across the heaven of English verse. The modern poet next read to this assembly the things that had been written against himself when he first blurred into the murk of our evening. He triumphantly concluded : " What was said against Swinburne they have said against me ! " Then there arose an aged writer of reviews, a man whose hair, whose voice, and whose Aura were all three of delicate silver. He said : " Yes ! But in what they said of him they were wrong ; in what they said of you, they were right."

This was not an epigram, it was a paving-stone ; and it reminded me of that line in the Epic of Roncesvalles, " Christians are right and Pagans are wrong."

So in the matter of Speakers. I have seen the action of four ; but of none would I say even that they had talent, saving in this case alone, where I have used another word. . . .

So we drifted down the narrow entry and out into the open sea ; and all that afternoon, under a wind now slightly lifting, now falling again, we crept eastward and a little south, making more way as the sun declined, because the wind was shifting westward on to our quarter ; and of that I was glad, for I desired to look into Port Madoc, which I had not seen since I was a child. I had vivid memories of it during a wonderful journey overshadowed by that air wherewith the Creator blesses childhood, lending to everything an active flavour of the Divine ; which is in three things, Clarity, Magnitude and Multiplicity of strong emotion.

For the Divine reveals itself in a special multiplicity, in an infinite variety. All that there is in colour and in music, and in line and in affection, and to these added other raptures innumerable, such as we know not of nor can conceive—that is to be at last our beatitude : that is the fulness of being. In childhood our innocence permits us some little glimpse of such things ; but with the passage of the years they are lost altogether.   The light in the lantern goes out, and the living thing within us fails, and is stupefied, and dies.

So Musset and old Pythagoras and Mr. Tupper. If any man doubts the Fall of Man (and I see from the papers that two belated bishops and one dean are still shaky on it, through some Victorian influence upon their minds, not only of bones but of chipped stones), let him consider this decay of heaven within ourselves as the maturity of our manhood develops. The more we are of this world and the more we know of it, the further are we drifting from the shores of the Blessed.   Which shores also the poet had in mind when he wrote, sang, crooned or what not :

" Sing to me of the islands, oh, Daughter of Cahoolin, sing,
　　　　Sing to me of the West,
　Sing to me of the girth loosened and the lax harpstring
　　　　And of rest.

" Beyond the skerries and beyond the outer water,
　　　　There lies the land.
　Sing to me of the islands, oh, Daughter of Cahoolin, oh, High
　　　　　　　　　　King's Daughter,
　　　　And of the over-strand.

" I desire to be with Brandan and his companions, in the quiet
　　　　　　　　　　places
　　　　And to drink of their spring.
　Sing to me of the islands, oh, Daughter of Cahoolin, and of the
　　　　　　　　　　blessed faces.
　　　　Daughter of Cahoolin, sing."

But if you tell me that that is not the way to spell " Cuchulin," I have two answers, each of them stronger than Hercules.

The first is that the poet spelt it as he felt inclined, that is, by ear ; for poets excel not, as is commonly believed, in speech but in ears ; as you may see by their profiles or sidehead views; and as it is his spelling your action lies against him, not me.

And the second answer is, that one ought never to be bothered with the pedantry of quaint alphabets and the spelling tricks of outer men. Cuchulin is, or was, or should be, pronounced " Cahoolin," and there is an end of it. But as to whether he ever had a daughter, or if he had, whether she could sing, or even whether that Irishman existed at all, I hold all these things to be perfectly indifferent. . . .

. . . . .

We cast anchor in the very midmost of that solemn bay with its half-circle of huge mountains looking down upon an empty sea. The giants were dim in the haze, but the more enormous, and I revered and worshipped them.

We so cast anchor because I had to wait for the tide. I could not run up the long, winding channel through the sands of Port Madoc until the flood should be with me, and that would not be till the gloaming, between eight and nine o'clock that night.

Therefore did we lie thus in Harlech Bay, gazing at the great hills of Wales. There is no corner of Europe that I know, not even the splendid amphitheatre standing in tiers of high Alpine wall around Udine, which so moves me with the awe and majesty of great things as does this mass of the northern Welsh mountains seen from this corner of their silent sea.

Few can recall it, for few visit that corner of the salt. It leads nowhere but to the harbour of Port Madoc. No man beaches a boat to-day under Harlech ; no man to-day sets out from that shore for Ireland beyond. The halls are in ruin. There is no more harping. No flight of sails comes up eastward out of the sea like birds. Even the sailors have forgotten Gwynnedd. To-day the only sailors familiar with the solemnity of which I speak are those who ply in the small boats of the Slate Trade, or who, like myself, have employed a curious leisure in searching out new things here in the seas of home. For all my life I have made discoveries close at hand, and have found the Island of Britain to be infinite. But who in our times knows where to look for vision ?

Indeed, this lack of fame applies to perhaps half the greater visions, even of the modern over-frequented and travelled earth. Men know half of them to satiety, but the other half they never see. Every one has wearied of the Bay of Naples, repeated a thousand times, but what of that lonely field by the flat Adriatic sand whence you may see the dark eastern Fall of the Gran Sasso, tragic, with storms about it, dominating a deserted shore ? Everybody has his bellyful of Gavarnie, but what of the valley of Araxas, which proclaims so terribly the glory of God ? Where are the pictures of that ? Who has drawn it ? Yet it is but half a day from Gavarnie.

So it is with this awful parade of the great mountains standing on guard over the northern corner of Cardigan Bay, seen from the silence and the flat of ocean, towering above its glass ; and all that late afternoon and evening I adored them until, with the last of the light, and a westerly air which was but the suggestion of a breeze, we groped north anxiously for the opening to Port Madoc channel. How I should make it, even upon the flood, in the darkness, I knew not ; for the sands there are miles wide, and this channel (which I had never yet made) shifts continually. But God sent me a pilot.

He hailed us out of the half-darkness from a small

boat, and asked us in the dialect which I will call
" Anglo-Welsh " (after Anglo-Catholic, Anglo-
German, Anglo-Indian, Anglo-African, and the
rest), " Whether we would not have a pilot, ah ? "

Nor was he a pilot, as the event shall show ; but
at any rate he belonged to that shore, and would
have more knowledge than I. So I gave him the
helm, and went up forward to look out over the bows,
as the " Nona " glided slowly along the flood into the
channel which they call " The Water of the Smooth
Lake " (" Afon Glaslyn "). For half an hour of that
very slow gliding all went well. The darkness had
quite fallen. There was no moon.

The gliding stopped ; there was a slight thrill.
She had hit Wales : an under-water, advance guard
of Wales. The man at the helm was not apologetic,
he was not humble, but he was at least subdued ;
and he said, " Her will float soon, so her will ! " I
forbore to reproach him, not from kindness but from
cowardice.

The flood lifted her foot, she swung off, and we
went on again up the darkness, with the least of
little airs to give steering-way.

So for a quarter of an hour, covering perhaps a
third of a mile : then again, rather sharper this
time, came the honest thrust into the sand, and,
what was more, she had run up against it so high
this time that she was careening a little ; she was
taking it very hard, as the high-brows used to say
of their beloved Prussia after the Armistice.

This time it was a good half-hour before she
floated, and all that time the culprit was silent, nor
did I reproach him. He at least had some vague
memory of where the channel might be, and that I
certainly had not.

As we lay there, waiting for the rising water to

lift us, a clear sound of hammering rang from the black shore, far away, over the vast expanse of sand. It meant something to the pseudo-pilot, for he called out in loud, sing-song tones five or six words in the Welsh language, wherein I distinguished the word "Afon," which means "water"; and his very distant Kymric fellow, there unperceived in the night, answered with a distant cry. What they said I know not; perhaps the unjust man at the helm was asking at what hour she would have water enough to lie higher up.

She floated again (it was now deep into the night, and the dim stars, through the haze overhead, watched our misery). The "Nona" glided on.

. . . .

To be coming thus into a very shoal fairway, after dark, and to be in the hands of a pilot who was quite clearly one of God's Three Welsh Fools—one of the Triad, one of the Three Great Fools of Britain—was a strain to the temper, a strain to breaking point. It was no good my taking the tiller, for I had no idea of the channel, and only saw now and then, straining my eyes forward, a little blob on the darkness that would be a drum-headed buoy slowly drifting past as we lifted on the young flood.

I used to think that the irritation against fools was irrational and purposeless. Where it is written in Holy Writ that one should tolerate Fools even with gladness, I thought that this was a general rule of conduct. But now I know it to be a counsel of perfection and, indeed, like so many things in the Old Testament, a counsel generally to be avoided. For the strong exasperation against fools is, I am now sure, an instinct implanted in us (or, as fools themselves would say, "evolved") whereby we defend ourselves against such accidents as this perpetual

bumping which the " Nona " was undergoing on the
sands of Port Madoc. Our anger against fools is
a natural faculty of conservation, like the sensitive-
ness of the nerves of the skin ; and in those countries
where fools are too much tolerated (of which England) many little disasters proceeding from such
tolerated fools combine to make a great one at last
and to break down the State.

It is high time that a new book were written on
Fools, like those of the sixteenth century, which are
so excellent, and which you have in Latin, in German,
in French, and in English : " The Praise of Folly,"
" The Ship of Fools," " The Fool's Paradise," and
others. If I had the leisure, it is one of the many
hundred books which I should like to write myself :
" The Fool, sociological, biological, and patho-
logical, with many portraits and an appendix on the
newly discovered Giant Fool of Aphasia." As I
have not the leisure (and never had it) I bequeath
the idea to other and younger and wealthier men,
just as some years ago I bequeathed them the idea
of a Cad's Encyclopedia.

Among other chapters in this book I would have
one on the Fool and the Label. For I maintain that
Labels are the great support and sustenance of the
Human Fool.

Labels help the fool to do what little dull thinking
he manages to get through. He knows whom to
respect and whom to despise and what wine to
choose, and so on—all by the label. And then again,
labels are very useful to the Fool by getting him
taken for more than he is worth. Any number of
my friends have said to me at one time or another,
when I was having my laugh at the politicians :
" A man does not get to a position like that (Secretary of State for Drainage, or Prime Minister, or

what not) without abilities." Now this error shows
how useful the label is to the fool. For a matter of
fact I can testify, if any living man can, that the
politicians who get their share of the swag are of all
degrees in the matter of intelligence. Some have
first-rate abilities, especially among the lawyers ;
many are of the ordinary second-rate, fifty-eight per
cent., β *minus* or Wandsworth intelligence ; and
quite a large proportion are Plumb Stuffed Fools,
true Fools Absolute and of the Nadir ; Rooted
Fools. I knew one Fool Secretary of State who, in
his Whitehall office, used to look at his official documents with a sort of tragic stare, as men look on the
dead, and slowly wag them up and down in front
of his face with a hopeless gesture. Then he would
call upon his permanent official, who would explain
to him what they meant, whereupon he would use
one after another of the great Fool Phrases which
are the furniture of the Fool's Mind, such as " Yes,"
" I see " ; " Quite," " Precisely," and then again
" Yes." Having done this, he would sign his
name to a number of papers which meant no more
to him than so many Chinese tracts, and with a
groan he would go off to spend his £100 a week at
Brighton.

Even in those trades where you would think there
must be activity of brain for a man to advance at all,
your Fool drifts forward somehow. You find him
quite high up in armies, and as for his number in
the great cheating professions, notably Share-
shuffling, it is prodigious. Half the wealthy Share-
shufflers I have known have been fools animal, fools
crass, fools to be driven blindfold or led about on a
halter ; but to do that great modern profession
justice, there is a minority of Share-shufflers as keen
as needles and as wide awake as ferrets. They have

no more luck, however, than their duller brethren, for fate rules them all, and alternate wealth and poverty is as much the rule with them as with the stupidest men. I will bargain that if you were to take samples of Share-shufflers out of three sacks, the House of Lords, Monte Carlo, and the gaols, you would find the same percentage of Fools in each sample.

Which leads me on to say that never was an old proverb of less accurate modern application than the proverb about the Fool and his Money. You will have heard it said that the Fool and his Money are soon parted. That was true enough for the yokel at the fair, but in this modern city life of ours it is just the other way. The Fool of Inherited Money (not the Gambling Fool) holds on to it with fish-hooks. It is the intelligent man, with many interests and (by some freak of nature) a generous heart, who squanders his hoard. But your Fool gets his legs round the money bag and crosses his ankles on the other side, clasps it higher up with both arms right round it and fingers tightly interlocked beyond ; digs his teeth into the mouth of the same and, screwing up his eyes, clutches it all over desperately with the rigour of death, making himself wholly one with the beloved object. From this attitude nothing can move him save the lure of a plausible fellow promising to increase his wealth. I have seen a clot of fools thus hanging on to money bags, all pressed up together like bats in a steeple, when a repulsive over-dressed young adventurer would slither by singing a light song of great wealth to be made in some scheme of his devising ; and, behold, the Fools would turn their round heads ungummed from their money bags and listen in rapture to that song, and many of them would even hand over their bags to the young adventurer, never to see their gold again. But I say that, save when they are thus tempted by their blind avarice, Fools are not easily parted from their money.

However, this harbour- or pilot-fool of mine was not, I think, troubled in this regard, for had he been a Fool of Wealth he would not have been blundering to get the " Nona " up-channel in the dark.

Five separate times did we touch and wait with increasing anger each time till the flood released us, but at last we came to the pool, and to reasonable deep water, and to a quay.

There did we put out our warping ropes, and springs, and the fenders alongside, and there did we give money to the Fool as a reward for all the pain his folly had given us.

For this also is the rule in human life ; that when you suffer anything you must pay a good price for the entertainment.

It is true of bad cooking, and of bad wine, and of a painful illness, started or continued by doctors, and of all the intolerable noisy hotels, full of insolence and maddening bells.   It is true of all the bad things of the world.   Nor does it follow that all cheap things are good.   Far from it !   But all good things are cheap (except caviare), and the way to get good things is to look for them as you would look for a penny which you had dropped in the straw of the (once again !) dear old omnibuses of my youth which were pulled by horses, and had standing at their door a guardian of the poorest of the people, foul in speech, grimy of skin, unshaven, bloodshot, from the gutter —but (oh, believe me !) a better citizen of a better time than ours.

"Nona," cruising and voyaging "Nona," wanderer over the seas of Britain, how in the solitude of your companionship my mind does lead me from one thing to another !

But that's all one. It is time for sleep.

. . . .

The new day having come, we got the half-ebb a little before six o'clock, and threaded away down the Channel for the open sea.

I ought, I suppose, to have stopped in Port Madoc, and renewed the memories of my childhood. But a fig for the memories of my childhood, at six o'clock in the morning : At six o'clock of a May morning, and a nice little leading breeze, all cold and merry ! The memories of childhood and the contemplation of the Divine are for the evening ; they go with candle-light, and with a wine I know, and with friends of twenty years. But, so help me He that made me, when I find the morning wind blowing well for the salt and myself freshly roused from a good sleep, I am full of nothing but the coming of the course and an eagerness for the line of the sea against the sky and the making of a further shore.

It ought to be more dangerous to float down on the ebb without a local trickster, than to come up upon the flood. But fortune served, and the swirl of the ebb plainly marked the channel under that heartening light, with the glory of the new day shooting over the tops of the great and solemn mountains eastward, by the land.

Therefore, without misadventure, we came to the last marking buoy and took the sea ; running easily with the wind nearly aft, but a little on the port quarter, so that all was well.

The great field or marsh before Harlech stretched there to landward ; and, on its splendid defiant height, the old castle watched us as we went ; the place where they hid poor Henry the Saint when the true Plantagenet was pacing for his blood.

Here is a landscape inhabited everywhere by things not of this world ; by the gods of these hills whom our God has ousted ; by the memory of great men dead and their wraiths, I suppose ; and by the troops of the Empire, marching up the inland road, and by the chieftains, and by the very saintly men who cast their spell fifteen hundred years ago over the islands and the rocks of Lyonesse.

So we sailed on and on, heading over to the Atlantic southern corner of Wales. Then, far away in the midst of the sea, we heard the tolling of a bell. . . .

The tolling of the bell was not only mournful (and at the same time terrible), but had in it an odd quality of message ; as though it were not of the world through which we moved. For a bell is a land thing, and even in salt water we think of it as sounding upon a buoy near shore, or as the companion and regulator of human things, like the bell on board ship. For Mr. Masefield is very just when he notes how the clang of the ship's bell by accident in the swoop of a ship down the great waves of an Atlantic storm, has an unnatural call : being rung without the aid of men's hands.

Now this bell, as I heard it plainting away deeply, unable as yet to see the thing on which it swung, mixed up its noise in my mind with the great story of St. Patrick : a story I had designed to write many years ago in Arras, where I went to see the manuscript which most vividly recalls him. But of that task I found myself incapable. However, I did visit his staff in Rome.

For the bell thus swinging on its buoy far out to sea, swings on the western edge of that strange, long,

undersea road which they call the "Sarn Badrig"
(which means "The Causeway of St. Patrick")
and cannot but awake the great story of the coming
of Europe to Ireland.

How right they were to call that sunken ridge
pointing straight to Ireland "The Roman Road of
Patrick!" And how its sudden cessation symbo-
lises the break, the wound, the rupture, by which
this island was cut off from that : more than two
hundred years ago. The ridge ends suddenly in
deep water and continues no more. But the bell
tolls on, appealing.

St. Patrick is the second of those witnesses which
remain to us of the more than natural quality of
Ireland. The first is the old Pagan story of the
western harbours from which the dead were ferried
over by night to their felicity. The second is that
undying phrase in the *Confessio*, where St. Patrick
himself says that at night and in dreams "He heard
the voices of the Irish calling."

It is gloom upon the mind to remember that the
magnitude of the task set to Britain (a Roman land)
in the matter of Holy Ireland, has been so missed :
as though a man having to encounter a mountain a
little before the day thought it no more than a slight
hill against the dawn. Here was the difficult land,
—but inspired—which Agricola said (and he knew
his business) he could have mastered for Rome and
right order with one Legion. That Legion was not
given him, any more than the Divisions were given
that might have made the break through before
Cambrai. Would that the officials at Rome had
listened to him! Here was Ireland that most
difficult of subjects, most intriguing of friends, most
tenacious of enemies, set up against the western
shores of Britain, of Roman land ; and through all

those centuries nothing was done to enrich the subject, to acquire the friend, to reconcile the enemy. But I am weak enough to believe that this failure also was in the Providence of God.

The mountains look upon the mountains : the mountains of Britain to the mountains of Ireland ; from the east to the west, over a magic sea. But they look in wrath and remain sullen giants. Nor is the battle concluded.

As we sailed past the bell very slowly (that Mark having come into sight) we discovered it to be enclosed in a sort of great cage which swung with slow dignity and bowed backwards and forwards upon the large swell, unaffected by the light breeze which gave us our two knots through sluggish water. My companion said to me, brutally enough, " How would you like to be shut up in that cage, and left there to the night and to the wind ? "   I answered " Not at all," and in this I told the truth.   But the bell did not repine, for it was fulfilling its function, expiating its sins, pursuing its end, and consonant to the will that is behind this world.   It tolls there beyond the sea-ward end of the Sarn Badrig to warn mariners of that long ledge submerged : barring the sea ways.

My mind returned to that great Causeway, that shelf of rock and shingle behind us, just hidden by the waves, pointing westward into the deep, mile after mile, like some drowned giant's pier ; the beginning of a bridge, as it were, between Britain and the Other Island ; the marriage of Britain with the older island, whence the dead are ferried over to their repose.

But that Causeway was never completed ; that bridge was never built ; and the weight, the future consequence, of such a failure lies not upon Ireland, but (alas !) upon England.

For how many years did I not see the tragedy
played out !

I knew its roots as well as any man. I knew that
the gulf was a gulf of religion. I knew that the
riddle was without solution for men whose eyes
were cast downwards ; who did not admit the
unseen powers ; who could see nothing but the
mud and wealth in which they stood—yet I mar-
velled that the dreadful affair should drag on so
long.

To the one set, to those sham " Liberals " and
" Unionists " of the wretched money game at
Westminster, it was a lucrative jest. They cared not
for Ireland at all, and not too much for England.
They treated the martyrdom of Ireland as a counter
in their play. To do them justice, they thought that
England could never suffer. To the others, to
those of Ireland, the struggle was (as they thought)
a battle always lost.

In the beginning of their effort, the men who had
organised a political caucus for Ireland and had
attempted, by what they called the " Nationalist "
Party, to get some settlement by way of the Parliamentary morass, were sincere ; yes, at first, flamingly
sincere. Parnell I never met ; but Davitt I knew—
and a man more heroically sincere I have never had
the fortune to meet and respect. To the very end
the effort of the Irishmen at Westminster retained
some dwindling element of truth. And this I say
though I know that many Irishmen to-day may
laugh at me for saying it. But it is true. Down to
the very end, sunk as they had grown in the sodden
Westminster habit, and conventional as had become
the repetition of their demand, some conception of
a goal to be reached at last still inhabited these men.
I knew them and I can testify to it. Right up to

1914—it sounds laughable, but it is true—the group at Westminster which called itself "The Irish Party" did, in some fading way, still hold the idea of a "Parliamentary settlement." It was true of John Redmond and his brother : I may fairly say that his brother died for that idea.

They really did think (to me it was astonishing ; to the younger Irish, to many of them at least, incredible) that a solution was to be reached through the working of those then undermined, moth-eaten, now crumbled falsehoods of the professional politicians : that the farce of voting is " the voice of the people " ; that the House of Commons is " a mirror of England " ; that " the nation rules through its representatives "—and all the rest of the absurdities bred by the grafting of French Democratic attempts on to the decline of English aristocracy.

It sounds not possible that *any* Irishman, even after a lifetime at Westminster, could be so deceived. But, I say it again, I knew these men. I can testify to the truth of what I have said. They did right up to 1914 still faintly hope. I knew them as friends and as opponents. They were my opponents when I took my share in defending the Catholic schools in 1906, and they were angry at my going to see the Pope in that year, to lay before him what I thought to be sufficient amendments to Mr. Birrell's Bill (for they regarded the Catholic schools in England as their private domain). What is enormous, these men, Redmond and his party, thought that their Westminster method could still achieve something after the manifest betrayal of Ireland by the politicians labelled "Liberal" upon the outbreak of the Great War.

It is a process I have watched over and over again

in the course of my short but too long life ; men not seeing what (one would imagine) should be apparent to a child.

These men did not see that you cannot get strength out of rottenness ; nor justice, nor truth, nor generosity out of moribund institutions (such as is now the House of Commons), which, after a certain stage in decline, no longer live save for personal intrigue.

I say nothing, therefore, against them, in spite of their failure, and I revere their memory. The Irish in good time will give to the last protagonists in that futile attempt a due position in their annals ; and specially to William Redmond and his brother, John Redmond.

For writing this I may be assailed from either side ; but it is true.

Anyhow, I saw the tragedy going on before my eyes, as a man on a shore-height may see a boat making straight for rocks under water, apparent to him, but of which her steersman knows nothing. I saw it in the years when I watched it as a young man from the gallery of the House of Commons ; I saw it during the two Parliaments in which I sat ; I saw it when I had left the place in disgust. I saw it in the last four years before the Great War ; England, still drifting hopelessly on to the Irish reef : till she struck.

I saw, year after year, from my boyhood to my middle manhood and later, the Parliamentary poison eating up the Irish effort and the English face turned away from Ireland, failing to understand its own doom. For England, a seat of vision, might have understood the opportunity and the peril had the Irish themselves used pen and word directly. But the wrong instrument was used : the broken and now useless instrument of the Commons.

I saw the politicians whom the Irish sent over,
or rather, who had the machinery of the Irish
protest in their hands, grow fonder and fonder
of the Westminster drug and degradation. I saw
them half in doubt, at last, whether it were not
better to remain in London half enjoying what had
become second nature to them, the wretched
pomposities of the House of Commons. They
should rather have nourished the flame of their
country. Yet they were honest men, and at heart
and at root were Irish to the end. But they thought
that England was to be made to understand by the
use of a machine, the Parliamentary machine, which
was already worn out. It was their fundamental
error. What man desiring to move men would
waste his time in Parliament ?

If a man may boast of a small personal experience,
I myself told them what would come. But they
would not believe me. They thought me fanatical
in this—and to the end. They put their trust
in the slime of the Lobbies. It swallowed
them up.

I saw the end ; or rather the beginning of the
end—for the true end of the Irish quarrel is still
hidden, and will be perhaps for us, here in England,
very terrible. I saw the professional politicians
carrying their silly labels of " Liberal " and " Union-
ist," footling, on the very edge of the war precipice in 1914, at a game for avoiding the Irish issue,
and (as they dined together) arranging tricks to
put it off on one side. I saw their vast relief
when they were given their chance to the threat
of a mutiny against the salvation of England and
Ireland. And I saw—I lived to see—the contemptible capitulation : the Parliamentary puppets
(Lord Chancellors and the rest) shouting on a

Wednesday that "They would not rest until they had taken the last arm from the hands of the last rebel," and on the following Friday, at the bidding of their financial masters, surrendering to Ireland for ever : Ireland that might have been the bulwark of England. . . . It is done.

.   .   .   .

So we sailed slowly on, past the end of St. Patrick's Causeway, past that mournful great tolling bell which hangs there in the middle sea ; imprisoned in its cage, expiating the too careless sins of its youth. The lamentable sound of it, the unsatisfied appeal, followed us over the deep. So we sailed on, with our nose for the Atlantic headlands of the south, and for the corners of Wales, where they face the Cornish and the Devon seas and Ireland also, beyond, with the great ocean rolling in between.

.   .   .   .

High as are the mountains on this shore, yet by a trick of the air they were soon out of sight.

That is a thing I have never understood. High land which ought to be plainly visible, and even over-hanging one, disappears like this at sea magically on a clear day. When the weather is thick, one expects that ; but the curious thing is that one may see clear air all around and a sharp horizon, nothing but sea and sky, and yet know perfectly well that the empty heaven at which one is gazing is really full of great hills close at hand. I do not know whether this happens in the clearer parts of the world. I have never seen it off North Africa or California. But upon the coasts of these islands it happens continually, and it is one of the hundred things which, I think, has made their inhabitants familiar with mystery and amenable to the unseen. For those of these islands, British and Irish, have always been remarkable for the sense of mystery ; and among them none feel the effect of mystery more strongly than such as sail upon the sea.

It was an astonishing thing to sit there, at the end of the afternoon, just past the end of St. Patrick's Causeway, heading for Strumbles light below the horizon, with a slight air, now from the north-west, giving the boat steering way and no more, with the tiller lazily pushed a little up to keep her course, and looking over the rail to the left, eastward, and seeing nothing there but an horizon of empty sky ; yet knowing very well that the sky was not empty, but that the enormous mass of Cader Idris and the enormous mass of Plinlimmon stood guarding the sea. It was like the continual experience of this life wherein the wise firmly admit vast Presences to stand in what is an apparent emptiness, unperceived by any sense.

As I thus looked over the rail musing upon the strangeness of such things, I remembered how, many years ago, in this same boat and holding this same tiller, I had wondered, after a too rapid passage across the Channel from France, under too much canvas and with too much wind, how near I might be to England. For one could not see the coast at all. The wind had dropped suddenly, it had grown dead calm, and the " Nona" lolloped on the big lump which the breeze had left. I had no idea, within ten miles, where I might be ; it is a ridiculous confession to make, but true. It was the height of the spring tides, and I only roughly knew the set of them in mid-Channel. While I was so wondering, I thought I saw some difference between the lower and the upper sky, as though the lower grey were faintly darker than the upper. In a moment the line was defined, and I found myself looking at the turn of the high land east of Folkestone, where it runs away inland towards the old Roman harbour of Lympne. I was not more than three miles from shore.

And as there is a concealment of reality at sea, corresponding to the concealment of reality from our experience in human life, so also at sea there is occasionally vision, corresponding to that occasional vision which you also have in human life : but vision is much rarer than the concealment of reality.

Once out near the Looe with an ugly thunder-storm glowering and lumbering down from the north, full of zigzags of lightning, I, in this same boat, was shortening sail rapidly to meet the gust when it should come. Even as I did so, I saw a fierce red light beating upon the Seven Sisters and Beachy Head, more than forty miles away. You could see every detail of those chalk cliffs. You could have touched them with your hand ; yet the sea in between was vague : and that was a vision of the unseen. I say that the sea is in all things the teacher of men.

·   ·   ·   ·

With the afternoon the wind freshened, and, as it freshened, went right round by north to a little east of north, whence it blew steadily enough, and gave us about four knots at the fall of darkness.

My companion had never held a tiller, but he was very expert at all sports, and I thought to myself, " I will see whether so simple a thing as steering a boat cannot be easily accomplished by a man at the first trial. Then shall I be able to get what I badly need, which is a little sleep." So I lighted the binnacle lamp, I explained to him the function of the lubber's mark, and gave him the point on the card which he was to keep on the lubber's mark. I said to him : " If it comes on to blow a little harder and the card swings, and the boat tends to yaw a little, don't mind that, but keep the lubber's mark on the average at the point I have given and that will be enough." He said that he understood all these things, and for the first time in his life set himself to steer a ship. But I, for my part, went down to sleep, confident that if it should come on to blow at all hard it would awaken me there and then, so no great harm could come. I slept for many hours, when suddenly I was awakened by my companion giving a loud cry of astonishment. I tumbled up on deck quickly, and I found him pointing at a light which shone brilliantly upon the horizon, dead on our bow. He said to me : " Look, look, there is a light dead ahead ! " I said to him : " Of course ! " and that it was the light of Strumble Head, outside Fishguard ; and I asked him what he would have expected. I had given him his course, and, naturally, he had lifted the light in good time. But he, for his part, could not get over it ; he thought it a sort of miracle. He kept on repeating his amazement that so clumsy a thing as a tiller and a rudder, and so coarse an instrument as an old battered binnacle compass, should thread the eye of a needle like that ; it was out of all his experience. It is true that he had not been disturbed by any current or strong tide, but even had he been so, he was bound on a clear night to make that light not much off either bow.

That things should turn out so gave him quite a new conception of the sea and the sailing of it, and he talked henceforward as though it were his home.

This corroboration by experience of a truth emphatically told, but at first not believed, has a powerful effect upon the mind.

I suppose that of all the instruments of conviction
it is the most powerful. It is an example of the
fundamental doctrine that truth confirms truth. If
you say to a man a thing which *he* thinks nonsensical,
impossible, a mere jingle of words, although you
yourself know it very well by experience to be true ;
when later he finds this thing by his own experience
to be actual and living, then is truth confirmed in
his mind : it stands out much more strongly than it
would had he never doubted. On this account, it
is always worth while, I think, to hammer at truths
which one knows to be important, even those which
seem, to others, at their first statement mere nonsense. For though you may die under the imputa-
tion of being a man without a sense of proportion,
or even a madman, yet reality will in time confirm
your effort. And even though that confirmation of
your effort, the triumph of the truth, should never
be associated with your own name, yet is it worth
making, for the sake of the truth, to which I am
sure we owe a sort of allegiance : not because it is
the truth—one can have no allegiance to an abstrac-
tion—but because whenever we insist upon a truth
we are witnessing to Almighty God.

A man who knows that the earth is round but
lives among men who believe it to be flat ought to
hammer in his doctrine of the earth's roundness up
to the point of arrest, imprisonment, or even death.
Reality will confirm him, and he is not so much
testifying to the world as it is—which is worth
nothing—as to Him who made the world, and Who
is worth more than all things. And, as it seems to
me, a man ought to do this even about truths not so
very important, but he should observe some proportion between them and truths of vital importance.
For instance, it is a truth of no very apparent

immediate importance to-day that any great poem
of the past must have been written by a poet, and
that those who think a great poem can be written by
a committee or pieced together out of traditional
ballads, think nonsense. It is also a truth that Great
Britain is no longer secured by sea power. It is also
a truth that the interests of this country were till
lately identical with the interests of international
banking and finance—and are so no longer.

All these three truths are true, but the first truth
touches no vital matter, while the last two truths are
of immediate importance ; and a man aware of them
should hammer away at them, and not neglect them
in order to pursue too constantly that other much
less important truth about old poems.

It is not often that one comes across men in a
modern lifetime intent upon the proclamation of
unaccepted, or of ill-accepted, or unknown truths ;
for such men must suffer. And few will suffer
to-day save for some reward. Very few modern
men value any reward that is not immediate and
material. Huxley, who sacrificed himself entirely,
both to false things which he believed to be true
and to real things that were true, I never knew.
But I knew Déroulède well, and Déroulède ham-
mered away all his life at the expense of ceaseless
insult and contempt, paying for the preservation of
his honour the heavy price of an unbroken isolation,
and dying without seeing any apparent fruit of his
effort. It was his mission to proclaim to his French
compatriots the elementary truth that, until they had
secured the defeat of Prussia in a war, they themselves were doomed to increasing decay, and Europe
to increasing ills. I visited his grave just after the
Battle of the Marne. It is in a little, somewhat
neglected churchyard, some three miles from the

house he had inherited : a place windswept and overlooking from beyond its walls a great horizon to the north. The season being late summer, and the war having left the little place untended, the grass was rank and high around the mound and the slab which marked the place where he lay. There, leaning against the wall, some one had put casually, as though by chance, in high dedication to his memory, the first of the frontier posts which the army had pulled up from the summits of the Vosges during the first ill-fated charge into Alsace.

I knew also one other man (who, for the honour I bear him and because he is still alive, I shall not name), an Englishman ; at the outbreak of war in South Africa he said to all who would hear him, and printed in a journal to which he had admission, the simple truth that this adventure would be the beginning of a decline in the financial credit of England. To discover whether he was right or wrong, look at any curve of that credit and mark the dates. He said to all who would hear him that from this adventure onwards we should find ourselves increasingly embarrassed, with increasing taxation, with an increasing uncertainty in our foreign policy, and in our hold upon the markets we desired to control abroad. His action was not that of the prophet, but of the reasoner. His unpopularity was extreme. He was the only public man who talked conscientiously and rationally in this affair of the Boer War, and who did not confuse his conclusions with that disgusting antipathy to their own country which marked the most of those who protested against the war. As for the enemy, the South African Dutch, he knew them and heartily despised them. The Outlanders he also knew, and thought them the scum of the earth. But he acted on no mood of

like or dislike. He was concerned with the future
of England and he reasoned. He talked a sort of
mathematical sense, and all his words were true ;
but he shall know no reward. Only, this remains
true also ; that all who heard him or read his writing
have secretly returned to those words in their own
minds, and have said : " He was right and we
were wrong."

There is another form of impressing the truth,
and testifying to it, and doing good by it, which is
the dogmatic assertion of truth by the old and the
experienced and the revered, to the young. It is
out of fashion ; it is invaluable. I can myself
testify to two such experiences which stand out
supreme among many hundreds in my own early life.
I am afraid they may seem trivial to my readers ;
I can only say that for myself they were as strong
experiences as any great joy or pain could be. One
was a sentence which Cardinal Manning said to me
when I was but twenty years old. The other was
one which the Master of my College, Dr. Jowett,
of Balliol, said to me when I was twenty-two years
old.

The profound thing which Cardinal Manning
said to me was this : *all human conflict is ultimately
theological.*

It was my custom during my first days in London,
as a very young man, before I went to Oxford, to
call upon the Cardinal as regularly as he would
receive me ; and during those brief interviews
I heard from him many things which I have had
later occasion to test by the experience of human
life. I was, it may be said, too young to judge things
so deep as sanctity and wisdom ; but, on the other
hand, youth has vision, especially upon elemental
things ; and Manning did seem to me (and still

seems to me) much the greatest Englishman of his time. He was certainly the greatest of all that band, small but immensely significant, who, in the Victorian period, so rose above their fellows, preeminent in will and in intelligence, as not only to perceive, but even to accept the Faith. Not only did his powerful mind discover, but his powerful will also insisted upon all the difficult consequences of such an acceptation. He never admitted the possibility of compromise between Catholic and non-Catholic society. He perceived the necessary conflict, and gloried in it.

This saying of his (which I carried away with me somewhat bewildered) *that all human conflict was ultimately theological :* that is, that all wars and revolutions and all decisive struggles between parties of men arise from a difference in moral and transcendental doctrine, was utterly novel to me. To a young man the saying was without meaning : I would almost have said nonsensical, save that I could not attach the idea of folly to Manning. But as I grew older it became a searchlight : with the observation of the world, and with continuous reading of history, it came to possess for me a universal meaning so profound that it reached to the very roots of political action ; so extended that it covered the whole.

It is, indeed, a truth which explains and co-ordinates all one reads of human action in the past, and all one sees of it in the present. Men talk of universal peace : it is only obtainable by one common religion. Men say that all tragedy is the conflict of equal rights. They lie. All tragedy is the conflict of a true right and a false right, or of a greater right and a lesser right, or, at the worst, of two false rights. Still more do men pretend in this time of ours, wherein the habitual use of the human intelligence has sunk to its lowest, that doctrine is but a private, individual affair, creating a mere opinion. Upon the contrary, it is doctrine that drives the State ; and every State is stronger in the degree in which the doctrine of its citizens is united. Nor have I met any man in my life, arguing for what should be among men, but took for granted as he argued that the doctrine he consciously or unconsciously accepted was or should be a similar foundation for all mankind. Hence battle.

The truth Dr. Jowett gave me came thus. He asked me the political question which was always uppermost in his mind, and which he believed all young men should consider. It was, " Under what form of government is the state of man at its best ? " I answered as all young men should answer, " A Republic," to which he answered gently in his turn, " You cannot have a Republic without Republicans." Now that, for terseness and truth and a certain quality of *revelation*, was worthy of Aristotle. It is the full answer, historical and moral, to every honest man who desires, as most honest men do, democracy, and who wonders why it is so hard to attain. But I had never considered that answer ; and I think if I had not heard these half dozen words I might never have considered it.

Democracy, that is, the government of the community by the community : a State wherein a man stands equal with his fellows, and has to suffer neither subservience nor the corruption of flattery and power : a State in which office alone commands, and not the being clothed with office—that is the ideal at the back of every man's mind who cares for right in public affairs, and who has within himself anything left of private honour. It is simplest put

by saying that democracy is the noblest form of
government. But the moment you begin to deal
with men, you find in varying degree, according to
the human material handled, a difficulty in the
direction of such an affair. You have experience
of the wickedness and folly of men, and if you add
to such growing experience the vast experience of
history, you find that, save in some few, and those
small, communities, the ideal of democracy must
break down in practice ; and that so far from
enjoying the noblest of social conditions, men
attempting democracy in great States are soon
suffering the basest forms of control by the rich.
That is because most men, though intimately
desiring a republic, are not republicans : when you
have great numbers, those worthy of democracy
are few. In the same way most men, though individually desiring peace within, have not the control
of themselves which makes such peace possible.

So much for the Master's excellent platitude.

It is strange that things worth saying and hearing,
guiding things, should always have that quality of
turning into platitudes, once they are familiar ; for
they were sudden revelations when first they came.
To me now the impracticability of democracy among
men indifferent to honour and justice is so clear
that I never pause to consider it, well knowing that
you cannot have the thing in any modern plutocratic State ; that even in small States it needs a
peculiarly admirable and rare temper in the human
material of them. But this conviction came slowly,
and all started from those few words.

And what has all this to do with the sailing of the
sea ? Nothing, save that it is during the sailing of
the lonely sea that men most consider the nature of
things.

The day broke long before we were anywhere near Fishguard breakwater. We must have done, I suppose, ten or twelve miles by the time it was broad light. Strumble Head kept on flashing, white and inept, under the daylight, and then went out. When it ceased there was no sign of land where it had been. Also the wind had fallen sluggish and we were not making three knots. But such as it was, it was steady ; and by mid-morning we saw all the coast quite plain, and, shortly after, the low black line of the breakwater which they have built out here to make their great artificial harbour of Fishguard. With the wind still falling we drifted rather than ran for the point of it and crawled in out of the wide sea. Even in that last hour, as we came in, we began to note a long heave gradually sweeping up out of the Atlantic through St. George's Channel, as though it had wind behind it ; but since it set north-eastward it did not affect the calm of the broad roads within the breakwater. We very slowly crawled to that inner southern part where boats of our sort could lie without interfering with the steam monsters, and there, after just twenty-four hours of the passage across Cardigan Bay, a run of seventy odd miles, we let go the anchor, and tying up our canvas in a very slovenly fashion we hailed the shore and got a boat to come out, seeing that I had lost my own dinghy during the tempest in Bardsey Sound.

The man who came out to us in the boat hailed us as he approached in the most beautiful English, either because we were now in that so-called " Little England beyond Wales," or else because he was indeed an Englishman, exiled to these parts ; or perhaps again he was bilingual and had acquired this perfect English as a classical and foreign tongue. It was a privilege and an honour to be rowed ashore

by such a man, for he was free of his conversation and
all that he said was interesting, true and well put.
He warned us against the people of the place—why
I do not know. He told us that where we lay was
good holding ground, and he gave us in that little
trip quite a lot of useful information about the
difficult passages between the islands and the mainland on the Points of Pembroke which we had to
pass on our way southward. He asked us as we
landed an astonishingly small payment for his services
and then he promised to meet us again at a fixed
hour to take us aboard. In all things this man was
worthy and a friend, for I could see in his eyes that
he suffered exile.

We came back to him after we had provisioned,
clambered aboard and made ready for one of those
empty days which pass so quickly on board a boat :
hours and hours during which nothing is done,
hours which on shore would exasperate every nerve,
but which here, on the soft movement of the sea, go
past as easily as sleep. For time on the water is
quite different from time on land. It is more
continuous ; it is more part of the breathing of the
world ; less mechanical and divided. There was
not a breath of air, so there was no question of
starting again during all those hours. The great
rollers outside were now at last beginning to affect
the harbour a little and the " Nona," with her too high
topmast, swung rather heavily to the slight movement ; but of wind not a stir. The falling of the
gradual darkness brought on a night brilliant with
stars and no moon. There we lay, sleeping and
waking, smoking, talking a little, vacuous, ready to
put up sail with the first hint of a wind and to get
outside. But all that night until morning again,
the calm continued.

How vast was that haven in the stillness : a mile of ebony water holding the stars and cut off like a lake from the deep by man. How admirable are the great works of man. But greater is God.

In the profound night and the silence I considered that wide space of shelter and the dyke man had made against the Atlantic Power.

For two hours I so pondered upon our strength and our nothingness, worshipping also the night until the stars had changed. Then I went down below and slept. But even with the dawn there came no breeze.

It was about half-past nine in the morning when there did come a draught from the northwards. There was very little of it ; it hardly crisped the oily lumping water of the great haven, but such as it was, we, weary of all this indolence, determined to take advantage of it and to set sail. So we took up the anchor and very slowly lay close to that breath of wind until we came to the breakwater ahead, and there we found the rollers outside large as though they were in the main ocean : so large that when we sank into their troughs there was no headway on the boat and the light air only caught her insufficiently upon the crests. Even as we thus attempted to make some way—lifted hugely up and down in a solemn sport of the sea, now seeing nothing but water astern and ahead and then, immediately after, the whole coast and its heights, and then down into the trough again—the little wind there was entirely failed us. We drifted aimlessly and in all the futility of such motion, up and down over the great swells and there even seemed to be a sort of slight drift ; it was, perhaps, only the set of the swell taking us against our course back eastward and northward.

We took council together and determined that

with the very first breath of air we could find we
would run back to anchor and wait for a wind worth
having. So we did, and a second day passed in
Fishguard harbour, as empty as the first, and a
second night ; and then it was I completed the
tune and first verse of a song called the " Chaunty
of the 'Nona.'" The whole of that time the calm was
broken by but few hints of very uncertain airs.

But just as dawn was beginning upon the third
day, when it was already so light that the sea looked
white against the black land, and before the first
touch of colour had made living the edges of the
inland hills, a heartening wind from those hills, cool
with morning, fresh and heavy, not too strong, a
friendly wind, a wind just suited to our course—for
it was a point or two north of east—blew down from
old Wales upon the sea.

Of this we took an immediate advantage and were
out at once, my companion steering for the breakwater head at a good pace, while I made the anchor
secure forward and then came back and joined him.
We rounded the breakwater, took her well out and
then gybed over with something of a clatter and a
shock and ran down for Strumble, under the growing
day. The great light was still flashing from its
tower, standing on an island off the head, and the
name of that island is Michael. Once we were
round that headland, the wind was fairly on our port
quarter and it was a merry race with a happy off-
shore wind all the way down to St. David's, so that
not only the day but also the old land and the much
older sea and the old boat, that was launched so long
ago, and we ourselves, were for the moment young.
So ran we down for St. David's and there, putting her
nose due south, I, holding the tiller, headed her for
that exceedingly dangerous millrace of a strait

between Ramsey Island and the mainland, called
Ramsey Sound.

It was full ebb. The water roared and thundered
over the rocks inshore for all the world as though we
were not upon the sea at all but upon the lower
reaches of a tidal river. Though we were running
under the lee of the land we were not too much
blanketed, and it was a comfort to feel the strength
of the wind on the boat and to know that one had
full way in such a pass, for these narrow sounds of
the Pembrokeshire coast are perilous to ships and
men. Here, in this very passage, lay two sets of
rocks to the right and to the left, called by the name
of the two perils attendant upon the wealthy young.
For the first set of rocks is called " The Horses "
and the other " The Bitches." These are rocks over
which, I say, the rush of the ebb made a noise like a
weir. We were through it in no time, at a pace
which, had she touched anything, would have been
the end of herself and of all aboard ; but there was
no danger of that because, as I have said, she had
full way upon her and was lively to the helm.
Nevertheless was it a relief to come tearing out of
this perilous corridor into the wholesome width of
St. Bride's Bay beyond.

Now, as I was coming through this ticklish
management of Ramsey Sound, I was too much
taken up with creening below the boom to make out
the water at the rush of the bows and to steer with
precision, I was too much taken up with the business
of exactitude under the strain, to turn to a thing
which, from the land long ago, had puzzled me.
That is the way in which one of the most ancient
roads in Britain comes down here to an open beach
just above the rush and the roar of Ramsey Sound
and stops dead upon the sands. That open beach

is to this day called *Porth Mawr*—"The Great Port." The ancient road here comes along the southern coast of Wales as far as Carmarthen and then branches, one branch coming up Cardigan Bay, which is called, I think, after St. Helena, the mother of Constantine, and the other coming straight along by St. David's. They call these old roads "Roman roads," and so I suppose they were, but still many of them were there in some form before this island entered the comity of Europe, before the Roman unity and order were finally imposed so that England became England.

Anyhow, there was a very old road of the first importance, running down that way and near it stands the see of St. David. Now the interest is this : it comes down to that beach above the narrow roaring river of Ramsey Sound. Why on earth does it strike the sea there ? It is true that antiquity pulled up boats on to the shore and might use the beach as we to-day use a harbour—though in our tidal seas a harbour was always better, I should have thought. But even if they thought the beach better than a harbour (which it manifestly could not be for commerce), why should they call it "The Great Port" ? There it lies on a most impossible bit of coast, leading nowhere and as valueless a landing place as you could get—granted a beach—anywhere in the island. Did the Ancients throw out great breakwaters and thus form a harbour ? That could not be, for surely, had that been done, there would be remains of such mighty work.

I leave it unsolved, as I and all other men must do this and all other problems, with the possible exception of the trisection of the plane angle, which I once all but caught hold of by the tips of my fingers during a long crossing of the Atlantic in a miserable lame steamer, too old for her job, in the year 1897, before the gods had left this broken world.

The "Nona" came therefore grandly out of Ramsey Sound with a sweep and dignified nod into the calm of St. Bride's Bay, but I knew very well that there was before me another trial, more difficult still, called Jack Sound, between Skomer and the mainland, seven miles to the south.

Lord, what a tangle of dangers are here for the wretched mariner ! Rocks and eddies and overfalls and shooting tides ; currents and (as you shall shortly hear) horrible great mists, fogs, vapours, malignant humours of the deep, mirages, false ground, where the anchor will not hold, and foul ground, where the anchor holds for ever, spills of wind off the irregular coast and monstrous gales coming out of the main west sea ; and, most terrible of all, Wild Goose Race.

I will maintain with the Ancients that there are some parts of the sea upon which a God has determined that there shall be peril : that these parts are of their inward nature perilous and that their various particular perils are but portions of one general evil character imposed by The Powers. For you will notice that wherever there is one danger of the seas there are many. If it is an overfall or a race then in that neighbourhood you will also have reefs, unaccountable thick weather, shifting soundings, bad holding and all the rest of it. Witness the western approach to the Isle of Portland, or the Bight of St. Malo, with the Channel Islands and their innumerable teeth ; the entry to the Straits of Messina and other places recorded in histories and in pilot books. Our moderns will have it that such things are chance and an accumulation of them a blind accident, but I hold with those greater men, our

Fathers. Some one here in these places, some early captain, first sailing offended the Gods of the Sea. Hence all the tangle of the southern corner of Wales, Jack Sound and Ramsey Sound and the Bishop and his clerks and, worst of all, Wild Goose Race.

I write without knowledge of the Wild Goose Race. I have never been through it ; neither have you been through death, you who read this. Yet, as we all know that death is a perilous passage and in accordance dread it, so I with the Wild Goose Race, well so named. My book told me that little ships like mine getting into that water were often dismasted and " even foundered." I like that word " even."

It seems that in Wild Goose Race a boat is taken up and pitched to heaven and let drop again, twirled round like a teetotum, thrown over on her side, banged off sideways with great stunning blows upon the cheek-bone and blinded all the time with cataracts of spray, the while the air is filled with a huge mocking laughter. Many races do I know, Portland Race and Alderney Race and Little St. Alban's Race, of which you shall later hear, and the Race round the Skerries of Anglesey, if you may call that a race, and the Race in Bardsey Sound. But there are many races, which, thank heaven, I do not know and which I do not propose to know, such as the Race of Ushant, and the very damnable races of the northern headlands, including that Great Mælstrom of which we hear so much and see so little, and which puts on great airs : but none of these, I am told, is comparable to Wild Goose Race, therefore did I let it alone upon this passage. Do not believe it when you read it in books that a race is made by anything so simple as a tide against a wind or a sudden precipice in the depths of the sea. It is made by the anger of those that rule the sea. And yet of races there is one that has always treated me kindly, and that is the race off the Start. I have been through it I know not how many times and always was the sea there either quite smooth, gentle, purring and domestic ; or an honest running sea, parallel and ordered. But, perhaps, whatever governs the Start Race had received from me without my knowing it, some courtesy. I take this opportunity to thank whatever Powers govern that little corner of the watery world for their kindness.

I have often seen pictures of these Powers, horses and men and women with fishes' tails and scales, and Gods without scales that ride in chariots over the sea. I suppose in that world, or in those circles, the scales are a badge of service, making the link between the immortals and the dumb fishes of the sea ; just as our highbrows make a link between the rich masters who rob the modern world and the millions who work. Only there is this difference, that our highbrows have no scales ; they have nothing in common with the dumb millions who work. But I will not pursue this metaphor lest I should offend Mr. and Mrs. Able, who themselves indeed live in western suburbs but, upon the other hand, are perpetually in the houses of the great.

Where then was I ? Why, coming into the quiet and amplitude of St. Bride's Bay, but having before me the terrors of Jack Sound. For it is true of the sea here as everywhere, that it is the symbol of life, and of our ceaseless duties, and of death. We must never expect long quiet in the business of our living, nor any long security in any passage of the sea. But I must say that this run across St. Bride's Bay was very genial upon that summer noon, only there came with the early afternoon those ominous patches

of an oily look to windward, the falling of the breeze ;
the sea still running, and yet the canvas not always
over well filled : briefly, the renewed menace of a
deadly calm. That calm fell upon us suddenly
enough, just at the moment when we might, with
the last of the ebb, have run through Jack Sound.
It came upon us at the mouth of that forbidden
passage, and left us idle and foolish, pointing anyhow
and seeing, to our despair, the marks upon the
distant shore slowly moving backward as (alas !) we
drifted n rth.

Truly, indeed, did the immortal trio—Swift,
Arbuthnot and Pope—exclaim in chorus : " What
is mortal man but a broomstick ! " Never are we
in half a gale of wind but we pray crapulously for
calm. Never are we in a calm but we whine
peevishly for wind. What, Dog, would you have
the weather cut out for you like a suit of clothes ?
Is all the universe to arrange itself simply to your
convenience, as it does for the very rich—so long
as they keep off the sea ? Will you not be content
with sailing unless just that wind plays which is
exactly trimmed for your miserable barque, neither
too strong nor too light nor too far forward, so that
you have to beat, nor so far aft that you fear a gybe,
or pooping from a running sea ? Will you never
repose in the will of your Maker and take things
as they come ? Why then drift round Skomer like
a fool !

Which, indeed, was what the " Nona" did, for as
it fell dead calm, the set of the sea took her in the
most amusing unaccountable way on a jolly little
voyage of exploration. The sea took charge. The
tiller was not worth holding, the helm swung idle, and
the canvas hung like the flabby muscles on the face
of an Opposition leader towards the end of the third

hour of a speech from the Front Bench to which he has had to listen, sorely against his will. It hung loose and inept, like the hands of a poor man, waiting orders in the presence of a rich man, or, like the mind of a sceptic, when he considers the ultimate nature of good and evil—let alone beauty. The sea took charge and trolled the little boat along, keeping her just so far from the shore, as who should say, " See, my child, how remarkable is the Island of Skomer ! Come with me, I will show you every cranny of its outer shore." So were we taken off round Skomer by the tide in that calm, further and further from Jack Sound.

When they had played this farce with us long enough, the Powers halted the sea, as is their fashion every six hours, and we found ourselves close aboard a large ketch which lay at anchor off that Skomer shore. There was one man upon the deck, smoking a pipe and keeping his mind empty, as is the duty of all mortals in such few intervals of leisure as heaven affords us. He bade us not knock into him, and we called out to him (but not very loud, for we were at a familiar cast of but few yards) that if we came too close aboard we would shove off and do him no harm. We asked him who he was and where he was going. He did not tell us who he was, but he told us where he was going, which was to Cork, and what he had on board, which was a cargo of coal.

The lazy sun, halfway down the sky, looked indifferently upon us ; the quite smooth sea turned again in its perpetual come and go, and took us slowly back in so many hours, till we found ourselves again by evening where we had started, at the mouth of Jack Sound. What this current or tide movement was which had thus taken us nearly round Skomer and back again, I know not, but it was a journey that cost nothing, and, tedious as it was, we had at least learned another few miles of shore. It seemed, however, all of a set purpose, for the wind now blew again lightly but steadily from the north-east. The ebb was well on its way, and we could point through Jack Sound, and hope to be in Milford Haven, round St. Anne's Head before the late darkness of this day in early June.

So did we enter that passage.

Jack Sound in that evening light was a repetition of Ramsey, only more violent, for we were more in the full roar of the ebb. There was the same rush as of a millrace, the same cataracts of falling water over the landward rocks. We came out of it with the setting sun glorious upon our starboard quarter, and ran quickly for the end of Skokholm—another Scandinavian name—sure (in that steady breeze) of rounding St. Anne's Head easily before darkness, and dropping anchor in some cove of Milford Haven.

But nothing is ever certain at sea. We were, perhaps, a mile from the Head when there rolled up with astonishing rapidity from out the main ocean a solid bank of cloud, sweeping the level of the sea. I say cloud rather than fog, because it was so solid and so dark. It caught us like a cloak thrown over a man's head ; and, before we knew where we were, we found ourselves steering hopelessly by the card, not daring to keep too much out, lest we should lose the mouth of the haven ; not daring to keep too much in, lest we should strike : and nothing to prevent that but listening anxiously to the great fog-blast, which was now hooting regularly in its panic from the height of the headland.

What followed for nearly two hours was such an adventure as only wretched amateurs would indulge in, and amateurs in a craft which did not draw more than six feet of water. The wind, such as it was, had dropped, of course, with the fog. It gave us only enough way to creep eastward before it ; and what we proposed to do was so to feel our way in the fading light through that dense mist until we should hear the slight surge of water upon the rocks of the haven mouth to port, that is, on the north side of the haven entry. I had a large plan aboard, and I knew that there was water close up to the shore, and that it was plain enough going, with nothing hidden beneath the surface. So we gingerly put her head slightly round, when we made out the mournful menace of the fog-horn to have come just aft of the beam ; my companion took the helm, and I went forward with the lead, and also to call out to him to put the helm up whenever that might be made necessary by our getting too close. We faintly heard already the slight wash of the gently heaving water, and I saw, some few yards off the bow, little gleams of white through the mist, which were the foam sliding from the rock surfaces, as we slipped by. The "Nona's" movement was so very slight that even if she had struck a glancing blow, nothing that was not jagged would have harmed her greatly ; but we were preserved and did not touch.

We had this further good fortune, that, just as it grew quite dark, the sound of the slight surge to leeward receded and disappeared so that we knew we had turned the headland and opened the first bay of that long inland arm of the sea. Our chart showed us good depth and good holding ground, and a good berth for the night granted that there should be no other craft about. We heard none such through the fog ; no voices, no swinging spars, no movement at all. So when we had got well into the bight, we dropped anchor ; trusting to luck that, as she swung to her chain, she would not strike shoal ground nor anything near. Had we still had the dinghy I would have gone out and explored, and made certain and risked my chance of getting back aboard through the mist, but, having no dinghy, we had to take things as they were, and these seemed secure enough, for we were well out of the fairway. The first of the night was interrupted by that perpetual call of the great horn upon the headland, but before midnight the fog lifted, the sound ceased, and a profound silence fell upon the sea and the land. We had also the comfort of seeing that we had plenty of room to swing, with the shore perhaps a quarter of a mile away.

That night as I fell asleep I designed the second and third verses of the " Chaunty of the ' Nona.' "

The next morning we found, following the flood up the Haven, a very slight breeze from the west and north, not enough to allow us to beat up against the current ; so we passed the time till the beginning of the ebb, or rather till the flood should slacken, sailing slowly up that long fiord, Milford Haven, of which one reads so much in history, but which to-day, having no industrial hinterland, has half dropped out of men's memories. Two evils of the past are rooted in its landscape, for it was here that the first Tudor claimant, " the foul usurper, Henry Tydder," landed with his French mercenaries to try for the Crown, which he grasped in two weeks on Bosworth Field. And it was hence that the transports sailed for the Puritan orgy of lust, loot and massacre in Ireland under Cromwell's leadership. I wondered as I cruised about, watching the shores and the little town near by, what further fate Milford Haven might hold for England. Things go by threes—especially evils—what will the third curse arising from this inlet be ?

The wind freshened just as the flood was slackening, so we turned to beat out. It was well into the afternoon when we took the open sea, with the wind a trifle north of west, so that our last board out of harbour was a free run. We took her well outside so as to be able to set a straight course for Lundy and beyond, intending a passage to Bideford River, and the ending of this voyage.

The wind dropping somewhat, it was evening before we had well passed St. Goven's lightship, and all that night we went quietly over the seas with a gentle following wind until, before morning, we raised Lundy Light full and clear. But the wind failed us at dawn, falling first to irregular puffs, and at last, when we were about a mile and a half north-east of the island and pointing right for Appledore bar, it fell off altogether. Little patches of slightly-ruffled water, here and there, fewer and more distant one from the other, at last faded out to nothingness ; and we lay helpless, hardly moving, until the set of some slight current drew us half a mile further on into that strange piece of water called the Great White Horse Race.

What this may be in heavy weather or even in a strong breeze I cannot tell, for I have never been through it before or since. As things were, in that dead calm, it was a perpetual succession of fairly even, long, smooth, watery hills, with troughs astonishingly deep and rounded crests astonishingly high for a morning without wind. There was no way at all on the " Nona " ; she lay buoyant enough, but like a log ; broadside on and rolling damnably for hour after hour ; shaking her spars with every lie-over, as though to so many hammer blows.

Throwing the boom with a bang, although I had made it as fast as I could, and giving a violent jerk at the mainsheet each time she ended a swing. It was a miserable ten hours or so that we endured, gazing at Lundy from the top of each passing heave, and drifting there paralysed under the useless sky.

Lundy is one of those neat things which you get now and then in Nature, and which look as though they had been specially designed on a rather careful plan with one simple object. One would think Lundy could do no harm—yet I always remember the " Montague."

It is so placed that it gives shelter in any weather. It is a sort of little breakwater set up in the midst of the Bristol Channel, offering security to all craft, coming up or down ; for there is good holding ground everywhere about, and you can lie under the lee of the land whichever way it may be blowing. The only drawback of the neighbourhood for small craft is this same White Horse Race, in which we had been caught by the calm. Even in that oily weather, its great swells passed us halfway to the height of our jaws, and our topmast, excessive for the little craft, made her roll all the worse, while the motion was so jerky that at times I feared for the fastenings of the shrouds at the sides. But a larger craft would think nothing of this patch of sea and, save for it, all the water round Lundy is exactly made for security.

I have never landed on the island. I have heard many legends about it, none of which I repeat for fear that they are false. But what I should most like to know (only I have never met any one who could tell me) is whether the pleasure of isolation which these places afford increases with the years, or at last becomes intolerable ? I knew a man once

who, during all the latter part of his life, was torn
between the desire of possessing an island, and his
fear lest, once he had bought it, he should find that
he had purchased misfortune. All his friends told
him that islands were like those legendary objects
of bad luck which one man has to pass on to another
and which each new holder soon finds unendurable.
To be king of one's own land, to be quite cut off
from the complexity and futilities of the world, to
have a little country all of one's own, neatly bounded,
inaccessible if one chooses to make it so—that is
enough to tempt any one who has lived among men.
But I am assured by many who have not themselves
tried it, that after a very short experience in such
things one has no desire but to be rid of them. A
community might find it endurable enough and,
indeed, religious communities have often found it so ;
but not individuals, nor one family. Lundy, however, is larger than most, and perhaps the sense of
isolation is less.

When we had lain tossing in the White Horse
Race all through that morning and on to well past
noon, there came to our great joy, about half-past
one, a little breath, a little slant of wind, from off
Hartland Point. For all those hours we had had
no steering way at all, merely drifting and tossing
to the loud clapping of empty canvas. But now
the sails filled and, weary of the sea, we put her nose
round for Bideford River, with this pleasant little
breeze slightly blowing and coming right from the
starboard quarter, so that she sailed at her best.
The tide was at the neaps, there was little current,
we had a straight course to steer.

The wind rose, the sun was clear and shining, and
all the sea sparkled and was alive. It was a weather
in which to remember the little sacred places of the

shore ; the little towns with their own gods of the
sea, and springs tumbling through them from the
cliffs above : the little places that preserve their own
happenings. And one such place of which I had
very often heard was there, far off upon the starboard
quarter, and I knew it by the chart for Clovelly.

There are places holy to Apollo, Delian places,
protected tiny townships of the sea.

So from the tumbling water between Bideford
River and Lundy, that wooded coast, so isolated,
remote, sacred, appeared the touch of white in the
green which marked Clovelly. So looking on it
thus over the water that rushed by, and in the swirl
of the ship's way, Clovelly seemed what I had read in
books as a boy it was, and what I suppose it once
may have been, when England was England.

But England to-day from the land is a very
different thing to England forever from the sea.
Some years later I had again to seek Clovelly from
the land, and I shall no more forget it than did that
Northumbrian man whom God raised from the dead,
and whose experience is told us by the Venerable
Bede, could forget his glimpse of Hell.

I had come with friends in a motor-car, because
I had been told a man should see Clovelly before he
died. I had come from the noble isolation of
Hartland, where the great seas were running in
upon the rocks after a gale and thundering at the
doors of that good inn which faces ocean there. Our
road ran high above the sea, and as we came near
to the turning beyond which the cleft of Clovelly
would open below us, and its vision of peace, we
heard a murmur like that of bees swarming. As we
came nearer it was a confused clamour of human
beings, and as we came nearer still we saw the
dreadful thing in its entirety.

A great mass of chars-à-bancs were parked on the road itself, on the steep edge of the hill and cleft whence one looked down on the village and the sea below. There, blocking the ridge road, an immense mass of lost souls struggled and fought for the most part, or stood squeezed in a sullen despair. Their function was—not their intention, but the use to which the irony of Divine Vengeance had put them—their function was to form a solid wall by which all access from the village below, all further opportunity of climbing, should be forbidden. Meanwhile up that cleft swirled, surged, pushed, strenuously and unfailingly, one mass of packed, dark-clothed mortality, closely hemmed in by the cottages (I wondered that their walls stood the strain !), and looking from where we stood very much like black pressed German caviare, the acid stuff which is sold for the destruction of the race. This wedge had its base upon the seashore and was filled with a communal desire, with a mass mind, impelling it to attempt the height—a hopeless task ! For the char-à-banc crowd above could not have been pierced by cavalry let alone by an untrained infantry such as was this mob working hopelessly uphill.

So far so bad ; but worse remained behind. For on the calm sea of that bay were to be discovered three steamers, each of them looking like a piece of cigar-shaped board on which innumerable black ants had swarmed. Of these the one nearest to the shore was still discharging in its boats further human beings, who were fighting to land on whatever little strip of foothold could be found, while the two other ships stood by ready to re-enforce the attack.

So true is it that men desire beauty before all things and that great beauty draws all men to it.

The atheists, of whom some few stalwarts remain, strong against the pantheist flood ; those who despise mankind when they are healthy and when they are unhealthy despair of it ; the men who make nothing of life and think it immaterial whether man be or no—these are, in my judgment, of a clumsy habit in argument. For they talk in mere negations. But if they would breed (as is their intention) a proper contempt for the supposed Divine in man, a proper negligence of our fellow-beings and a right view of the whole insignificant human affair, they ought not to confine themselves to negatives, they ought to present vivid images, concrete and striking and say : " Look there and judge mankind ! " I suggest to them Clovelly on a holiday ; also the sands of Weston-super-Mare ; also St. Lazare Station in Paris ; the Frederick Street Station in Berlin, or Liverpool Street in London, just after office hours on a week-day. Or again, a crowd in Catalonia, outside the ring, when by some accident the bull gets loose.

There are other brilliant images all ready to the atheist's hand : a dining table of the rich, with some thirty guests, men and women, exactly alternate, like the red and the black cards in a patience, the wretched couples turning ten minutes to the left and ten minutes to the right, like jacks ; the wine of only one kind—yellow and acid with bubbles in it. Or again, they might give the same effect with the vision of any public vehicle, designed to hold twenty-four but packed with forty. Or again, they might do no more than distribute snapshots, judiciously snapped, of the men who are most talked about in this our day.

The truth is the atheists do not know their job ; for it has been clearly proved upon the thumb and the four fingers of the left hand that men cut off from the Divine are also cut off from reason.

So we sailed on, leaving that tiny white point of Clovelly far behind in its combe, dark against the afternoon sun, and ran straight for Bideford River, till we came to the fairway.

We had also a mark to steer by which was unmistakable ; it was a gate of dark smooth water in a mass of white surge. For rollers, though there was but a hearty breeze, through some mysterious process of the sea were bursting with violence upon the bar of the river as though it blew a gale. The bar looked like one tumbling wall of angry white, even from a long way off, and, between that wall and the east side of the harbour mouth, was this one narrow gateway of smooth water. We passed through it safely enough, steering by the leading marks, which are here quite clear, and brought up in the deep pool off Appledore, waiting for the tide to take us up to Bideford.

All that bit of coast is Charles Kingsley, with his violent fanatical genius (for it was no less) and his power of imprinting himself upon the place. Fanatical men are not usually happy; but I think Kingsley must have been happy, because he had the tide under him all the time. Everything in his own lifetime was going his way. The cause to which he was attached, the destruction of the Faith, appeared to be triumphing more and more ; though the slightest accident the other way (such as Newman's conversion) was an intolerable irritant to him. He lived in that part of the earth which he most loved, he enjoyed all its habits, he was supported by everything around. You could get no better and, at the same time, no more comic criticism of that Kingsleian mood than what has happed to the name

"Westward Ho," which Kingsley rendered famous. " Westward Ho " simply means the westerly of two landing places. Ho, or Hoe, is a wharf : but that " Ho " has been spread broadcast throughout the world of English as a sort of " Halloa," or " Yoicks," to call the adventurous overseas ; and not one man in a thousand, I suppose, but thinks of those two little letters as a hoot (perhaps he gives them a nobler name) ; as a call, resonant of the Elizabethan sailings.

One of the saddest things I know about the beach near Bideford River is the deadly hatred with which the Dons have persecuted poor, dear Kenwith. Kenwith is a place where a few boatloads of Danes landed in the Dark Ages, and were defeated by the English. The name is quite clear, the tradition is equally clear, and the description of the position is unmistakable. Therefore have the learned, as is their wont, insisted with the utmost virulence that the tradition, the name, the description, are all a popular error, and that the place where the little scrimmage really came off was miles away.

It is interesting to analyse the motives of this sort of thing. We are all familiar with it. The universities of all countries, but especially of our own, are a regular hothouse for breeding it ; but when one first comes across it, one is puzzled why it should come into being at all. Whence springs this lust for saying that the Gospel of St. John was not written by St. John ? That Homer was not written by Homer ? That the Battle of Hastings was not called the Battle of Hastings—although all the people who fought there called it the Battle of Hastings ? That William the Conqueror only had a handful of men there—though his secretary, who saw them, and read all the documents connected

with them, gives us fifty thousand ? That Julius
Cæsar's Gallic War was written by his tutor—and
all the rest of the nonsense ?

The powerful force urging Dons to make fools of
themselves in this way seems to me to come from a
convergence of three currents. First of all there is
the vanity of the learned man, who has all the better
opportunities for action because few have any knowledge at all of the matter, and he is fairly safe from
criticism—or thinks himself so. His fellows will
not give him away. It is clearly a flattering thing
to think that one is right where all the world has been
wrong, and, in a time like ours, when there has been
accumulated such a mass of special technical knowledge, people are ready to swallow almost any assertion, because they know not what new evidence
may have appeared.

The second source is that very human thing, the
love of the marvellous—though it is the love of the
marvellous appearing in a very degraded form.
Your pedant says : " All the apparent evidence, all
tradition, all that you would call common sense,
would make out Little Muddipool to be that same
Little Muddipool where the treaty of Little Muddipool was signed. It is called in plain words ' The
Treaty of Little Muddipool,' and its last words are
' Made by us at Little Muddipool.' But *I* tell you
that it was not Little Muddipool at all, but a place a
hundred miles away with a different name. ' The
spirit at work there is exactly the same spirit as that
which says : " Common sense and your own
experience will tell you that the bishop must have
crossed the river either by a bridge or by a boat. *I*
tell you that the holy man sailed across it on his coat.
What do you think of that ? "

And the third cause is a negative one. The

perpetual substitution of hypothesis for fact (which is the great mark of Dons to-day) ends by getting men into a state of mind where they can no longer weigh the proportions of evidence : they can no longer distinguish between the certain, the probable and the absurd. Thus, it was but a little time ago that an Oxford Don came out with a miracle. He said he had discovered any number of classical passages containing concealed anagrams, furnishing the most astonishing information ; for instance, that Euripides, when he was a little boy, wrote the plays of Æschylus. A stopper was put on him, however, by a man, who wrote to the *Spectator* (of all papers), proving that the said Don's name was but thinly concealed in an anagram of the opening lines of the " Iliad," so that he must have written that excellent poem, not when he was a little boy, but long before he was born—and so much for that.

Another pleasing thing about Bideford River is the startling contrast between Appledore, on the business side of the harbour over against the sea, and Instow, all so genteel upon the further shore : Appledore frankly a lair, and Instow a desirable resort. Appledore for beer, Instow for wine ; and the English talked in the one almost incomprehensible to the other. I have sometimes thought that whenever the foundations of society shall be shaken, the strong men of Appledore will sail across (you can almost walk it at low tide but for one thin channel) and storm and loot Instow. Pretty well every modern set of human habitations has this contrast of rich and poor quarters, but when there is water flowing in between them it is the more striking : with hard work on one side of the stream and the fruits of it in leisure upon the other.

My voyage was over. I had brought up in
Bideford River before the long bridge of Bideford,
and I made all quiet for the night, and for a long time
to come. For there would I leave the " Nona " in
charge, till I could take her out again.

Swaying in the cabin that night also, I finished
writing the " Chaunty of the ' Nona,' " of which if
any man say that it is a vile piece of verse, I am ready
to agree with him, but if another man say that it
heartens him, and fills him with the sea, why, I am
ready to agree with him also. It is all one. Bideford River is the end of my passage and a place of
rest. We come to death at last, as is our due, and
we come into port out of the sea, and all things reach
their end.

I have always thought it a very ridiculous thing
to bother too much, after thirty, over literary fame :
if it comes, let it come, but for God's sake let us have
no publicity with it, for to be pointed at and known
is to live in a glass cage. And very much do I
applaud those men who do what in youth I myself
desired to do, but was unable to do, that is, to write
consistently under a false name, and carefully cover
one's tracks. I wanted to write verse under one
name, history under another, travel under another—
but fate was too strong.

Of the men who have done this in my time the
most successful was Dodgson, the mathematical Don
at Christ Church—that is, of The House. He had
calculated well ; and the immense fame of Lewis
Carroll and of " Alice in Wonderland " left him
private and secure.

Mention of that book also makes me consider how
false is nearly all literary fame, or, rather, how great
an element of falsity there is in nearly all such
fame. " Alice in Wonderland " is a very remark-

able book, as are, indeed, other books of Dodgson's, though not all. But a large element in its vast diffusion was its consonance with a particular "drawing-room" mood of a particular day. I shall be called blasphemous, I know, but I am perfectly certain that Alice will not long survive the ease and unquestioned security of the England of her day. For every implication in morals, and even in humour, with which Dodgson's books are crammed sprang from that security and that ease. Nor is there a stronger symptom of so abnormal a passage in human affairs as was the English gentry's generation of 1833–1899 (abnormal, for normal men live under a strain and a peril, and in active defence against the barbarian or the menacing enemy) than the delight of Dodgson's vast audience in nonsense : in the humour which is founded upon folly as contrasted with the wit that is founded upon wisdom. Even the facile composition of odd childish words, which had a slightly reminiscent sound, was sufficient to delight that generation. But when the terrors and the heroisms permanently return the sawdust will run out of such things.

And, after all, what is the possession of literary fame ? Can dead men use it ? Does any man possessing it, unless he be asinine in his vanity, think himself the true creator of some really high line his pen has happened to set down ? Is there any writing man with a true judgment of great things in writing who does not doubt his own achievement ? Or is there any who, when some particular piece of verse or rhetoric whch he has written convinces him of its merit, does not admit to his own soul that not *he* was the true author, but rather some force working through him ?

Again, does not any writer who is also reasonably manly prefer any one of man's virtues to an accident of verse or prose? Who with stuff in him would not rather be a brave boor than a cowardly poet?

So much for literary gents. Excluding my own self, I should like to see them all driven aboard an immense barge, and the same towed out to sea and there scuttled. Their absurd little quarrels, their posings, their insufficiency, the chaos of their minds— all these things are a burden, and there is not one day's riding upon a horse or sailing upon the sea (let alone still better things which, for the honour I bear you, I will not mention here) that is not worth the whole tonnage and shiploads of their printed stuff, save here and there a piece of lyric verse, or here and there a good run and rhythm in half a page of prose.

But, I say again, that's all one. Here am I in Bideford River, at anchor and come to the end of the seas, leaving her, the "Nona," my companion and my home, my very loyal boat, under the tutelage of the long bridge of Bideford, which is notoriously the end of the world.

.   .   .   .

Now a day came when I had some freedom again. So I set out at once from Devon with one companion, and finding all on board as I had left it, I set sail to leave Bideford River. I proposed to myself to explore the outer sea beyond Hartland, which till then I had not seen, though now I know its character and its harbours familiarly enough.

The tide so served that it was evening when I set out, nor was it easy to shoot the channel at the bar of Appledore, in spite of the strong ebb, because such slight wind as there was had too much north in it.

For the same reason we had to beat all that night,
fetching up towards Hartland Point in two long
boards ; helped at first by the tide, but later, of
course, finding it against us. It was daylight again
before we came to the headland, and opened the
coast beyond.

The Ancients made a solemn and special sanctity,
it seems, of this barrenness and strength and height
of Hartland. The Romans called it the Point of
Hercules. They felt, I think, that when they
rounded it, they were coming into another sea ; for
they were much alive to the mystery of things. If
they thought this of Hartland, that it was a boundary,
they were right. Within Hartland, you are under
the wing of England, and in homely water ; outside
Hartland, you have all the West before you, and the
power of Ocean. And so with us that morning.
Even as the wind died down there came a mighty
succession of slow heavings, which grew more
regular and defined until at last the smooth water,
just crisped here and there, by mere breaths of air,
ran in giant folds—parallel, regular, unceasing,
enormous. All that sea, I say, is odd, and I have
felt spells upon it.

The long rollers came prodigious out of the south-
west under almost a calm. There was not wind
enough to do more than give the boat steerage-way
—it was lucky we had that, for if it had been a dead
calm she would have rolled broadside on and shaken
herself badly with that too-tall topmast of hers, as
she had done on an earlier day in the White Horse
Race. The rollers came on and on ; not the relic
of a gale (for there had been none anywhere), but
raised by one of those innumerable mysterious
influences which between them make the sea. They
lifted one after the other, hiding the horizon ; we

topped them, we sank into the trough ; they heaved majestically on, to thunder upon the savage grandeur of Hartland.

Our time has discovered so many things in the material world (and has grown paralysed to so many other more important things) that we profess to explain everything with perfect links of cause and effect. It is an occasion to use the phrase " We miserable sinners." For we shall never know anything at all compared with the unknown. What makes such waves ?

For that matter, why is one sea so different from another ? You measure the amount of salt, the weight of the water, the strength of the wind. Though you had all the factors we can measure, these three and a score of others (the pressure of the air, its wetness, its heat, and so on), yet you could never say why the difference between one sea and another appears. All measurable factors might be the same, and yet the seas quite different. You can, indeed, hardly describe that difference any more than you can describe the difference between two instruments of music, the flute and the trumpet ; or the difference between two materials in portraiture, marble and bronze. We only know that it is there. But our stupidly proud time misses such essential categories.

Why is it that what they call " The New World " is something utterly different in quality, taste, intimate soul, from the old ? We have here not only the conflict between England and America, but between Spain and the Argentine, and between England herself and the white colonies, and between the French and the French Canadians. It is not newness ; it is not lack of tradition ; it is difference of *timbre*—as violent as the difference between a railway whistle and the note of a thrush, or between wood and iron.

Modern men knowing a dozen out of a million causes reason downwards from the rules they have, instead of trusting their perceptions as their fathers did.

I take it that the great differentiations in human history proceed from these uncharted depths of cause, and that one civilisation splits apart from another through stirrings in the very root of the soul. Meanwhile, men prophecy and the future makes fools of them.

The great administrators of wholly foreign lands are men who have not pretended to understand these differences, or to combat them, still less to suppress them. They are men who have recognised the alien blood and, as it were, entered into it. That is government ; that is Empire : to get into the shoes of the governed.

In the strange, successful, perhaps ephemeral, adventure which has put our high European culture in command over the lives of others in the East and in Africa, not a few men have arisen, tested by circumstance and conforming to this idea. I have heard with respect the judgment of others upon half a dozen Englishmen, Scotsmen, Irishmen of the sort, though I have not seen their work. Russians have told me of compatriots of their own who have achieved such things beyond the Urals and the Caspian. Of Germans I never heard that any were so much as capable of beginning the great task. That the Spaniards changed half a continent we know. But the only instance that ever came under my own eyes, and that but for a few days, was the instance of Marshal Lyautey. Lyautey's Morocco is an astonishing affair.

It is true that there lay behind his great achievement more than a lifetime of foundation—the steady French transformation of North Africa. It is like a coral reef, solid, detailed, infinitely particular : the work of innumerable units, sacrificed, obscure, tenacious, creative, permanent. None the less, what Lyautey has done is a building by itself. It is like the new gothic of Brazenose or Magdalen at Oxford : one may say that there lay behind this also the multitudinous, patient work of a lifetime or more since Pugin began : or it is like Parsons' turbine, which came after so much experiment, but stands by itself all the same.

It is not belittling Lyautey's great work in Morocco to say that these things are only possible when there is frankly recognised the essential principle of personal responsibility in governing ; or (to put it in Colonial phrasing), "One-man control," or, to put it in Aristotelian terms, " MONARCHY."

There is no other working form of administration over multitudes of men, except the Aristocratic ; and the Aristocratic form of administration—which ruled for nearly three hundred years over Protestant England after the Reformation had destroyed Popular Monarchy and made wealth supreme—is only possible in those rare communities where men enjoy being governed by a clique and look up to, and revere, a special class whom they think of as their natural masters.

What Marshal Lyautey has done in the organisation of French Morocco has been based upon two foundations which, when they are absent from the effort to govern aliens—as one or both commonly are—make such government increasingly difficult ; until, at last, it has to be abandoned. The first of these foundations is *working with* the alien people whom one administrates, not *against* them, nor even *above* them. The second foundation is the deliberate investment of one's own capital and energy *for the benefit of the alien governed* rather than for one's own benefit : that is, the development of communications and of building, the extension of instruction, the improvement of waterways, afforestation—all manner of expensive functions which you can only get from a government directly concerned for the good of *all* the people and which will never be undertaken by the private home trader working for his pocket alone.

It is the absence of this sympathy with, and eager help of, the governed which prevents a trading community from ever biting into alien soil. For, in a trading community, the administration of a foreign dependency is directed to helping the home merchant or settler. The road is driven, the river is bridged, not primarily for the benefit of the governed, but primarily for the immediate profit of the governors. With this there goes a contempt of the governed, which is a dangerous sign, and later, that more dangerous sign, a hatred of them.

The foreign rule, therefore, gets more and more distasteful to the governed. For half a lifetime they wonder at it : then they grow restive, finding themselves despised to no purpose. Then they permanently rebel. At last the unnatural tyranny breaks down. When it breaks down the governors gradually depart and little impress of their foreign rule remains.

It was so apparently between Carthage and her dependencies.

But when the governors expend themselves for the good of the governed, an amalgamation takes place between the national spirit of the one and of the

other, and the superior trains and shepherds his
subject into a common civilisation. One of the
tests of success in alien government is to note
whether the governors despise or admire the
governed. If they despise them it is proof that they
are unfit to govern. If they admire in them what is
to be admired, all goes well. I found in Morocco
that a contempt for Islam (I do not say a difference
from Islam, but a *contempt* for it, a contempt which
would regard the Moor as a " native " and the
French as in some way a " superior race ") was only
to be discovered here and there among the worst of
the colonists. It was your half-educated, lower
middle-class immigrant who took this attitude and
gave all the trouble. The higher you went in the
scale, the greater was the liking for the Moor and
for his civilisation, the greater the desire to understand him and to know his past, the greater the
admiration of his art, his dignity, his faith. When
one got to the head of things, in the Residency-
General and in the Marshal's own household, there
was an understanding of the whole Moorish past
and present like the understanding which a scholar
has of his beloved text ; it was an intimate and all-
pervading familiarity.

I carried away with me from that glimpse of the
Atlas and of the treeless run of burnt land beyond
(for I travelled while the heat was still upon us)
vivid pictures in the mind. First of a vast tract of
dead upland, utterly bare, between Oudja and the
Moulouya (I had come from Oran). This tract
had about it the accursed inhuman effect of the
great American deserts in the west of the United
States : then, next in order, of Taza on the edge
of the hill fighting, and of the story I was told
there of two Moorish brothers. One of these would

fight under the French for six months and then desert. Thereupon the other brother would enlist in his place. So much was the object of each the pleasure of fighting and the advantage of pay, and so little the political idea of independence.

Nor could any one forget who has seen it (and it is now become or will soon become, a commonplace of travel) that great new road which I saw in its last making, but which was already nearly completed. It is driven right through Barbary like a stay, like a backbone, from the Bay of Carthage to the river mouth of Rabat on the Atlantic tide ; near one thousand miles in its actual trace, and following the great ride which the first Mohammedans took when they overwhelmed the west—when that horseman rode into the sea surf on the sands by the bar of Rabat River and cried out : " Had you not set bounds, O God, to the earth, with this your sea, I would ride for ever westward and continue to conquer in Your Name." A man may take his motor car on the boat to-day from Marseilles to Tunis and follow that strict and graded broad way uninterruptedly till he comes to the Atlantic and, turning south to Casablanca, ship it again for Europe.

The surprise of that Moroccan feat was the way in which it was handled during the Great War. When war was already certain in the last days of July, 1914, the Government in Paris, the politicians, sent orders to the Resident-General that all troops should be withdrawn to the coast, the interior to be abandoned, and reconquest (if possible !) to be achieved after the Peace. We who know what those words " after the Peace " have come to mean, know also that it would have been the end of the French in Morocco. It would have been the return to the old

pressure upon the Algerian frontier and evidence to
all Islam that Europe had failed.

What the soldier did was to maintain his garrisons
in spite of the politicians. What was astonishing, he continued the development of Morocco
during all those four years of mortal strain, as though
the peace had not been broken. Still was the railway laid, and still the new road completed, and still
were the buildings set up, and still was the wild hill
country contained by its ring of troops ; until, when
the curtain lifted in '19, Europe saw, not the
Morocco there had been when the Occident entered
on its great struggle, but another Morocco, wealthier,
stronger and more settled, with great new European
towns side by side with the Moslem, and with the
whole territory organised.

These new great towns are planned and are built
under a military rule—and that is very wise, for the
anarchy of individual mercantile effort would have
made the experiment break down. No house may
be built in the European fashion to jar against the
spirit of the place. Everywhere the roofs must be
flat and the outline preserved. Also the European
town is kept wholly distinct from the Mohammedan.
Thus in Meknes you may hear Mass in a chapel
which lies within the very thickness of the city wall
—it is the old chapel of the Portuguese prisoners
during the past of the great Sultans—but you may
not enter that chapel from *within* the city ; the door
faces outward, upon the country side of the wall.
Upon the day before I left Morocco, a soldier who
was driving me upon the heights above one of the
new cities in his car, said to me musingly, as we had
halted to look down upon the view of mixed Europe
and Africa and of all that vast new wealth : " It
is just ten years ago that the Sultan of the day,

annoyed with his brother, had him devoured by lions." Those who love contrast will not find it stronger anywhere than in this strange land.

But these distant memories of Morocco go ill with the presence of a Devon sea under the breaking of a chill dawn. Those African pictures in my mind, hot sand and palm, painted by memory in the night, grew pale and disappeared in the northern daylight, as do the coloured flashes of the headland lights with the coming of the day.

There was still no more wind than would just make the "Nona" feel her helm. My companion slept below. The heave of the sea grew less ; and then, to my disgust and dread, over the sea, already too hazy (so that the high land some three miles away was like a ghost), a fog came drifting up and enveloped us altogether.

I put her up a point more westerly, so as to be on the safe side, for I did not know what current there might be here, and I had to give the land a good offing. I did not want to come up through the fog in such calm weather to hear, close at hand, the treacherous murmur of slightly moving water upon rocks.

Of all experiences at sea in a small boat, under sail, there is none in these days of steam and petrol more trying (after a certain length of it) than being thus half-becalmed with barely steering way in a part of the sea where the great ships ply up and down, they themselves independent of the stillness that holds you fast. You can hear (as I did on that morning) the beat of the propellers, miles away or close at hand. You hear the hooting from time to time of a ship's siren—but there is nothing to tell you where your danger may be, nor upon what line it may be approaching you. Some with more

experience could, perhaps, have judged that these
occasional sounds were at such and such a distance,
each or none of them threatening ; but to me it
seemed as though every steamer in the Bristol
Channel was atop of us. I have no doubt that had
the fog lifted I should have had nothing in sight
but a couple of outward bound tramps halfway to
the horizon, and perhaps one small steamer in from
the Atlantic seas, and going up to Avonmouth,
rather nearer to our shore, so as to save the strength
of the tide. Indeed, when the fog did lift towards
noon, the sea was of that appearance, with not half
a dozen craft to be seen, and none near. But in the
white, cold blankness of the mist (with nothing
whereby to judge save the ear), the rhythmic beating
of the blades seemed anywhere close at hand; and
if the hooting of the steam whistles was dull and
dim, that seemed due not to distance, but to the
blanketing of the dense cloud. It rose at last, first
in patches and wreaths, then altogether, and a pale
sun showed over distant land.

There is one thing that has always puzzled me
about the Devon and Cornwall peninsula, and that
is why the entry into it, up to quite late in history,
seems to have been from the north.

The deep harbours and secure anchorages are
to-day on the south. There is a whole string of
them ; and it is the south that faces towards the
main civilisation of the continent. You have the
profound inlet of Falmouth, you have Fowey, you
have the miles of inland water at Plymouth, you
have the Yealm and Salcombe, and the Dart and
Teignmouth. Yet the legends, and even the
history of Dumnonia are more concerned with
such shallow, small and difficult places as St. Ives,
Padstow and Bideford River. The wealth seems

to have been more on the north than upon the south, for you will note that the pirate raids principally struck there, and the shrines also, the ancient shrines, are rather on the north than on the south ; and on the north also is Tintagel, of which it was said by Tristram : "Blessed be Tintagel and all that dwell therein." The relics of the saints were established in the northern harbours. The seats of government were on the north : there, in the north, is the story of Arthur ; and when Cornwall communicates with Brittany in the early Dark Ages, men seem to sail round the end of the land— though the southern harbours are there, pointing right at the further shore.

Did that peninsula swing as on a pivot axis ? Did it deepen to the south during the long, hardly-recorded ages ?

.   .   .   .   .

I knew nothing of these harbours of North Devon and Cornwall, not even by hearsay. I read up diligently in my "West Coast Pilot" that river which seemed the best for entry along these coasts, and hoped to make it before evening. But the wind died down altogether, and we drifted aimlessly enough back upon the flood, then down again on the ebb, through the night, and all through the morning and the noon, and on into the afternoon again of the second day.

It was full evening, and the sun within an hour of its setting, the air much warmer now and the light mellow with a powdery gold, when a strong breeze came up out of the very sun, as it were; out of the glory. The "Nona" heeled to it, and was now to be handled at will, making a good run a little north of west, with the opportunity for beating as we chose.

We beat up towards the river mouth, sure, as we thought, that the wind would hold, and that we could easily run up the stream and so to the town beyond before darkness. What we had not reckoned with was a sheer cliff lying along the river mouth to the west, overhanging it and cutting off the wind. On the eastern shore was an immense stretch of half-covered sand, bearing a name of disaster, and famous for wreckage. Having lost the wind we could no longer manœuvre, and, what was worse in that narrow passage, we found that the tide did not run true to the sea-tide outside.

We had counted upon the flood making ; but, whether because there was more water than usual in the river, or from some odd effect of the wind, or because locally it is always so (though the " West Coast Pilot " told us nothing about it, nor the chart either), the river was still running out violently, and there seemed no sign of an upward-going stream before darkness.

I had almost determined to let her drift out again, catch the sea wind when I got beyond the wall of the cliff, find anchoring ground well offshore, and wait there for the day, when there appeared, coming down the river at great speed, a white motor boat, large and exquisitely apparelled, splendid with burning bronze, regally accoutred in unspotted gleaming mantle of the foam-colour, of the cloud-colour, of the snow-colour, and a line of gold all around. It was indeed a boat apparelled, not only as to itself, but as to its two humans ; and shameful did the " Nona " appear, homely, draggle-tail, sordid, even after so very calm a passage, when contrasted with that dandy of the inland waters. Alas ! That dead wealth should dig such gulfs between mortals and that poverty should lessen virtue !

But, to be just, it is not only wealth that breeds these fine sights, it is also a certain temper in the owner. And I knew very well that though I had three million pounds and some odd pence over I should never have a tidy boat. I could not sleep in such a thing.

Anyhow, there she came, thundering down the tide. I had thought she would pass me in her rush of speed, and I held up until she should have done so, for it would have been dangerous to have tried to go about with such a weight of movement coming on us, and our own course half out of control, dependent only upon occasional slight splashes of wind from over the cliff. But the motor boat slowed down, and its owner asked us if we wanted a tow up to the town. We met him with gratitude : he was of that very considerable class known as the Good Rich, with whom are the Penitent Thieves, the Reformed Drunkards, the Sane Professors, the Womanly Furies and all other candidates for heaven. We threw a line aboard him and made fast, and so went up just as the darkness came, and dropped anchor in the pool under a neat little city, which lived by the traffic of that difficult waterway with its strange tide. But, then, all tides are strange.

My companion and I sat in the hatch that evening under quiet stars, smoking pipes, watching that most pleasant of sights, the home lights of a little harbour town, and their trembling reflections in the water, the slight swaying of the masts of fishing boats moored by the quay. We wondered together at the way the tide had behaved when it tried to baulk us of our entry, and we decided before we slept that it was better never to reason upon tides, nor even to accept print upon them, but to take them blindly as they came, for " No man living can

understand the tides," said my companion, and, as
he said it, he sighed ; and he was right.

No man living can understand the tides. And
the mystery of the tides is as good a corrective as
one could find to our deadening pride in exact
measurements, and to the folly of attempting to
base real knowledge upon mere calculation : our
pretence to a universal science, and to a modern
omniscience upon the Nature of Things.

The bungling of landsmen in the matter of tides
begins with Galileo. That worthy had a talent for
getting off the rails and he bungled on the tides as
he did on comets. Then came Newton. Why does
the tide flow every twelve hours on the average,
instead of every twenty-four ? If it be true, as I
suppose it roughly is, that the moon is the main
puller of the tides (helped and hindered a little by
the sun, and certainly by other forces of which we
know nothing), then there ought to be a tide every
twenty-four hours. Put a lot of fluid round a solid
sphere, and set a pull, working from some point
well outside the fluid. It looks as though the fluid
would heap up towards the pull. It being discovered that the fluid did *not* heap up only towards
the pull, but also on the other side of the solid
sphere, away from the pull, the mind of man
could not rest without proclaiming an explanatory
dogma, and we were told (by Newton among others)
that the pull, not only heaped up the fluid towards
itself, but also dragged away the earth from the
water on the far side. Indeed, Newton worked it
out and proved that it was so.

If the phenomenon had been the other way about,
if the fluid had behaved as one would expect it to
behave, and had heaped up only on the side towards
the pull—oh ! believe me ! a formula would have

been discovered to explain *that* with just as much ease as the formula which has been drawn up to explain the real state of affairs.

But this original false dogma is not of very much interest compared with the immense complexity of the tides, and the inability to follow them with any sort of completeness by reason of that complexity.

For the tides behave in the most inexplicable fashion. They follow, of course, certain habits, which we know (from the observation of liquids everywhere) to be in the nature of a liquid in movement. They pile up higher as they rush up funnels. They are checked by ridges, they form eddies—and all the rest of it. But they are continually playing anomalous tricks ; and any one who tries to work up a theory of the tides makes a fool of himself : still more does any poor sailing-man do so who uses science to discover what the tide may be doing in a place he has not yet tried. He makes not only a fool of himself, but also, very probably, shipwreck.

Why should a tide run three hours late inshore along the Bight of Sussex ? We are told it is an eddy. Of course it is. But why an eddy of such extraordinary retardation ? The main Channel tide runs from headland to headland. It is " true," as the phrase goes, at St. Catherine's, and again at Beachy and so on to Dungeness ; and if you are going up Channel outside, you carry it with you " true " all the way. That it should be a little retarded in the Bight of Sussex one might understand, but that Bight is very shallow (it is only fifteen miles from the deepest point by Shoreham to the outer line), and yet you have this three hours' difference ! The tide still runs hard to the west along shore, three—anyhow, two and three-quarters —hours after it has turned eastward outside.

Who can explain why there is nine hours ebb on the easterly shore of Portland and only three hours flow ? It is a monkey trick, designed to prevent the poor sailorman from sneaking in just under the Bill : it only gives him three hours out of the twelve in which to do it, with Scylla on his left, and that most abominable howling Charybdis, called Portland Race, on his right. And if he comes up to the Bill at the end of his three hours' limit, he has his heart in his mouth for fear that he should find the ebb stream catching his bows the moment he is round the Bill, and driving him headlong into the heart of the Race.

And what about the double tide of the Wight and Poole, the *gulder*, as they call it—the mystery of the Dorset and the Hampshire seas ? In the days of my innocence I used to believe what I was told : that the double tide in Southampton Water was due to the water coming in first through the Needles channel and then around by Spithead later. It sounded reasonable for Southampton Water. But when I first made Poole, and found that they had a double tide there as well—and even out beyond St. Alban's Head—my philosophy was shaken, and my scheme of things fell heavily to the ground. Why on earth should there be a double tide on that coast ? Who could explain it ?

The enormous tide at the end of the funnel of the Bristol Channel is reasonable enough, though it is a little odd that it should be so very much bigger at Chepstow than at Gloucester. But how will you account for the prodigious heave at St. Malo ? Why does the flood come up Arun River like a racehorse recently invigorated with a bucket of beer, and at Newhaven hardly move at all up the Ouse ?

I have stood outside the old piers at Newhaven

in a little boat, with a northerly wind, expecting the
first of the flood to help me to beat up, and waited
for the quarter flood, and the half flood, and, later
than that, and still have seen the sluggish surface
water running out to sea against all the tidal laws
that were ever written down : running out to sea,
though the level of it steadily rose.

But there is no end to the mystery of the tides.
Why is there a tide at Venice ? It is not much of a
thing, but it is there. And, for that matter, there
is *a* tide in the Lake of Geneva. Here, again, the
learned come barging in and tell us all about it.
Closed basins (they say) like the Adriatic, even
quite small ones, like the Lake of Geneva, have
their little tides after the fashion of water swung in
a basin. The explanation is given in some simile
like this : " If you shake a basin slightly, the
water will begin to swing with a regular movement
back and forth." So it will. But who shakes the
Lake of Geneva ? Or who catches the Adriatic
at either end, and gives it a regular balance up and
down, exactly so often, every so many hours ?

All this questioning sounds like the Book of Job ;
but, note you, that I, for my part, am with Job, and
against the scientists. For Job, or God, or whoever
it was who set the catechism, put the questions and
was careful to avoid the answers, and for my part I
will do the same, not only in the matter of the tides,
but for the whole basketful of things on which the
scientists have been pontificating with increasing
uppishness for the last two hundred years, until at
last they have led us to the morass wherein we are
sinking. When they pontificate on tides it does no
great harm, for the sailorman cares nothing for
their theories, but goes by real knowledge, and I by
my sworn authority, the Admiralty texts, the like

of which for excellence the world has not : "High water, full and change, six hours, thirteen minutes after Dover. The stream is barely perceptible in the first three hours of the flood, but runs very strongly in the third, and through three-quarters of the fourth hour ; after which it slackens. There is no perceptible stream in the last two hours of the flood." Or again : "On rounding the Devil's Point the tide is lost." There is no theorising, no mumbo-jumbo. The thing itself, reality, is stated; and it is true. There is not even a passing wonderment as to where the tide goes to when it is lost. The "Channel Pilot" tells you the truth. You stick blindly to its text and you are saved.

There are many parts of the sea where the tide goes round like a clock, and no one can tell you why. Instead of the stream setting first east, let us say, with the flood and then west with the ebb, it goes all round the compass. It sets north-west with the beginning of the flood, then north, then north-east, then east, and so on. Looking all round about itself like a performing dog, and slowly and ceaselessly revolving. It behaves not like an eddy, but like spokes. It is perfectly incomprehensible.

There is also this about the tides, which we all know to be true, and which we can see at work any day, but which I defy any man to rationalise : when the tide runs up a narrow river—or, indeed, any river—it will be still running up, say, ten miles from the mouth, when it is running *down* again, say, five miles from the mouth. What happens in between ? Slack water, of course. But *how* is there slack water ? How can the running *down* be going on at one point and, immediately beyond, the running *up*, without a division ? How can the water go on running up from a reservoir below which it is running down ?

It does so, and it is all in God's providence, and I accept it as I do teeth, or any other oddity. But I will not pretend to explain it.

The sea teaches one the vastness and the number of things, and, therefore, the necessary presence of incalculable elements, perpetually defeating all our calculations. The sea, which teaches all wisdom, certainly does not teach any man to despise human reason. I suppose there was never yet any Kantian fool or worser pragmatist who would not have been cured of his folly by half a week of moderate weather off the Onion. No one can at sea forego the human reason or doubt that things are things, or that true ideas are true. But the sea does teach one that the human reason, working from a number of known premises, must always be on its guard, lest the conclusion be upset in practice by the irruption of other premises, unknown or not considered. In plain words, the sea makes a man practical ; and the practical man is, I suppose, as much the contrary of the pragmatist as the sociable man is the contrary of the socialist, or the peaceable man the contrary of the pacifist.

And, talking of pacifists, there is nothing more pleasing to note than the excellent unconscious patriotism of the men and women who solemnly propose that patriotism is the ruin of the world.

There is a delightful irony in observing how intensely national these anti-nationalists are ! It is a profound and satisfying thing to watch. Any one can get a good laugh out of the patriotism of men with no nation, or, at any rate, with a nationality very different from that which they profess. It is a common jest, the sham patriotism of the nomads. But far more subtle and penetrating is the fun of watching your genuine pacifist, who believes the divisions between nations to be evil artifices, soon to be conjured away.

Nowhere are these international pacifists more national than in England. They have all the English spontaneity and love of adventure. They carry to extreme that English love of individual action which we nearly always find associated with their odd political blindness. They nearly all display some trick of clothing or food. They will drink lime-juice instead of wine, or wear elastic-sided boots, or think it wrong to smoke tobacco, or go about without hats. If they are men, they will have hair coming down to their shoulders, which is a very greasy habit. If they are women they will go about barefoot, save for the most absurd sandals ; and while they practise all these provincial follies they will be consumed with a passion for the general good of mankind.

If you wanted to get a specimen—I do not say of the average Englishman, for he is certainly not that —but of a being in whom the English characteristics are to be found most deeply marked, this pacifist is the very man whom you should choose. All the English conceptions of right and wrong, all the English habits of thought, all the sheltered English attitude towards the great outer world, all the local errors, and much of the local generosity are there present to the full.

I cannot help thinking it a strength to England that the pacifist or internationalist in England should be so intensely English. It prevents any disruptive effect, and it, therefore, prevents the rivals of this country taking such folk seriously.

The French and Italians are far less happily circumstanced in this regard. In those two countries—and, I suppose, in Spain also, although

there I have less knowledge on which to speak—
the internationalist *is* an internationalist, bearing but
weakly the common marks of his own people, and
willing to act not only against his country politically,
but also in all his being, morally and spiritually. A
French or Italian internationalist and pacifist will
not only sympathise with the enemies of his country,
nor only give them actively all the help he can,
but he will particularly attack the soul whereby his
country lives, its traditions and character. If he is
French he will hate wine, if Italian, macaroni. But
does the English pacifist hate tea? The unrooted
man is a very dangerous type, and in England
happily unknown. To read anything said or written
by such men as Mr. Wells or Mr. Snowden is to
read something by people who evidently think of
international peace as something closely connected
with cricket, teetotalism, and the use of Bible
language—coupled, of course, with a reverent
agnosticism—which means a wearied puritanism.

I have spoken of their courage, and certainly the
courage of the typical conscientious objectors during
the War was an arresting thing.

One of the most famous had been a fairly close
acquaintance of mine many years ago. I had
known him to be a man of eccentric nature, hardly
mad. But I could not have believed he would have
stood up as he did to the martyrdom which he was
made to suffer. The violence of his protest against
all violence was an admirable thing.

A lesser form of the paradox in these people is
their hatred of the French, and their passion for
Prussia. This love of Berlin would seem to be
compounded of two elements, partly a natural
desire to support the losing side, but much more
the strong religious sympathy they have with the

Northern German in Europe, and the hatred they feel (very naturally !) for the Catholic culture, of which the French are the chief representatives.

They preached a universal similarity. Yet there were very few of them who would not have joyfully watched the most bloody war against the French at any time after the Armistice, and none of them would have doubted one moment of the issue: for they had prepared for war in the best of all possible fashions by refusing to arm. Such men are confident that their country must be victorious, for, in their childish minds, anything strange and foreign seems naturally weak, and doomed to extinction.

You see, I plead for the fools. But although I like these eccentrics for their sincerity and for their spontaneous virtue under persecution, yet I cannot associate with any of them long. They make me nervous—and I think this effect is due to something insane about them. . . . Anyhow, they are national, and that is always to the good.

I have noticed that this kind of fanatic, like every other kind, is in two species ; the species which too clearly thinks out its own insane theory, and the species which remains perfectly muddle-headed.

I had a long talk lately in the ruins of the town of Rheims with one of these people. He was drinking a sort of special fizzy coloured water, which he had imported, and which he worshipped because no man could become drunk thereon. He was doing very noble work in helping people who had lost their homes. He was a " Helper "—and all the rest of it. He was also occupied in spreading the Gospel, under the reservation, of course, that it was not true ; at least, as he was careful to explain to me, he " was not emphasising the miraculous element." This person had a great deal of money, but could none the

less reason closely, and he had evidently thought out
his subject completely.

He said to me that, by his principles, if he were
attacked he ought not to defend himself ; and he had
a well-constructed answer ready for the obvious
objection that people with so strange a creed would
soon be destroyed, and that, therefore, all their
predication would have been in vain.

He told me that, upon the contrary, the example
of non-resistance would spread ; and he pointed out
that, in fact, throughout history, sacrifice was fruitful,
and particularly self-sacrifice. When the body of
those who had refused to resist had grown to a
respectable size, all European society would be
changed ; the possibility of attack would be dissolved in an ambient medium opposed to it, and
would disappear. He was also ready with an answer
to the general objection that his philosophy applied to
only one form of human conflict, and left untouched
all the other and really more serious forms.

I pointed out to him, for instance, how, in societies
like that of modern England, where recourse to
physical combat between private citizens had been
crushed out by an all-powerful police, there was the
more opportunity for injustice and oppression and
unredeemed insult. His answer to this I thought
curious and worth noting. He said that men did
not resent insult very much, and that as for such
oppressions as swindling them out of their goods,
or cutting them off from all useful information
through a control of the Press by a few adventurers, these evils were superficial, and soon cor-
rected themselves. He said they did little permanent harm to the human beings who suffered
them, but that physical violence on a large scale,
as in war, was quite another matter.

I asked him whether he approved of the holding down of subject peoples for produce—as, for instance, for copra or cocoa. He said that he did not ; but I found him very wobbly on that point. He took refuge, for a moment, in hypocrisy, and said it was for the good of the oppressed ; but he was disturbed.

The man who takes up the cause of subject peoples against his own country is usually of a very different type from the internationalist or pacifist. He is usually a man with a particular romantic interest in that one particular part of the world, and he is usually either a man of independent position through birth and wealth (who feels himself, there-fore, fairly immune from the Law Courts), or a hanger-on of such. And I have noticed that these cranks begin by what is no more than an affecta-tion ; but, like all humbug, this affectation brings its own punishment in the shape of a sort of ingrow-ing false sincerity. Such men *almost* get to believe in themselves. It never quite comes off. I have never known one of these men, even in his latest days, to be really, fully, and homogeneously sincere. For instance, I have never known one who would hesitate to make money out of the English rule in some part of the Orient while denouncing that rule with fervour, and (no doubt) heartfelt indignation.

There is another curious little point about this sort of people: they are always very proud of being mixed up with the British administration of the dependency in question. They love to point out in conversation how their very opposition has brought them into contact with this, that, and the other important Administrator and his class. Usually their birth has made them familiar with that class ; for, until lately, the controllers of dependencies were

drawn in the main from people of family or from
their dependents, and your pro-native crank must
be himself of consequence to survive. Were they
poor and weak they would be broken.

Upon the whole, I think these anti-Englishmen
are an advantage to the State. You may be perfectly certain that they will never go to the length of
doing anything active to the hurt of England, and
they lend variety and criticism to the external action
of England. They make the rivals of England
admire a social structure in which such internal
strains (which foreigners always exaggerate) are
rendered innocuous. If they do any harm, it is by
inflating, through reaction, that growing and very
dangerous vanity which the public schools and
universities have so much encouraged in our
generation, and through which most men have come
to feel that Fate is necessarily upon the side of their
country, that no national disasters need be feared in
the future, nor any precautions taken to forestall
national decline. The Englishman who says that
he wants England out of India, inflames, by reaction,
the fatuity of the Englishman who thinks himself
in India as one of a Chosen Race.

These pacifists or internationalists of Britain have
strongly in them the English hatred of cruelty,
and they have in high development the national
habit of short cuts in thought ; as, for instance,
when you may hear them say that war is wrong,
which is as much as to say that a house on fire is
wrong.

This habit of taking short cuts in thought is often
called, not only by foreigners who are unused to the
English habit of mind, but by Englishmen themselves, an incapacity for clear thinking. I do not
quite agree. As it seems to me, the essential

characteristic of this way of speaking and thinking
is not its lack of lucidity—for, though that is
evident enough, it is not the essential. The essential
is the taking for granted of a great many things
which are not expressed. This habit of taking
short cuts in speech is in some way a habit common
to all this group of islands ; for the Scotch have it,
too, though not so strongly marked as the English ;
and the Irish have it very pronouncedly indeed : it
is far more marked in them than in the English,
and is the root of the " bull."

For instance, when a man says that war is wrong,
he is saying something which, as it stands, is manifestly nonsense. But if we expand the phrase it
has full and definite meaning. He means " for one
organised community to attempt destruction and
physical pain upon the organisation of another such
community with the object of gain or increase of
power is wrong." And so it undoubtedly is. Or
when he says that war is silly and not worth while,
he again means (when we fully expand his phrase
for him) that such action is commonly so expensive
and hurtful, even to those who successfully use it,
that it is a bad speculation. In this, indeed, he is
not so certainly right as in his first proposition, for
most victorious wars in history have handsomely
paid the victors; but my point is that this kind of
talk, whether about war or anything else, is not *due*
to muddle-headedness ; though it goes with muddle-
headedness. It is due to a clotting of thought
through compression.

One phrase which I very often hear (and which,
as it stands, is apparently a piece of bestial unintelligence) may further my point. It is the phrase :
" Some religion ought to be taught in the schools."
It is obvious that this phrase as it stands is a

contradiction in terms ; for the word " ought " can only apply to a moral good ; and if such and such a religious system is of good effect, then an opposite and contradictory religious system will be of evil effect. If I think it wrong to murder, if my religion teaches me that murder is a great moral evil, then I teach children in schools that this is so. But if my religion is that of an Oriental body I have heard of, called Thugs, with whom murder is a high religious act, then I teach an opposite set of morals. Both religions cannot be good. One must be good and the other evil. But when you hear people say, " Some religion should be taught in the schools," what they mean is that " the general Protestant ethics of the English people should, on their broader lines, be taught in the English schools." They take for granted that every one using the word " religion " means English Protestantism. Having taken that for granted, they shorten their speech in the fashion I have just quoted.

. . . .

And really such wandering of the mind over this, that, and the other, as I have thus indulged before sleep, in the pleasant little cabin of the " Nona " (pleasant to me, odious to the pernickety, for it is a hugger-mugger home) watching between the open skylight and the combing a little belt of nightly sky with stars, is a poor adjunct to the scent of the sea, and to the Devon air. To the devil with all reasonings and counter reasonings and abstractions and argufying : I am for sleep.

. . . .

We woke early next morning to the noise of the loud clapping of water upon the bows, and I put my head out of the skylight to see little dusty clouds going too quickly across the heaven, and a freshening breeze blowing up from a little south of west, so that all the harbour water was dancing and alive. But the glass was high, and there was no reason why we should not take the sea again, only we must wait for the ebb (which would come in about three hours' time, nearer nine than eight o'clock). For, in that blanketed part of the river down below, we should never get the "Nona" out against the flood. Nevertheless, I asked my companion whether it might not be wise to take another man, for we were going down the coast, where the rare harbours were shoal, and not easy to enter, and also small, and lay so that, with such a wind, one would have to beat up to them. An extra hand, such as we had with us during the never-to-be-forgotten business of Bardsey, would be an advantage. Such a hand, therefore, after minute enquiry and searching questions, did we ship ; then, all things having been done in their order, and sail set with the second jib and two reefs in the mainsail and one reef forward, we got up the anchor and let her down for the sea.

The hand we had shipped (promising him his journey home by rail within three days at the most) was very well got up in sailor fashion, with his jersey and his peaked cap, the latter worn a trifle to one side, after the fashion of those who are daring, and challenge Æolus. His trousers, it was true, did not spread out at the bottom, like elephant's feet or the mouths of bells, as do the trousers of sailors upon the stage. On the other hand, he would give them a hitch from time to time—a gesture symbolic of the Main in Drury Lane. He had nothing to do as we dropped down river, for all was trim. He sat and smoked, and watched the water before him with wistful eyes. I think he was by nature a man sad or saddened ; and he was very silent.

On the bar there was no end of a lump, and, as we were blanketed by that high cliff, the " Nona " took it uneasily, chucking up and down with flapping sails and rolling damnably, but in a few moments the strength of the ebb had swept us far enough out to catch the wind again, and we set a course full-and-by ; right out for the open, for the large. For we designed to beat in again after a few miles, and so make our way down Channel toward the Cornishmen.

There was certainly quite enough wind : " All the wind there is," as an old Irish sailor said to me once during an Atlantic gale so abominable that he and I could not walk against its icy, sleeting December fury, but had to crawl forward tugging along the rail by main force, all up the windward side. . . . That was a passage worthy of remembrance, for we took three weeks between Europe and the Delaware, the engines and the old frame quite unfit for their task ; and in that cheap passage also, I learnt from a stoker two songs : one called " The Corn Beef Can," and the other called " The Tom Cat." They are of the great songs of this world.

A man should learn all the songs he can. Songs are a possession, and all men who write good songs are benefactors. No people have so many songs as the English, yet no people sing less in these last sad days of ours. One cannot sing in a book. Could a man sing in a book, willingly would I sing to you here and now in a loud voice " The Corn Beef Can " and " The Tom Cat," those admirable songs which I learnt in early manhood upon the Atlantic seas.

There was more wind, indeed, than I liked. We

took in the third reef, and went about to the starboard tack, after we had run out so far that we thought we could fetch, upon this tack, the next harbour. As we came near to that town, and saw its roofs far away appear and disappear again behind the crests of unpleasant seas, the " Nona " heeled suddenly to a much too angry gust. I heard a crash coming from below, and with it the voice of my companion crying, " Come down quick and help ! "

The crew (if I may call him so) was sitting forward, hunched up, clutching the weather shrouds, and not happy. I called him to come and hold the tiller, while I should go below to help, and I warned him that she was pulling hard, although she was under three reefs, for we had nothing forward now but the third jib. He looked over his shoulder in a very ghastly way, and shook his head from side to side, as though despairing to be heard in such a wind. I was within a few feet of him, and I bawled : " COME AND TAKE THE TILLER ! QUICK ! " but again he miserably shook his head, and clung to the shroud. Then did I, commending myself to St. Elmo (which is a false name, for his real name was Peter, and even Gonzales, and he was the man who was so shocked to find all the Galicians lapsed into a Pagan darkness and living in open fun) struggle to make some shift of keeping the tiller up with my right arm stretched back, while I craned my head down below the cabin door to see what was going on downstairs.

The stove had got adrift in the lurch. There was oil all over the place, and a mass of crockery, and everything on the weather side had leapt to leeward, and some little of it trailed in the oil of the floor-boards. It was not more serious than that ; for, luckily, the stove was not alight. I shouted to my companion that I could not leave the tiller. I bobbed up my head again and found that even in that short moment she had almost swung into irons. I put her round just in time, and we raced and flew, breasting the seas for that further little misty harbour town.

The "Nona" is like those women who are peevish and intolerable under all conditions of reasonable happiness, but come out magnificently in distress. I lie; for the "Nona" is never peevish and intolerable. What I mean is that in easy weather she is a little sluggish on the helm, and has one or two other small faults, excusable after the fortieth, the fiftieth, year: for she was launched before Plevna, though it is true, a year or two after Sedan. She has her mortalities; but in a sea-way she is magnificent. With her few inches of freeboard, her old-fashioned straight stem, her solid grip upon the water, she takes the sea as though she belonged to it, and so she went that day, riding in high-bred fashion, worthy of all praise, and praise she received from me as she leant over and took the combers one after the other. I gave her perpetual encouragement : for no boat will do her best unless she is sufficiently flattered.

Thanks to that increasing wind, the passage was short enough, and what we had said would at most take three days was accomplished between a morning and an evening, for it was still broad daylight when we passed outside the group of rocks of which the chart warned us, and stood within a mile or two of the now distinct houses of that little harbour town, all full of Cornish men.

But the wind still rose, and for the wind to rise when day is falling is a very bad sign. I had no desire to ride it out in the open, and I proposed to get in under the lee of the land (for there was a sort of point there), and not to drop anchor till I could be sure of plenty of water in the harbour later on, when I should make for it on the flood.

My companion came up on deck, from settling things below, and we cast about anxiously for a place where the anchor might be let go.

It was not an easy calculation. She was driving pretty fast. One had to get well under the shelter of the low point, and yet to leave plenty of water beneath one in which to swing. I asked him to go forward and get all ready, and the Crew would help him. But the Crew did not do so.

The sea being now calmer (though the wind was still rising) because we had come under the lee of the point, the Crew did, indeed, stagger forward ; but he still held on manfully by the forestay, and looked curiously on my companion's activity with the anchor as at a novel and a pleasant sight. Beyond that he did nothing ; but I think he was proud of keeping his legs so long as he could grasp that forestay. It is no use to argue nor much use to command in the face of imbecility.

I shouted to my companion to let go the chain when I thought the right moment come, and at the same instant brought her up sharp.

The anchor took the ground. We were in, perhaps, five fathom of flood water ; for it was full evening, though still light. When we had so lain for a quarter of an hour or so, taking stock of everything around, I asked my companion whether we could not, with the last of the light and the last of the flood, make harbour. The wind was still rising, but we should be running before it towards the not distant pier. Rounding that stonework, we should shoot right into the wind's eye, when it probably would be broken by the hillside of houses

beyond, and, even though we did not know how far
the harbour might still be dried out, we should be
in safety, with plenty of water beneath our keel for
an hour or two more, while we enquired where we
should berth. So we decided to risk it, though
perhaps wiser men would have ridden out the night
where we lay.

She certainly took a great deal of water aboard
during that short mile or two, with more and more
breakers as we got further and further from the
protection of the point. Once, when she buried
badly, I was afraid the sprit might snap, for I had
not housed it. But she carried through all right
(though the sprit bent like a willow wand), and we
rounded in the gloaming, shot past the pier end,
and dropped anchor immediately inside.

A man hailed us from the shore ; we threw him
a rope, and he showed us where to berth in water
that would just or nearly float us, even at the lowest
of the tide.

The Crew was no longer indolent, now that he
had left behind him the pitiless waste of the seas and
felt once more beneath his feet the solid strength of
England. He did what he was told in fastening
warps and putting out fenders. Then came the
moment for payment : wage and the railway fare
home. Before he went over the side I asked him
gently whether he had ever been to sea before.
He said : " Oh, yes, in a manner of speaking." I
asked him whether he had ever handled a tiller.
" Not by rights," he said. " Not in such a boat as
this." I asked him whether he had any fault to find
with the boat. He said " No, she was a very good
boat so far as he could see, but he did not pretend to
understand these things." He went over the side
into the darkness. He was and he remains a mystery.

Was he a Charon man who pulled a ferry from shore to shore ? Or was he a man who lounged about on the quay, dressed as his companions were dressed, but timid of tumbling water ? Or was he a vision ? Or a detective ? Or an actor ? Or one of those writing men who pretend to go to sea in boats, but never do ? I cannot tell. I never saw him again.

This episode of the man in sailor clothes with the hitch, who knew nothing of the sea, started my mind upon two ways, which, as they diverged, I could not both follow.

For first it made me think of how we judge by immediate indications—and the taking in of people through this method is at the basis of most commercial successes ; even this poor fellow had made some shillings by it. But also it led me to consider how astonishingly in the modern world we live side by side and know nothing of one another.

There was certainly never a time in the history of Christendom, nor of the Paganism that went before it, never a time in the history of our race, when we Europeans (I cannot answer for the Asiatics or the niggers) were so split up, one small set of men knowing nothing about another small set of men at their elbows.

The worst form it takes, of course, is the division between rich and poor, which is quite a modern thing, and an abominable one—the product, I suppose, of what people call " democracy."

Mr. Wilfrid Blunt and I would often talk of this in connection with my own dear county of Sussex. He was much older than I, between twenty-five and thirty years older, and he could, therefore, remember a simpler and a better time than that into which we have descended ; yet he confirmed me in my

judgment that, no matter how fond a man might be
of his county, or how long he might live in it, he
would never, if he were of the wealthier, cultivated
sort, know the lives of the poor people about him. I
had lived among them on and off all my life, and so
had he; and I certainly loved them with all my
heart, and so did he ; but as for knowing how they
live or what they really think, there is a gulf dug
between us. It ought not to be so.

Apart from this modern separation of the rich
from the poor, there are any number of side separa-
tions. It is only by an accident that the writing or
teaching man knows anything of business, though
the commercial man more often knows something
of writing. But the greatest anomaly of all, the
one that has puzzled me most of a hundred such, is
the complete ignorance of what the Catholic Church
is and means—the ignorance even of what its
doctrines may be. One would think it should be a
mere matter of encyclopedias and text-books—easy
for any one to look up. In nations of Catholic
culture, of course, the Church is thoroughly well
known, even by its worst enemies ; but in nations
not of Catholic culture the absence of all contact
with, and of even elementary information upon, this
essential thing, is stupefying.

Here is the corporate tradition which made
Europe : the Thing which is the core and soul of
all our history for fifteen hundred years, and on into
the present time : the continuator of all our Pagan
origins, transformed, baptised, illumined ; the
matrix of such culture as we still retain. For any
European not to know the elements of that affair is
to be in a blind ignorance of all his making, and,
therefore, of his self. Yet it is perfectly true that
the Englishman or Scotsman, cultivated to excess,

saturated with the knowledge of all he thinks there is to know, fatigued and cynical after too much sounding of the world, says things with regard to that great affair which show him to be as little acquainted with its essentials as he might be with another planet. He has many Catholic acquaintances ; he probably has some reading of his own country before the death of Elizabeth ; he is certain to have read Shakespeare—a writer who wrote for and in a Catholic England, and a writer whose whole atmosphere is Catholic. He may justly pride himself upon his knowledge of the architecture, or even the institutions of the Occident before the great sundering of three hundred years ago. Yet, when he is dealing with this mighty business, he says things more grotesque than anything said by any Colonial about that very governing class to which he himself belongs. He produces an effect, when he touches upon the Faith, which—I say it honestly—is as startling and as comic as the effect produced by those ingenuous millionaires from the backwoods who come barging in among the London subtleties of ancient wealth.

And if this is true—as it is true—of the old governing class, who have some few of them direct family traditions connected with the Faith, nearly all of them relatives, and every one of them friends and acquaintances who are Catholic, it is, of course, still more true of the average writing and speaking man of lower birth upon whom general opinion depends.

Now and then one comes across a man who talks or writes with some knowledge, if not of what lies beyond the boundary, at least of the boundary itself ; but it is exceedingly rare. The latest example I know of the thing is the preface by Mr. Bernard Shaw, written for his play, " Saint Joan."

Here there is a clear recognition of the boundary
between the Faith and what lies outside : between
the garden and the heath, or marsh.

He is writing there of the voices which St. Joan
of Arc heard, and which determined her mission.
He points out that people often hear voices through
a morbid faculty of projecting what they have themselves imagined. It is well known that that may
happen to any one ; and most people recognise that
such a phenomenon is within themselves, and has no
value of reality. Indeed, pretty well every one has at
one time or another vividly heard not-present sounds,
whether through the recollection of a loved voice
or through some other emotion of fear or violence ;
and it is only a question of degree whether you call
the impression " hearing " or no. He also points
out that in the case of diseased people this imaginary
stuff takes on a false reality, and that many lunatics,
criminal and other, imagine themselves to have heard
voices commanding them to do this or that—usually
something very unpleasant, nothing half so fine or
sane as conducting a triumphant war.

All that is perfectly true. Then he comes to the
specific point of St. Joan's voices, and he says that
having been brought up a strong Protestant (and,
indeed, a strong Protestantism is the note of all his
writings) he cannot accept the idea that these voices
were real.

Now, there you have a perfectly clear and lucid
statement of the boundary between the Catholic
world and what lies outside it. The specific
difference between the Catholic and the non-
Catholic—so far as Europe is concerned—lies in
what is roughly called (it is a conversational term,
and I do not accept it as accurate) the " acceptation
of the supernatural." The Catholic does not

believe that every one who hears voices hears real
voices. He does believe that it is possible for such
voices to be real ; and he, therefore, believes that
this thing, philosophically possible, has also had,
now and then, a real historical existence.

In the same way, he does not believe nine-tenths,
or ninety-nine hundredths, of the miraculous stories
which have grown up out of distortion or mere
wantonness, or (for the greater part) out of
the gradual substitution of direct statement for
allegorical or fictional statement, turning fairy tales
into fact ; but he does believe that the miraculous
—that is, an irregular suspension of the order of
nature—is philosophically possible. He, therefore,
believes, when the evidence is sufficient, that it
has historical existence in certain examples. For
instance, I certainly believe that the blinded man of
York had his sight restored to him by St. Thomas
of Canterbury ; but I don't believe that Mahommed
went to the moon on donkey-back—if, indeed, that
mysterious mount of his *was* a donkey, which the
best authorities deny. The Catholic not only
believes that certain historical examples, which are
of faith, were real and took place (as, for instance,
our Lord's walking on the water—and St. Peter's
less successful effort), but he also believes in general
that the phenomena called miracles continue actually
to happen throughout history : that they go on
to-day.

The same principle of division runs through the
whole of thought. In the matter of the development of religion, everybody outside the Catholic
body talks as though the development of the Catholic
religion were a human process. They answer the
famous question : " Is religion of God or of man ? "
with a hearty affirmation of the second hypothesis.

In this mood they examine such a story as that of
the Mass, the Papacy, or the doctrine of our Lord's
divinity. They take it for granted that all was
man-made. In this mood they interpret (usually
with guesses of the wildest sort, which the much
stricter and more rational Catholic scholarship soon
disproves) the origin of the Scriptures, and in particular of the Gospels. Now the Catholic admits *all*
evidence in these matters : that is a matter of course,
for if you exclude any evidence your conclusion is
vitiated. But the difference betwen him and the
others is that he regards the action at work as divine,
willed, and, to repeat a word I have used, " illumined." That is why the Catholic thinks of the
modernist as a man of warm hear, but of poor
intelligence.

Here is an example. The man of warm heart,
with a strong sentimental attachment to his Scriptures, to familiar views, has his mind shaken by the
discovery or even the suggestion, that his document
is not wholly authentic. His intelligence must tell
him—if he would use it—that a document cannot
be an authority superior to the body which gave it
its claim. But his intelligence falters. Now the
Catholic, accustomed to the theory of authority and
having decided, let us say, upon evidence sufficient
for his judgment, that such and such a text was not
part of an original manuscript, could never on that
account abandon the doctrine consonant with that
text. He believes a doctrine to be a divine, a supernatural thing, communicated, revealed to the world
by an authority which still lives, and to and of which
he is at once a subject and a part. He says, upon
an accepted authority, " This is so." The presence
or absence of one piece of documentary evidence does
not affect reality. I have never thought the evidence

against the " Johannine Comma " so strong as that in its favour: but, though it were proved unauthentic to-morrow, what possible effect could that discovery have on the reality of the Trinity ?

The Faith is an attitude of acceptance towards an external reality : it is not a mood.

Now, of all this the men who elbow the Catholic Church on all sides in non-Catholic communities, such as England, remain as ignorant as they are of Sanskrit—with those few exceptions of which I have spoken. They seem to think that they have in their midst a body of men who go on strangely, either because they refuse to listen to common reason, or because they have a sentimental attachment to some old-fashioned tradition, and will not openly admit its absurdity. In this they resemble the simpler type of bucolic republican, who does not know that there are any arguments for a monarchy ; or the still simpler mind which believes that the earth is flat, and thinks that those who call it round are finicky people playing a subtle game in which they do not at heart believe.

Perhaps the best test of the difference is to be found in the doctrine of the Fall. The Catholic, with his acceptation of the supernatural (I again apologise for the term), accepts, upon an authority which he has discovered sufficient (on the statement of a Person, the Church, whose voice he has recognised to be divine), a doctrine that man, as man, was created superior to his present natural state ; that he was created to be supernaturally happy. Where, when, and especially *how*—in what mode— he cannot say. It is a mystery. He, therefore, accepts the doctrine that man, by a rebellion against the will of God, did at some time lose the super- natural powers, the supernatural life, the supernatural happiness, and fell into his natural state, as we see him to-day : of this world, and yet the only exile therein. What that process was whereby he existed with beatitude inhabiting him we are not told, nor in what place, nor at what date. But we are told, and we accept it, that a certain process, a certain sequence, due to the human will, took place ; a rebellion of that will, and a consequent loss of the supernatural life which was our inheritance. That doctrine no more clashes with any proved historical, or probable prehistorical, process than the discovery that William Wordsworth grew up from childhood to manhood proves that he was never a poet, or that he never ceased to be a poet. But the man who rejects the supernatural ignorantly distorts (many popular preachers of heretical theory to-day distort) the doctrine of the fall of man into something very different. He thinks it means that man was once in a particular place and time— Mesopotamia about 4,004 years ago—behaving like a gentleman, and then, following the advice of his wife, sank to be a perfectly horrible creature, tainting everything he touched. Naturally, a person informed by this childish idea—born, without reason, of a book—on finding what seem to him proofs of development from a simpler to a more complex society, and on waking up to what everybody might know by the use of plain common sense, that men progress from one stage of art to another more intricate (until they crash, and begin all over again), is thrown off his basis. He begins to make a new religion and a new mythology for himself, to talk of an "Ascent of Man" ; he thinks himself a summit and a glory—and at the same time he rids himself of morals. It will be interesting to watch the end of the process.

In connection with all this—though the connection is strained—I have often wondered to myself, and especially at night-time upon the sea, how long the mystic Catholic doctrine of human equality would survive in the non-Catholic world. It has survived so far because it is flattering to the many. Only a very small number of men are conspicuously rich or talented, or (for those who love publicity) public ; it is naturally an attractive doctrine for the obscure, untalented, poor mass, that—not in the sight of their Creator, for they no longer accept one, but in some incomprehensible way—we are all equal, and that in some odd fashion which they cannot discover, but which they have felt in their bones, the rich or talented or advertised man is really no better than themselves. You find the doctrine lingering most tenaciously in the popular conception of justice. Men would still be shocked, even during the present decline of morals, at the open admission that a man, important for wealth or public position, should be admittedly and overtly immune from the criminal law. In practice, of course, he is so. But so much of the old Catholic dogma of human equality survives as forbids—so far—the open admission of privilege.

But flattering as the old Catholic doctrine of equality is, I do not think it can survive much longer outside the Catholic body. It is in a high degree mysterious, and I am amused to find one man after another suddenly making the discovery that it is not a patent truth, apparent upon the surface of things.

I remember once sitting next a very worthy man at a banquet in the United States : it is now nearly thirty years ago. This man explained to me laboriously enough, but very privately, that the statement in the Declaration of Independence " Men

are born equal " seemed to him great nonsense.
For he had come to observe that they were of
different stature, muscular strength, and even intelligence—in which last conclusion I supported him.

There is another Catholic mystery to which the
non-Catholic world still uncertainly clings (I do not
think its tenure is at all secure), and that is the
mystery of immortality.

That also is consoling, and to some even flattering.
It can be used as a soothing drug on condition that
you do not work out the full theology of it, and admit
the double doom of beatitude and damnation. But
the repetition of this old Catholic doctrine as a dope,
by which may be evaded the menace and reality
of death, does not seem to me to have enough stuff in
it to endure. Yet there are many men and women
still living who can remember the time when the non-
Catholic world did still accept the full doctrine.

Indeed, a living friend of mine has recited to me a
verse learnt in her childhood, which ran somewhat
as follows :

> " There is a dreadful Hell
> A place of aches and pains,
> Where sinners must with Devils dwell,
> In fires and shrieks and chains."

But that is all over. All that is left of the doctrine
of a life to come is a very vague mood of comfortable
assurance, dissipated at once on the approach of peril.
It will not last, apart from the great and only true
philosophy of which it is the last poor relic.

.   .   .   .

I wonder, indeed, how much of Catholic doctrine
will survive, and what part of it—if any—in whatever of Europe continues to reject the present
advance of the Faith ? That some great section of

Europe will lose the last savour of Christian culture, and that soon, is probable ; for already the half-educated are abandoning it all over the north. That the rest will return to full doctrine is probable. For already the thirst for it is apparent, and the stronger minds are so returning. But what will follow where it is wholly abandoned ? We know what heavy weather property is making to-day, and, as for marriage, it has nearly gone by the board. The doctrine of justice is cloudily remembered, but mixed up in some muddled way with the idea of playing a lawyer's game, and so sodden with sentimental frailties, and rough-edged with cruelties and sale and purchase, that one can make nothing of it. For instance, outside the Catholic world, it is an accepted idea that if a man accused of murder be under grave suspicion, but not definitely proved guilty, he must, indeed, be condemned to some horrible punishment, such as imprisonment for life, but not to the punishment for murder. And it is an approved idea that punishment should not be vindictive, but only deterrent, save where the vindictive side of it is the vengeance of the great against the weak. And it is an approved idea that the witness in a legal case may justly be confused and harried in order that the truth shall be concealed; and that capacity of so confusing and harrying a witness is the great test of a man's moral aptitude to administer justice. And it is an approved idea that a lawyer may do his utmost to have an innocent man condemned, if only he be paid highly enough. But the breakdown of the idea of justice is only one department of the great change. There are a score of others to be surveyed ; notably the novel doctrine that a man's wealth is the test of his value in the State.

Well, what will come out of that welter, that

corruption into which the decomposition of the
Christian culture is now dissolving ?

What I think will spring out of the filth is a new
religion.

I think there will arise in whatever parts of
Christendom remain, say, two hundred years hence,
cut off from the advancing restoration of the Faith,
some simplified, odd, strong code of new habit,
comparable to the sudden code of habit which
Arabia constructed on the ruins of Christian doctrine in the East. Whatever refuses to accept
the Catholic restoration will sooner or later develop a
new religion, because human society cannot live on
air, and to men of our strong western blood the
substance of a doctrine and a ritual are especially
needful. This conception of a new religion (and,
therefore, an evil one) arising out of the rottenness
of the grave of truth, seems to-day at once fantastic
and unpleasant. Unpleasant I admit it is ; fantastic I do not believe it to be.

.   .   .   .   .   .

From that Cornish town I had the next morning
to make my way back to London ; and Stephen
Reynolds, whom I met, got her round the land sately
to the ports upon the southern side, whence later I
resumed this cruise: Stephen Reynolds, that
strongest-souled and most sincere of men, who
desired and did good all his life. It is the meeting
with such men, and the comparison of their public
label with their true function, of their false renown
or lack of renown with their certain standing in the
eyes of their Maker, which lead all wise men to a
perfect contempt for the modern world.

Does any one remember him now of those who are
reading this ? Perhaps one or two, perhaps no one.

He loved the poor : he understood the sea. He
was a brother and a support to sailing-men, and he
had charity, humility, and justice in equal poise.
But the truth is, I take it, that our world is no longer
fitted for governance by, nor even for advice from,
its rare great men. It is fitted for governance by
those who boast so exact an admixture of folly and
of vice as makes them reasonably consonant with the
stuff they have to govern. As for those who are
too good for us, or too wise for us, why, the sooner
they are out of it the better for them. And so it
is the better with Reynolds. . . .

But I wish that I could come across him again in
this world, somewhere at the meeting of sea and
land, and talk with him again about the schools of
fishes, and the labours of those who seek them along
our shores, and the souls of sailormen.

. . . . . .

I confess to a complete ignorance of going round
the land, that is, of turning the point of Cornwall,
and of passing from the northern to the southern
coast. Three times have I set out from St. Ives
with the firm intention of passing the Longships,
and putting her round up-Channel. Never have I
done so. For the Seven Gods, or one or another
of them, forbad it. Had I ever fallen so low as to
put a motor into the " Nona, " she would have gone
round like a bus or a taxi ; but under sail alone it
was forbidden me. Each of those three times I
started with a light wind and was becalmed ; and
at the end of the each of those calms I drifted back
so far upon the flood that I sickened of the attempt.
St. Ives is a very long way from London, and a still
longer way from Sussex, and a man cannot spend
his life indefinitely taking that immense journey

back and forth for nothing. And that is why I
sent the " Nona " round the land.

I have never made Newlyn. I have never gone
into Falmouth, so there is still something left for
me to do. I have, indeed, seen all that coast from
within, and walked back and forth across the last
peninsula of England, and compared Mounts Bay
and its rock with the towering brother island upon
the further shore : for every such sea-girt height is
dedicated to St. Michael, being a natural perching
place for winged things. The two Mounts are little
models of the two national histories : each begins
as a monastery ; but one becomes a king's prison,
then derelict, then a sort of national showplace ; the
other becomes a country house.

You may trace a parallel in the fate of the
Templars in the two capitals. The secret society
of the Templars, with its gigantic wealth and
universal conspiracy, was suppressed (to the salvation
of Europe) six hundred years ago. Their centre
in Paris fell to the King, became in its last stages an
appanage for younger sons and cousins of the
Crown, then a prison. It was at last destroyed in
the very beginnings of the new Paris under
Napoleon. Its memory has almost disappeared.

The Templars' centre in London passed gradually
to the lawyers, and now fulfils, among other functions, the very useful one of preventing cabs from
getting too quickly from the Embankment to Fleet
Street.

As for the two round churches, the mysterious
symbols of that great, now dead, freemasonry (which
for a moment threatened all our lives) that one in
which the Mass was preserved, has disappeared
from that capital of Europe where the Mass has
perhaps most power. But that from which the

Mass was driven out is still carefully maintained in its externals, and stands there still in the midst of London—dead.

It was upon this coast of Cornwall that I once, to my shame, wholly misread the outline of a headland, not from sea but from land.

Standing upon the shoulder of the Lizard peninsula, and looking eastward upon a clear summer's day, I misread the Dodman. Now from land this is unpardonable, because one has on land points of reference, and, indeed, had I been careful, and with a map before me, I could not have made such an error. But from the sea it is a thing that happens very much oftener than sailing-men are willing to admit.

I remember once, many years ago, coming in from far outside, and making sure of a point of French land, which I thought I knew by heart. I saw a characteristic dip, and, in front of it, the nearer lump of land which I knew for an island, and then there was a gap, or " V," which I could have sworn to be the harbour town I knew. It is true that I was surprised to find it lying so far over my starboard bow. I had thought it to be right before me, but I trusted my eyes rather than my reckoning. As we drew nearer I found all that inference in error. I had, indeed, failed in my reckoning somewhat, but it was the other way about, and the place I was looking for lay more than twenty miles to the eastward, and, when I first saw land, my harbour was hidden below the last horizon, over the port bow.

One would think that the outline of a headland, once one had known it from a particular side, was an unmistakable thing, and one would think that the same would be true of a characteristic range of hills seen lengthwise, or even of the entrance to a valley harbour.

After all, the same sort of thing is at once recognisable by land : a man does not mistake the Wrekin, or the Malvern Hills.

But at sea, for some mysterious reason, you never can be sure ; and that is why such pains are taken in the elaborate descriptions and plans of sailing directions, and in the little pictures which they make in the official books. It is not only a matter of what is called to-day " visibility," though it is true that the thickness of the air makes a great difference to one's judgment of distance. No matter what the conditions, the most absurd mistakes can be made, and are made continually, and that by practised men. It was only the other day that I mistook Grisnez for the end of the cliff some miles to the east of it above the flat of Calais. You would think that Beachy Head, seen from up-Channel looking westward, was unmistakable ; for it has the exact outline of a hippopotamus, with its little ear and fat forehead and snout, and there is a long flat before it, so that anything rising up, one would think, was bound to be Beachy Head, but it is not so. A man who has been knocking about the Channel at night, and does not quite know where he is, except that he is somewhere off the Sussex coast, may (it sounds absurd, but it is true) take Fairlight in a haze for Beachy Head, or (coming eastwards) he may catch in a dull dawn the low cliffs beyond Newhaven, and, if the thick air hides Beachy from him, he may take these for that headland.

Much more excusable, and yet much more common than mistaking the outline of hills, or a headland, is the mistaking of a light. All of them have carefully marked spaces of time, a flash for so many seconds, or a change of colour, or what not. But a man cannot always be bothered to time these things, and in a little boat under a strain he may not be able to do so. But the very commonest form of error in this, as in everything else, comes from an absolute and false certitude. You say to yourself, "There is no doubt at all that that light is such and such a light." You have been waiting to pick it up, and when you pick up a light you are certain it is that light, unless the timing of it is quite grossly different from what you expected. But you may be quite wildly wrong. I suppose no one will believe me when I tell them that I have known St. Catherine's mistaken for The Hogue.

But there are more absurd cases still. Many years ago, a ship called the *Mohegan* struck the rocks called the Manacles, which are inside Black Head, in Cornwall. She was going down Channel, and there would seem to be no question of danger in the matter. The Lizard light is there, staring plain enough ; one only has to keep it well on the starboard bow going down Channel, and one is sure to miss England. One cannot hit the Manacles so long as the light is well off one's starboard bow, for they lie inside the Point. Therefore, when the *Mohegan* struck, she must have had the Lizard light on her port bow, and the look-out man, and the man steering, and the man setting the course, and the man in command on the bridge must have known perfectly well (one would think) that the situation was impossible. Yet strike she did, and no one has ever really explained how it happened.

There are some of these mistakes which cannot be avoided, and which are explainable, not by any failure of the human reason, but by a very natural confusion between similar things. Thus, any one runs a risk at Dungeness on account of the two lighthouses there ; I mean any one going up-

Channel, and aiming at giving that point a very close shave.

Dungeness grows out to sea at a certain rate, so that, at long intervals, a new lighthouse has to be built to mark its extremity. Though it grows outwards thus into the Channel, the end is steep-to, and there is plenty of water right up alongside the land. Therefore, any one going up-Channel makes for the lighthouse direct, intending to pass within a few yards of the shore, for this shortens an up-Channel course. Also, if you have the tide with you, you have a strong stream there to help you.

Now, about one hundred years ago, they built the old lighthouse where Dungeness then was. That old lighthouse is now about one mile inland. It does happen, and I am witness to it with hundreds of others, that the modern lighthouse on the extreme end of the point may be obscured by day, when the old lighthouse is visible. In that case a man tends to steer for the old lighthouse, thinking it to be the new one, and he is aiming, of course, right on-shore when he thinks he is just going to miss the point.

The worst mistake of this sort I myself ever made was mistaking the Varne Buoy for the South Goodwin Lightship. It is not so impossible as it sounds. The weather was thick ; I had been drifting for many hours without much wind, and with no certitude of where I was except that I was somewhere in the Straits. I looked up-weather, to the north-east, and saw in the brume what looked like a hull and a pole. I could not be quite certain whether there was a ball on the pole or not, but I certainly took it for a lightship ; and, judging from the time that I had left the French harbour, and the sort of pace I thought I had made in my little boat, and tricked by the weather (which was much thicker

than it looked) I made sure that this apparently
distant object was the Goodwin. It was not till I
came within a hail of it that I knew it for what it
was—the Varne Buoy, not a hundredth the size of a
lightship.

I suppose that the regularity and certitude of
modern mechanical life on land tend to make men
exaggerate the fixity of evidence. When men dealt
more with the caprice of Nature, they were more
ready to admit two things which modern men under-
estimate : the possibility of marvel and the falli-
bility of the senses.

Different periods take quite different standards in
such affairs. Our own time prides itself on a
specially clear vision of reality, and ridicules the
credulity of the past. Yet I notice a hundred
things in which I could imagine posterity stupefied
at our inane credulity. We accept, in everything
which does not immediately concern us, a bare
newspaper statement made anonymously. We
accept it as we accept the evidence of our own senses,
or more ; we accept it although it is unvouched for,
unproved, untested. We accept it—to be brutal—
because it is printed, and because it is printed on a
large scale.

There is a whole mythology of " prehistory,"
which has grown up, mushroom-like, in less than a
lifetime, which pretends to explain the unknown
past of man, and which has already become more
fixed and sacred to the multitude than any mythology
accepted by our fathers. Not one of the millions
who accept that mythology could give you even the
briefest account of the supposed steps of evidence
upon which it reposes. In this process the strange
mechanical, universal, influence of what is called
" popular education " plays a very great part, and

whereas the half-educated man was always a danger, to-day he is a catastrophe.

Or, take not prehistory—which is a mere imposture—but recent, recorded, real history. Millions of children are told that the American Colonies revolted because they were unjustly taxed by England ; that after a long struggle they won, and that they won because they were right ; because they had the same qualities as our own sacred selves, being of our own sacred blood ; that the trouble ought never to have arisen, and was only due to the folly of a few misguided and pigheaded English gentlemen who happened then to hold political power. I will bargain that—above the labouring mass—this is the attitude taken by nine men out of ten in England to-day towards the American War of Independence. On the top of that all are told—or given the impression, at any rate—that England soon repented of her error, and came to regard the United States as the noblest of her children.

They are not told that an expensive war had been waged by the Mother Country in defence of the Colonies ; that long and difficult negotiations had been undertaken to see how that expense could be shared ; that certainly a majority of the colonists—and probably a large majority—were on the side of England, and against the rebels, and that the final defeat of England was mainly due to the intervention of the French, and especially to the more close concentration of the French fleet. They are not told that the English people regarded themselves as perfectly right, that they continued to detest the Americans with the most vivid hatred for a hundred years afterwards, or that the policy of pretending a friendship with America is quite recent, and only grew up after the strength of the new country was apparent, when the long agony of the Civil War had turned in favour of the North. Worst of all, they are not told that this pretence of identifying the United States with England is being carried on against increasing odds, as the United States became less and less English in tradition, in blood, in morals, and everything else.

The false legend is swallowed whole, and it is a very good example of how mythology can have a direct practical effect for ill. Our general opinion is only now beginning to be shocked by the foreignness of America, and is still bewildered by the refusal of Americans to regard themselves as English. You can always be certain of middle class and lower middle class support in England (I do not say popular support, for the populace are quite indifferent to the whole affair) for any foreign policy which takes for granted that America is but another England overseas.

I saw a very good example of this at the beginning of last year, 1924, when I was watching opinion at home and abroad upon what were then called the " Expert Committees," and later, the " Dawes "—that is, the two Committees sitting in Paris to decide whether the Germans had concealed large assets abroad, and also to decide what the Germans could pay by way of reparations.

For three solid years the international financial powers which directed our policy in the matter of German reparations had denied the accumulation of German wealth abroad, and had persistently clamoured that the Germans could never pay more than a small fraction of the sums claimed of them, if that. From the same sources there had been in England a persistent clamour for " expert " examination of the question under American direction, and the basis of this last demand was the certitude that America would only act in the matter as the willing helpmate of England. The Committees met, but the initiative for calling them together was American ; the American delegates, and behind them the American Government, were the deciding forces. When the reports came out there was a stupefaction, gallantly concealed ; for those reports, insisted upon by the American delegates, completely contradicted in every point the propaganda of the past three years. They insisted that the Germans had accumulated vast sums abroad, especially in the United States, and that Germany could soon pay indefinitely, at the rate of £125,000,000 a year. The result of having nourished these illusions upon American relations to England was that the foreign policy adopted officially by the British Government was thrown out of gear. The English Governments (acting in this respect differently from the way in which the English public as a whole would have acted), had supported Germany to the fullest of their ability. They had postponed all efforts of reparations, they had insisted that all demands to obtain payments by force were illegal ; they had refused to help their Allies to obtain such payments; their Treasury spokesman had told everybody that Germany had nothing concealed abroad to speak of, and certainly could not pay on any considerable scale. They then asked for a Committee of Experts, took it for granted that American pressure on this Committee would be in their favour, openly pledged themselves beforehand to accept the Report, and were bewildered, when the Report came out, to find it opposed to them.

Those who govern us have been compelled to

accept the Dawes Report—even to set it working—
and they watch anxiously its coming effect upon that
balance whereby England lives. They are caught in
a trap. Had they known a plain, modern historical
truth, that America is a foreign country, they could
have preserved an independent national policy. It is
now too late. America has mastered us.

. . . . .

The next port from which I have taken the "Nona"
after the turn of the land is Fowey, for, though I have
gone into Mevagissey once in my life, it was but in
an open boat, sailing across St. Austell's Bay ; and
there, in Mevagissey, I did not learn what I had
always desired to learn, and what to this day remains
a mystery to me, and that is, the history, nature and
fate of the busy little buzzer, the Mevagissey Bee.
It was in the port of Boston, in Lincolnshire, that I
first heard of this animal, having then not yet arrived
at my thirtieth year. Perhaps I had heard its name
before, and had not noticed it ; but it was there
that I was first struck by the account of its strange
demeanour.

There lay in the narrow river a very large, hideous,
and dirty steamer, and I could not see how she
would have room to turn, for she was pointing
upstream, under the distant benediction of that
marvellous great tower. I said to a sailorman who
was leaning on a post, and looking moodily at this
steamer (which may have been his ship for all I
know) : " How will she get out of this ? " To which
he answered : " Starn foremost, like the Mevagissey
Bee." I asked him what that Bee was, and by way of
answer he lurched away. I have asked many men
since, and no one has been able to tell me.

Fowey, then, I say, is the most western port to
which, or from which, I ever took the " Nona." And

Fowey is a thing by itself. One may say of it what Mr. Barry Pain said in his review of that ought-to-be-most-famous book called "Delina Delaney" : "This is a thing which only happens once in a thousand years."

Fowey is the harbour of harbours, and the last port town left without any admixture of the modern evil. It ought to be a kingdom of its own. In Fowey all is courtesy, and good reason for the chance sailing man. For your provision, or your transport, or your mooring, you pay no more than you should, and whatever you may need in gear is to be had at once ; and in Fowey have I had a sail made for me in, perhaps, one-sixth of the time it would have taken anywhere else along the coast eastward. It was a jib, and it fitted. In Fowey, also, there is security from all winds, good holding ground, and, what is best of all, an air in which all other places may be forgotten, and in which the cares of this crowded island melt away. I suppose when the crash comes, and the ruins have been more or less cleaned up, Fowey will remain to carry on the traditions of a better England. I hope so. There is no fault to be found with it. Now, can this be said of any other town except Leominster ? I think not. I have never sailed into Fowey or out of Fowey without good luck attending me. I have never had to beat in or out of Fowey ; I have always had a leading wind. I have had light airs, of course, outside, but I have never been becalmed. The last time I left that blessed land—to which, perhaps, I never shall return—it was under so gallant a north-west breeze, so clear a light in the first of the midday tide, that the career along the coast to Plymouth Sound was like a song.

It is unreasonable, but those stretches of coast-

wise sea in which one has had good fortune remain
in the mind exceptional, and carry with them a sort
of false air of security, as though they were always
so. Men must have had the terror of their lives
time and again off that coast ; but to me it always
seems, when it returns as a picture in my mind,
sunlit, and framed in vigorous small seas, with the
attendance of a noble and a sufficient breeze. With
what pleasure have I not noted the speed she made
as she passed the measured mile by Polperro, and
how pleasant to see Rame Head growing perpetually
before one, until the "Nona" opened the majestic
breadth of Plymouth Sound.

As for Plymouth, I fear there is some evil of
perversion about that mood which makes so many
men (and I am one of them) disgruntled with
exaggerated fame. Modern legend has got a way
of selecting a few abiding places of its own, and there
trampling down the grass and all around with such
a multitude of repetition and exaggeration and
ready-made phrase as corresponds, in the things of
the mind, to the most intolerable mud in the things
of the soil. Is it print which has done this, and
steam—newspapers and the railway ? No ! So
much evil could not have come from material things :
its real source was in the degraded modern mind.
What with Drake and the Armada, and the Bowls
and the Rock upon the other side of the sea, which
failed to land upon the Puritans, and the perpetual
reiteration of all these things, I would rather see
Plymouth breakwater from the Sound, and so sail
past than look on the Sound from the Hoe. But I
admit that this mood is evil, and that it is something
of a perversion to feel such irritation against mere
wearisome repetitions. One has only to leave them
alone.

It is a heavenly piece of coast, all this southern bulge of Devon, with its little secret rivers and untainted towns. The people are good and the land. So, with reservations, is its sea even beyond the Sound. Though once, indeed, I did suffer off Bolt Head one of the two most abominable spills of wind I ever suffered—and the first was off Beachy Head by Birdling Gap on Whit-Tuesday, 1902, a day ever to be remembered.

For the air fell off Birdling Gap just like water out of a bucket, and nearly blew the "Nona" flat upon her beam. I let go the sheet with a run, but as it was she dipped, perhaps, a third of her mainsail, and nearly broke her lover's heart with fear. It is so sometimes with these high lands. The wind does not run true. It blows over them, and curls through a depression upon their edges, and curves, splashing down solid, in a bolt, on to the deep below. For, on that day by Beachy, all those years ago, the true wind was but just enough northerly to let me keep a course for Newhaven, hauled very close and saving every inch. But that gust came suddenly right on the weather beam, from far east of north, and nearly settled my then young craft and him that cherished and still cherishes her.

As for the spill off Bolt Head, it fell after a clear midnight, since the War, and it was more than a spill ; for it blew steadily for the best part of an hour and then ceased. But, like its younger brother off Beachy, it was peculiar to the high land ; for it came due northerly, whereas the main wind had east in it. I was watching the morning star burning like a sacred furnace on the edges of the black hills when Satan sent that wind and tried to drown three men. But we reefed in time—there were three of us, one for the helm and two to reef ; and when dawn broke, and the blessed colours of the east renewed the day, strange !—one end of the boom had three reefs down, and the other only two !

A coast of good memories : may it stand for ever in spite of petrol and every other evil thing. There might be no London at all, so kindly and so well guarded are all the men and women of its little harbour towns, and so uncrowded its hills. The Erne and the Avon I have never entered, but the Yealm I know : a difficult river in which to anchor, on account of innumerable moorings, a winding water in a wooded gorge, difficult also for wind. And Salcombe I have sailed in and out of—I suppose the happiest harbour in the world. It has many little beaches of its own, the homes of men standing separate upon them, far inland creeks, not too strong a tide, a bar, somewhat shoal, but always deep enough for the " Nona, " and a clear fairway to be fetched from within or from without, I take it, upon any wind ; for the harbour opens well inside the narrows, and the seaward shores open well outside them.

Upon this piece of coast, setting out once from Plymouth, there came to me an experience of no particular moment as history, but of powerful effect upon my mind. It marked, in a sort of mysterious omen way, or, perhaps, I should say in a sort of visionary way, the unleashing of the Great War.

It so happened that in that summer of 1914 I had had occasion to go from Hampshire to one of the western ports, where I was to pick up my boat, and take her ultimately into Plymouth Sound, and thence, when I should have the leisure, I proposed to take her out again, and stand eastward up the coast.

I was staying in Hampshire with a friend who had a house in the New Forest. It was on a Sunday

I set out thence. He sent me in his motor to Salisbury, where I wished to get Mass before going on by train. During the Mass, the priest, after his announcements, asked the congregation to pray for the soul of the Archduke Heir-Apparent of Austria, who had been murdered at a place called Sarajevo. I had never heard the name, and I had but a vague idea of who this archduke was, of his relationship to the Emperor, and of his heirship to the throne of Hapsburg-Lorraine. I came to the " Nona," where she lay, and sailed out with her into the sea for some days. I had no conception that anything could be brewing.

When I came to land again, and went up to London, I found the air to be filled with all the possibilities of that time. The Austrian Government had sent to the Servian Government a note, the like of which had not been heard in the history of Christendom. It made demands which no government claiming to sovereignty could accept. For my part, when I read the terms of the note, I was in no doubt that it was of Prussian dictation. I am in no doubt to this day that it was of Prussian dictation.

There are two ways of ascertaining the origin of such a thing. One is the material way, the consultation of the only available documents, and the only certified direct human evidence. The other is the moral way, when one says : " This can only have been written by so and so," or, at the very least, " Can only have been inspired by so and so." Thus, if I find upon the table of a doubtful, weak kind of a man—and a courteous one at that—a letter framed in the very terms and manner of a bully, constantly his associate, then, though the letter be in the handwriting of the former, and on his own paper, even if there were convincing proof that when the actual writing was done the man was alone, I should yet say that the real author was the bully, and not the gentleman. He may have learnt it by heart at dictation. He may have copied it from the other's draft. At any rate, it is morally certain that the one man, and not the other, is the true author of the thing launched—is the one responsible.

Now, in the case of this note to Servia, the whole thing is Prussian from beginning to end : the extreme arrogance, the deliberate provocation, the exactitude, the aridity and, above all, the unintelligence. And as for proof upon the other side, we have none, except what the various culprits chose themselves to give us.

As I went about London getting all men's views, as is my custom when grave things threaten, I heard many judgments passed upon the probable consequences of the note. The man whose judgment in European affairs I trusted most, one who had been largely employed in the foreign business of this country, and who also had a deep and solid knowledge of history, told me that there would not be war, even between Austria and Servia, let alone an extension of the peril.

The reason he gave for this was curious. He said that a document of that extreme violence would not have been issued if war were the object. The object was to make bargaining acutely necessary, and to get a further hold over Balkan land as a result of a long haggling. For very violent actions—of which this was the most extreme case yet known to Europe—the excess of offensive and inhuman brutality could only, he said, be used as a blind.

Though I then knew very much less of the European situation, I hesitated to agree with him as to the motive ; but, on the other hand, I certainly did not think there would be war. I thought Servia would yield in all save the very worst and most humiliating points, and that these would at last be waived.

Many other opinions of various colours did I gather in that interval, but only one foreseeing a war ; and to that one I paid no attention, because it was very foolishly expressed, and for the wrong reason. It was given me by a man who had travelled widely, and who was an expert in many languages, as well as a man of great knowledge in certain forms of mechanical construction. He had also a high scientific training. He had no public post. This man said to me there would be war, because Austria was known to be in a rotten condition, because upon the outbreak of war the various sections of her tessellated dominion would break apart, and the Servians, knowing this, and having the Russians behind them, would take up the challenge. The Prussian power, or " Reich," would be so alarmed at the prospect that it would attempt to stave off hostilities, or, failing that, to leave the Austrian Crown to its fate. Such was the folly and ill-judgment of the only man who thought that war was coming, among all those whom I consulted. It was a good example of hitting a mark by firing wide : like the duellist in the dark room who in mercy shot up the chimney, yet brought down his opponent.

For, note you, that though a great many men up and down Europe had said that Prussia was making for war, and that a conflict must come about in some near future, and though I myself had written it over my own signature (if I remember rightly), when, in 1911, Prussia raised her special war tax, and the

French were compelled to reintroduce the three years' service ; yet *this* did not seem to be the occasion—for it was too abrupt. There seemed to be no plot or plan ; and the season was already late.

I did not know what we know now, that Prussia firmly calculated on two things : first, the neutrality of England, and, secondly, a very complete and very rapid victory over the French, a decisive victory, destroying the whole of the French Army within a month of the frontier crossing ; a battle beginning as did Charleroi, but ending very differently from the Marne.

When I next had occasion to leave London, in order to find again my boat at Plymouth, and to take her out, nothing was decided. One might almost say that the suspense, such as it was, seemed less burdensome, and the sense of peril less acute. I came down by night ; I saw no morning papers ; I got aboard with my companion, and spent the whole forenoon before the slight tide would serve in putting things to right for the cruise.

We dropped out under a soft air, which soon died away. We spent the whole mortal day drifting down to the Mewstone, and then, in that exasperating calm, the turn of the tide took us up again towards the breakwater. It was not till the fall of day that a breeze arose ; I cannot remember from what quarter, but I think it was off the land—that is, from the north-east—but, at any rate, it served us; we could go eastward without having to beat, and we made out down the Sound. It was still light when we passed the Mewstone again. Through the last of evening and through all the darkness we ran along the coast to Devon for the Start.

I knew that the times were perilous, but I knew no more than any other man, in that odd week's lull before the storm, exactly how perilous they were. It was nearly a month, I think, since I had heard the priest read out, from those altar steps of Salisbury, prayers for the Archduke who had been murdered at Sarajevo.

When I had set out from Plymouth there was nothing but rumour, nothing certain. The Fleet had dispersed already some days past from the great review at Spithead, and was, as we were told, in the Atlantic at manœuvres. A night, a day, and now another night had passed ; I had heard no news.

Nothing was further from my mind than war and armament as the sun rose on that glorious July morning, right out of a clean horizon, towards which the wind blew fresh and cool. It was a light but steady wind of morning that filled my sails as I sat at the tiller with a blanket about me, and laying her head to the north.

We had just rounded the Start at dawn. My companion went below to sleep. I watched, over the quarter, the Start Light flashing pale and white in the broadening day, and at last extinguished. Then the sun rose, as I have said. Immediately after its rising a sort of light haze filled the air to eastward. It was denser than it seemed to be, for it did not obscure the low disc of the sun, nor redden it, but, as you will read in a moment, it performed a mystery. The little ship slipped on, up past the Skerries Bank, and I could see far off the headland which bounds Dart Bay. There was no sail in sight. I was alone upon the sea ; and the breeze neither freshening nor lowering, but giving a hearty line of course (along which we slipped, perhaps, five knots or six) made the water speak merrily upon the bows and along the run of our low sides. In this loneliness and content, as I sailed northward, I

chanced to look after an hour's steering or so,
eastward again towards the open sea—and then it
was that there passed me the vision I shall remember
for ever, or for so long as the longest life may last.

Like ghosts, like things themselves made of mist,
there passed between me and the newly risen sun,
a procession of great forms, all in line, hastening
eastward. It was the Fleet recalled.

The slight haze along that distant water had
thickened, perhaps, imperceptibly ; or perhaps the
great speed of the men-of-war buried them too
quickly in the distance. But, from whatever cause,
this marvel was of short duration. It was seen for
a moment, and in a moment it was gone.

Then I knew that war would come, and my mind
was changed.

The bright air was the same around me and the
heartening morning wind ; the happy course of the
"Nona," making for a known port with all in her
favour and something of youth in her and all round.
What that war would bring, its magnitude, its
character, was veiled from us all ; but the advent of
it, the mass of it coming, put a new face on everything
I saw and felt and heard ; on the steady breeze, on the
little lapping of the salt sea-water, on the strong headlands of England. So went I northward alone as
the day grew, until by mid-morning the breeze
having dropped somewhat and the boat running
more sluggishly, we lay abeam of the rock called the
Druid's Mare, and began to run up the coast for
Torbay. My companion wakened and came on
deck. I told him what I had seen.

.   .   .   .

These strong emotions, though they colour all
the mind, soon lose their edge, and we fell to talking
of the coast we passed, and of the chance of holding

the wind, which declined a little and was not so steady as we rounded the last headland. My mind turned nothing over of the possibilities of what was to come. It was later, when I had come ashore again, and had reached London, that I learnt of the prolonged hesitation among the politicians, men by their petty trade unused to and unfit for tasks of magnitude ; of the French President's letter and the ambiguous reply to it, drafted and published ; of the final voting when, by a majority of one, the Cabinet decided upon war. Had the virility of such a decision been known even four brief days earlier, war would not have come. But it was too late.

Among the nine who gave their votes in favour of the neutrality of Britain, some were actuated, as we know, by base, one, as we know too well, by the basest of motives : mere trivial personal ambition for success in the wretched tawdry game of professional politics, which was the only craft he knew. But some also acted from the noblest motives and rise for the moment above the fœtid marsh-mist of Westminster. These I shall always respect for the strength of their wills and the clarity of their convictions in so awful a moment.

Still more did I then, and do I still, respect them for the deliberate choice they made to accept what was certain to be a vivid, and might be a very dangerous unpopularity, when the first shots should be fired. These men were convinced that it would be to the advantage of their country if the Continental forces should be left to thrash out their own decisions. They were opposed, perhaps, to the majority of their countrymen at the time (it is not so sure ; for the mass of their countrymen had hardly had time to decide, so swift was the last rush of events). They would certainly be opposed, as they knew, to the vast majority of their countrymen in a few days. They were the more English, the more characteristic of the blood which they boasted, in that they took such a decision fearlessly. I can believe that to this day the best of them still thinks that his judgment was sound and that great evils now passed, and other evils dreadfully threatening us now, more than ten years after, would have been saved us altogether, if England had refused war. But the best instructed opinion, the opinion with the widest view, was opposed to them. War followed. With what full fruits only men now young can live to discover.

There is not perhaps in all history (of the sort which has full records behind it) any group of days on which men will debate more and will find it less easy to establish a permanent conclusion than those last days of July and first days of August, 1914. But there are certain structural lines supporting even the most confused and the most debated of records. Thus, men will never be exactly certain what Harold did at the court of William, nor of how the first directive events of that great quarrel lay. Men will never arrive at a fixed and general conclusion upon the initiative responsible for the revolutionary wars, nor even, perhaps, for the renewed attack upon Napoleon, or by Napoleon, after Elba. But these debates are, for all that, built round a solid skeleton of certain conclusions, and in this great matter of the Great War I do not think that posterity will depart from the general conclusion of our own times (which is certainly mine) that an early declaration of the British attitude would have prevented war.

It is a question easily confused with a totally different one, and the two must be kept carefully apart. The *right* of Great Britain to remain neutral should surely be admitted, not only in law but in common sense. In law there was no definite agreement with the French. There was no accepted obligation to support the French in the West or elsewhere. A great number of acts had been accomplished which could only have had such a support for their object ; the military situation had been studied, contingent military dispositions had been carefully planned in detail. The general policy of the preceding years, especially after Agadir, had pointed to the same end ; but the Government of this country had always, in the most insistent manner, affirmed and provided for its freedom of choice when the crisis should come. And the very fact that it had thus so continuously maintained that freedom of choice, and specifically asserted it, is proof that every other step, however obviously designed for common action in arms, was *not* to be given the interpretation of a binding alliance.

Since this great point in history involves a moral judgment quite as much as the mere interpretation of texts, it should also, I think, be laid down that, in matters of life and death, a nation, like an individual, has the right to stretch even a formal text to the very limits of interpretation.

I would say that even if a formal and solemn alliance had existed, any one holding authority in England at that moment and conceiving that participation in the Continental war would ultimately ruin Great Britain, had a right to seek for any phrase in the written pact which could save his country from disaster—and such phrases can always be found. I will go further: I will say that the certitude of disaster on such a scale would excuse even a breach

of faith : but I know that this is passing the bounds
ordinarily allowed ; and I only say it because there
seems to me an implied distinction between war for
a local object which could do no more than advantage
or hurt a country somewhat, and war of a sort which
this war turned out to be, wherein the whole structure of human society was imperilled.   In the same
way, if I have promised to help a man and to support
him in various details of his domestic life, even
though I have taken good consideration for my
services, I have the right to fly from his house if it
catches fire in order to save my child from being
burnt to death.   A vast difference in the scale
between the reasonably expected effects of a compact
and the suddenly discovered real effects would seem
to release a man from the obligation of that compact.
But in this case there was not even a definite
compact.   Therefore, no one could advance a moral
plea against the hesitation which our politicians
showed in that grave moment.   No, what is to be
advanced against the politicians who so lamentably
bungled that affair is a charge drawn from the
intellectual, not from the moral side of our nature.
They acted stupidly, as indeed their trade leads
men to act : for professional politics is a trade in
which the sly outweigh the wise.   It was bad judgment to leave the matter in doubt to the last ; and
the decision was deferred and deferred again,
simply because your professional politician, always
absorbed in a wretched personal intrigue, blinked
and was bewildered by a great issue suddenly
thrust upon him.

You will often hear it said war could not but come
when once the three great Continental Powers had
mobilised.   It has been repeated that the act of
mobilisation—of full mobilisation—renders war

necessary. The statement is untrue. Certainly the French mobilisation did not, even up to the very last moment, render war necessary ; and the same is true of the German.

Again, it is still said by fanatics that the Russian Government intended and provoked the war. And many men not fanatics, but ignorant of Europe, or at issue with Christendom, repeat the myth. Those who plead in favour of Prussia and of the German general staff (they are numerous in England to-day) still pretend, as do all the German writers, that the mobilisation ordered from Berlin was but a reply to the earlier orders issued from St. Petersburg.

History will not accept that. There is altogether too much against it. There is the connection between the *Lokal Anzeiger* and the German general staff. Still more there is the nature of German mobilisation, which was so designed that *preliminary* orders were, to its general scheme, what *final* orders were in any other country. The Prussian scheme of mobilisation may be compared to a loaded gun. If I know that a man has his gun loaded and he aims it at me, my then loading mine is not a provocation.

Much more is there, against so strained and distorted a piece of special pleading, the truth obvious to any one, even the most superficial, who had seen Germany since 1911 : the whole mass of that population supported its government in a determination for what was believed would prove a short and highly lucrative campaign, and one not only highly lucrative, but settling for ever the security of that great experiment which Prussia had not quite consolidated by her series of rapid victories a lifetime before.

But though the German mobilisation was indeed

proof of the truth that Prussia and her subjects desired war, that war so eagerly desired was a Continental war only. The Continental war envisaged at Berlin excluded the factor of English intervention. Not that it was believed such intervention would make any great difference in what was assumed would be an immediate and crushing victory in the West, but that sea power continuously exercised could not but have given pause upon what Berlin thought would be the probable result of the struggle in the East. Granted an immediate and certain German victory in the West (as a fact it failed), there would still be an eastern campaign which the German general staff believed to be necessarily prolonged and which they dreaded ; blockade during *that* trial they dared not face.

Two men, I think, deserved well of their country at that moment, granted that an entry into the War sooner or later was inevitable. One was Mr. Winston Churchill, who upon his own initiative mobilised the fleet ; and the other was Lord Haldane, who convinced his colleagues of the nature of the peril and who, it should be remembered, had made possible the co-operation of Britain in the War by his scheme for mobilisation. All that followed was based upon the work originally done by him at the War Office at a time when, to the great bulk of his countrymen, the idea of such a conflict was still quite unfamiliar and its enormous implications incredible.

For the rest, it is neither generous nor wise to pick out any particular set of misjudgments ; for the whole of Europe, all its culture and all its intelligence, was at fault in estimates of the War. You may say of all the mass of stuff that has been written since the Armistice that it can be graded in

degrees of intelligence according to its admission of
the unexpected and the fortuitous throughout those
terrible years. The less intelligent the writer the
more he ascribes this or that development to a plan ;
the more intelligent he is the more he admits
factors independent of our wills and our intelli-
gences : factors proceeding, as our fathers would
have said, and as I believe, consciously from a will
above humanity or (as it is the modern fashion to
affirm) coming into human affairs from no god, but
blindly—at any rate, factors external to human
direction. In the individual actions can be traced
clearly enough what measure of conclusion their
success involved, or what lack of it their failure was
due to. But, in the general lines of the turmoil, it
is not so. Here and there a chance guess proved
right, but it was no more than a guess, unless we
except Lord Kitchener's warning that the War
would last at least three years : he gave it when
most men thought it might not last three months.

It is with regard to the Great War as it is with
regard to every set of campaigns in history ; if you
omit that which was not subject to any human will
and intelligence you omit nine-tenths of the factors
that make for the final result—and that is why
every great captain has put his trust in fortune and
in a star : a destiny of his own. For great captains
know what part fortune plays in their trade.

I remember Boulanger saying, when I was a boy
of nineteen : " *La guerre est une chose aléatoire.*"
It was one of those enormous truisms which make
one shake with laughter, and, coming from the lips
of such a man, it was particularly comic ; he, with
the short stature which he owed to his Welsh blood,
with his middle-aged hesitations, and his ludicrous
incapacity for the *rôle* into which the popular anger

against politicians had unnaturally thrust him, and his very natural disinclination, being what he was, to accept risk. I saw him in Portland Place, and it was there that I heard him discourse in such fashion. Young as I was, I hugely enjoyed the unconscious meiosis of such a phrase. Yes, indeed : *la guerre est une chose aléatoire !* Would that this fortuitous character in it were confined to its immediate operations ! But they stretch outward over a lifetime at least and, in some great effects, for much longer.

As I write this, it is more than ten years since the dice of that "*chose aléatoire*" were thrown, and no one can even yet determine what interests in Europe have, upon the whole, most suffered ; though (alas !) the larger lines of the result are already apparent.

Some day, I suppose—but a good time hence— one of the mob of witnesses to what went on in Paris between the Armistice and the Treaty of Versailles will write us an amusing book full of truths, made up of anecdote without much comment. Or perhaps, better still, we shall have a highly readable book from the pen of a man who was not there. We had a glimpse of such possibilities from a witness in a few sentences of Mr. Keynes', which were very illuminating ; but Mr. Keynes' book had not for its object an historical relation, but rather financial propaganda, so that the part dealing with the comedy of small men in big places was too short. If he had confined himself to the words and gestures of parliamentarians suddenly confronted with the task of diplomats I think he would have produced something memorable. One or two other pens have dealt with that comic affair, but none sufficiently, nor at any length.

I was not myself present. I was continually

between Paris and London, I had many friends and a few relations engaged, and I heard a mass of stories from many who were witnesses. Of that mass of stories, not a few sounded probable, and quite a reasonable number were vouched for by witnesses whom I could trust. I have had quoted to me, for instance, the excellent story of a Prime Minister pettishly complaining that he would not be bothered about the Dalmatian coast because they had not yet come to consider the Baltic. And the same man curiously moved a squat forefinger along the River Save upon the map, saying with a would-be-important smile, " Now here is the Upper Danube." Really in this I have some sympathy with the little fellow ; for when I first went to school I always thought it a shame that the Save, running in a straight line with the lower Danube, should not carry the same name. I thought there was something irregular about the Danube taking its great bend past Budapest.

Then there was that other story of the indignant politician who, upon reading the French word " *demander* " in a memorandum, indignantly protested against this insolent use of the word " demand."

Poland was a subject of ceaseless blunders. One politician vaguely thought it a Province of Russia ; another was surprised to hear that Danzig had ever been a Polish town ; and the same man was contented to express his simple conviction that it was no use setting up Poland again seeing that such a State could never last.

That they should get mixed up about their figures is pardonable ; there were more naughts than a man could count. Still, there is all the difference between 125 milli*ard* francs and 125 milli*on* francs : but I am assured it was not always easy for every member of the august group to carry the distinction clearly in his head, especially in the morning. Would that some more than human power had suddenly descended—or lacking such a Being, a corporal and four men—and taken the politicians forcibly into three rooms, put paper and pen before them and bade them write down, under heavy penalties, all they could remember of Europe. It would have been a pretty examination !

Now parliamentarians such as these are ridiculous, not only by the absurd disproportion between their nominal powers and their capacities, but more by their ambition—which swells out to bursting the little vessel containing it. They have not talent, save for intrigue against fellow politicians : they cannot speak or write, let alone *do* anything worth hearing. None the less would you find, if you could take the tin lid off their hollow minds and look in, a froth of insane vanity, bred of years of speech-making ; a more than kingly assurance bred of knowing no control and of immunity ; and (what is astonishing in men of such calibre) ambition itself. A paltry ambition to be sure : an ambition to fill the newspapers : but still, ambition.

Yet if there is one thing I have noted more than another in the few men worthy of admiration in this our time (men worthy of admiration through their capacities as well as through their characters), it is the absence of ambition.

There could be no better commentary upon the days in which we live. For it is reasonable and normal that men of great capacity should have ambition to exercise it in government, in the ordering of their fellow-men. It was a chief quality always looked for by our fathers in those who rose high, and

were worthy so to rise ; nor were they disappointed.
Ambition of old was a mark of greatness. But
to-day it is the mark of the capable man that ambition disgusts him. That mark is most notable in
Mussolini. It is most notable in Foch. It was
notable in most of the commanders of armies ; in
the admirals of fleets. It was most notable, of
course, in the saintly eminence of Mercier. It was
notable in almost every one I had the privilege to
meet and watch during and after the struggle, who
had been capable of doing something great in that
time.

It is not difficult to discover when you speak with
Mussolini that his interest is in his job, not in his
name. It is apparent to all that the great work of
the Cardinal Archbishop of Malines is remote from
all personal motive—and ambition is essentially personal. As for Foch, it is manifest not only in his
every gesture and expression, but in the life he has
lived after saving Europe. But this novel feature,
the absence of ambition in our greatest men to-day,
goes further. It has been notable in our chief
discoverers in physical science—all can bear witness
to that—it is even becoming apparent in the best
writers ; though writers are among the vainest of
mankind.

All men of real capacity in this our time seem
to be agreed that the peculiar odour of modern
success is a thing for a decent man to avoid. It is
becoming a sort of habit of the mind throughout
the West, that is, throughout civilised Europe to-day,
in such few men as can do some great work, to do
it silently and apart, and to disconnect it wholly
from immediate renown.

Conversely, you will have monstrous advertisement
surrounding the mere name of a man incompetent,

and usually thoroughly dishonest as well, because he is athirst for publicity of the modern sort, and loves it, and because he is quite content to serve those lumps of wealth and vulgarity, who, through their possession of the mob newspapers, can grant or withhold publicity.

Here is a situation thoroughly diseased : the spur of ambition withdrawn from those who can do. It cannot last. How it will be resolved I do not know, nor does any other man ; but that it cannot last is apparent. The mere force of competition, the mere mathematics of the world will see to it that blaring incompetence shall not permanently wield even nominal power ; and it holds more than nominal power to-day.

I was interested, among the many things I heard from the more advertised civilians of the Great War, to note two things ; the first was a rooted conviction in the most advertised parliament men that things and people foreign to their experience were inferior to them. We know, of course, that that is the natural instinct of the schoolboy, and of the very simple good person without experience ; but the astonishing thing was to find it in men whom one would expect, in spite of their origins, to have become a little polished by long conversation with their fellows, a little trained by responsibility. Before the end of the conflict one would have thought that even your politician must acquire some judgment from so much vivid and informing experience. Not a bit of it ! It went off him like so much water off a duck's back, and you may hear him to-day, six years after the Armistice, peddling the same inanities as he peddled in 1913.

The second thing I noticed was the alarming difference between politicians and the soldiers in the sense of reality. I say alarming because, after the

war, Europe, instead of continuing the rule of
soldiers as it should have done, returned to its vomit ;
and the miserable parliamentary figures of the old
degraded day put on again costume and grease paint,
filed back upon the stage, and began to play their
old antics as though nothing had happened. The
French, who ought to know better (for they have
found parliaments out), behaved disgracefully in this
matter. You may take up any French newspaper
to-day, and find yourself appalled with the recurrence
of such names as Caillaux, Briand, Herriot,
Loucheur, who ought never to have been mentioned
again after such an experience as the Great War.

Italy has done better : but only under the stress
of a threatened dissolution. Society in Italy had to
reach the point of acute peril before that reaction
took place which saved the country ; but what a
fine reaction it was, not only in its virtues, but, what
is more important, in its spirit ! What a strong
critical sense Italy has shown ! What intelligence
in rejection of sophistry, and what virility in
execution ! May it last ! But will it last ? Even in
Italy ?

Everything good in this world is doomed to
perish, and I cannot tell how long this excellent
experiment will stand, or whether it will take firm
root, and make Italy all that it desires to be, and all
that Italy should be—seeing the strength of the
blood, the industry, the intelligence, and the warmth
of all that people. But, at any rate, it is good to
visit a society still under such an impulse, and to
feel that, in one section of Europe at least, things
are going well.

I made a sort of pilgrimage to see Mussolini, the
head of the movement, and I wrote about him for
the Americans. I had the honour of a long con-

versation with him alone, discovering and receiving his judgments. What a contrast with the sly and shifty talk of your parliamentarian ! What a sense of decision, of sincerity, of serving the nation, and of serving it towards a known end with a definite will ! Meeting this man after talking to the parliamentarians in other countries was like meeting with some athletic friend of one's boyhood after an afternoon with racing touts ; or it was like coming upon good wine in a Pyrenean village after compulsory draughts of marsh water in the mosses of the moors above, during some long day's travel over the range.

One thing, however, struck me in his comments which was, as I thought, extreme and ill-founded ; and that was his complete contempt for all majorities. Mussolini laid it down to me that the conception of majority government is as ridiculous as it is immoral, and should be fiercely combated as a lie and an evil *in itself*. I do not agree ; it seems to me that the rational basis of majority government stands firm upon certain conditions.

The right of a majority to rule is, indeed, an absurd doctrine as we hear it commonly stated. I do not mean the doctrine of majority government under what is called " the representative system," for that is not majority government at all : it is mere oligarchy in the hands of an intriguing caucus, and perhaps as base a form of oligarchy as mankind has ever tolerated. I mean real majority government ; the reference of a question to the body of the governed, and the taking of a decision according to the superior number of votes recorded on the " Yes " or " No " side. Such a test used as a universal decider is ridiculous. What would a majority vote do with Bimetallism, or the appointment of admirals ? But there are conditions in which a decision by majority is just, and they are surely these :

(1) When the question arises from a homogeneous community ; (2) When there is an active popular demand for its settlement ; (3) When the matter under discussion is reasonably familiar to all ; (4) When it concerns all, or nearly all, directly, and in much the same degree ; (5) When the majority is substantial.

You must be dealing with an homogeneous community—for in one made up of various races, or fundamentally different religions, a majority means nothing towards a decision. It is a mere affirmation of discord. You must have a real and popular demand for a decision, and it must proceed from the people themselves : not from a body claiming the right to frame the question : a vote on matters of no popular interest—as a vote on Welsh disestablishment in North London, or on mining regulations in Brighton—is a manifest abuse. Even on a burning matter, discussed by, known to, and affecting all, no small majority can possibly be decisive, or make an accord—for a half is not the general will. But when a community of one stuff votes by a large majority in favour of something they both understand and desire, and that something close to their own lives, then that majority is of true effect.

Under those conditions the moral argument for majority government seems to me unanswerable, for under those conditions you have the will of the community really expressed by the majority. Now the community is ultimately sovereign ; for if the community be not sovereign, what else can claim sovereignty ? It is the old dilemma of Suarez, the great Jesuit doctrine, as absolutely secure as a mathematical conclusion ; ultimately, the community is sovereign. But unless these conditions are present, and unless all of them are present, the majority is *not* the community, and to call it so is either a delusion or a trick. It is always immoral, usually fatuous, and occasionally disastrous.

By what right shall fifty-one men out of a hundred, who have no particular taste for the drinking of tea, who, upon the whole, dislike it, but not earnestly, forbid the other forty-nine to drink tea, when those forty-nine feel tea drinking to be a very necessity of their lives ? For what reason shall fifty-one men— of whom perhaps only one knows anything upon the subject, outvote forty-nine of whom perhaps five know something of the subject ? Decide (for instance) upon the annexation of an Asian islet ? How can you trust fifty-one white men to legislate for forty-nine black men, or, to put it more strongly, fifty-one black men to legislate for forty-nine white ? Who does not know that in such a case only organised force could decide ?

Mussolini's reaction (as the Americans would call it) was, I think, against the ludicrous abuse of the doctrine of majority, which has brought Europe to its present pass; for there is nothing so wicked or so senseless or so degrading, but a majority (to the honour of our race it is generally a sham majority) can be quoted in its favour.

There is a very deplorable instance of this to-day in French politics. A small but active caucus in France hates the Christian religion. Its members are afraid to make a frontal attack on that religion, because such action would endanger their skins, but they will take any measures which will, they think, indirectly weaken its influence. Particularly do they desire to restrain the activity of the religious orders, and, so far as they can, to prevent those orders from having any corporate existence at all. The mass of the people are, in varying degrees, attached both to their traditional religion and to the more popular and active forms of the Monastic Institution : that is, the teaching and nursing religious orders. The contemplative orders they do not come in touch with. Most men and women in the nation would leave things alone, and that with a bias towards religion. Very many are almost indifferent. More, though preferring to go on as their forefathers went on, do not put it—religion—in the forefront of their lives. Many more think it of some importance, but are far more actively concerned with their material interests. A small body, quite as small perhaps as the anti-Christian caucus on the other side, are active in defence of religion. After a wearisome, meaningless rite of making marks on bits of paper, the said rite (confused by a hundred legal and personal interests, and conducted by the wire-pulling inherent in all such performances) throws up some five or six hundred members of a Parliament, nearly all of them intriguers moved by a petty appetite for money or for notoriety, or both. Of these it may be that fifty-five out of the hundred follow the anti-Christian caucus, and look to it for salaries and jobs, forty-five are organised on the other side. Or the numbers may be the other way. When the fifty-five turn up on one side, the whole vast organisation of the religious orders in France (most of which are beneficent, the rest certainly doing no harm) is suddenly imperilled and shaken ; its members are exiled, its goods are stolen and spent riotously by the lowest sort of politicians, and their hangers-on, its accumulation of wealth dissipated and destroyed. Then another chance majority comes along in four years, and offers a restoration which can but only be most precarious : a restoration of their natural rights to these infamously (and ridiculously) harassed men and women, but a restoration liable to be ruined in another four years.

After the war there happened to be in the French Parliament a vague uncertain majority more or less pledged to traditional things. The politicians most prominent in that gang approached the Carthusians who had been exiled, and had taken up a new home in Tarragona, and offered them a chance of returning to the Grande Chartreuse. These exiles very wisely refused, for they said : " How do we know that after all the expenditure of re-establishing ourselves in our ancient foundation—venerable for centuries, peaceable, remote—we may not at your next ' elections,' as you call them, find ourselves turned out ? " They were very wise :—But what a commentary upon a system of government ! Think of it ! Here is a great House with its roots right back in the beginnings of the Middle Ages, with its oaken traditions, its reserves of strength available for itself and all men ; doing nothing which could be construed as perilous under any system of common morals, either to the State or to any individual. Merely because a clique of anti-Christians hates them, this doctrine of artificial majorities can turn the whole community out of doors at a moment's notice, exile its members, loot its fortune.

Nor let it be said that these things only happen in countries like France, to which the disease of parliaments is unnatural and of alien importation ; they happen in one form or another wherever the parliamentary fraud is at work. In countries which have

lost dogmatic religion and have only vague opinion
left, the parliamentary evil takes another form, that
of a perpetual restriction against common liberties ;
or it takes the form of putting finance secretly within
the power of inferior men, who fill their pockets
at the expense of the commonwealth ; or it takes
the form of treason in time of war—attempting to
make peace with the enemy behind the back of the
people and their allies. Or it takes the form of
saving the enemy after his defeat. There is no form
of parliamentary activity which is not deplorable,
save in aristocracies.

For, in aristocracies, which are of their nature,
governments by a clique, a Parliament—which is a
clique—can be normal and natural. In communities based on the idea of equality, and of action by
the public will, they are cancers, under which such
nations always sicken and may die.

I can bear the thought of them no more. I must
get back to realities and to things loved.

I must return to my "Nona."

.   .   .   .

We came to Berry Head and opened Torbay.

It is with Torbay as with the Fowey coast. I
have known it only under such weathers as leave a
hint of heaven : never have I opened Torbay in
passing Berry Head but it was morning, with the
young sea delighting in a leading breeze ; and once,
a draught to last for ever, I came up under such a
dawn and with so tender a dying crescent in the
sky that I spent an hour in Paradise.

What are those days of glory ? They are not
memories : are they premonitions, or, are they
visions ?

They are not memories though perhaps Plato
thought them so, and our modern Pantheists, with

Wordsworth for their spokesman here, called and believed them so.

I will hope that they are premonitions, hints granted beforehand of a state to be attained. At the worst they are visions of such a state lying all about us, the home of the Blessed, which we are permitted to glimpse at for a moment, even those of us sad ones who may never reach that place.

As for those who call such joy illusion, they are of that great *Schola Stultorum,* that new herd of fools peculiar to our day ; they who have made the discovery that Something comes out of Nothing, who pour quarts out of pint-pots and give emptiness creative power.

Neglect them, but ask yourself as I do when such rare moods are granted, whether they be visions or premonitions, and hope that premonitions they may be. For certainly they are the supports of this life, and we creep from one to another like travellers from Inn to Inn, and when they fail us the world will be no more endurable.

Such thoughts I had—and have had repeatedly—in this run of water under a morning sky. It is inhabited, is all that air and sea, by something beneficent—at least, I have always found it so.

.　　　.　　　.　　　.

But there are pictures more definite and of the hard past which come into my mind every time I round Berry Head and see Torbay before me. And of all such thoughts that crowd upon me when I pass the point, and open that deep recess of water, two stand out most vividly. It was here on the southern shore of the Bay that the Dutch, and other mercenaries of William of Orange, landed for the destruction of the last poor remnants of English Kingship; it was here that a Catholic priest discovered the first ancient human relics, and thus started our modern controversies.

This last is a most interesting story and little known. Here is what would seem to have happened:

There is a cave near Torquay into which the water, passing, I think, through limestone, leaves a deposit. Under this deposit a Catholic priest in the place, a certain Dr. McEnery (I suppose, an Irishman, but I have not read sufficiently about him) found a number of human bones ; associated with them were barbaric implements and the remains of animals, some of such tropical kinds as can no longer live in our climate, others wholly extinct.

He came to the very just conclusion that he had here evidence of an antiquity for man, far removed beyond the bounds which had been set by the idolators of the written word of Scripture. He started that ball rolling which has bounded down so devious a course through our time, until to-day the grossly ignorant talk of an imaginary being, whom they call a " cave man," and the half-learned can bamboozle the public at will with the pretence that they know all about what they call the " pre-history " of our race.

That man, as man—I mean man as we know him (not imperfect man)—has lived upon this earth for very much more than ten thousand years, we are now pretty sure ; and we owe the first step to this same Dr. McEnery—whose name no one hears. The later discoveries in the Somme Valley we also owe to another priest, and that is as it should be.

What a turmoil so simple a discovery aroused in biblical countries, to be sure !

But that turmoil was but the forerunner of something prodigious : nothing less than the shaking, splitting, and at last the collapse of all the foundations upon which had been erected half the modern culture of the West.

For one may say that the modern culture of the West lay after 1600 in two halves, increasingly different one from the other : the Catholic culture and the Protestant.

Now, on the Catholic culture, physical discovery of any kind, in geology, or biology, or chemistry, can have no effect, save that of some slight expansion, that is, some addition to the general powers of its members ; just as the learning of mathematics at Cambridge will not transform, but only somewhat extend the general culture of an English public school boy. The culture of an English public school is founded upon a system and tradition which mathematics do not affect one way or another, save somewhat to increase them. The Catholic culture is founded on a philosophy which physical science does not affect.

In the Catholic culture of Europe, and especially among the French, who are the leaders of all our discussions, the opposing camps were upon the one side those possessed of Catholic dogmatic theology, a strong metaphysical structure, and, on the other, those sceptics who denied and ridiculed the claims of such a theology, standing upon the platform of what they called pure reason ; and this ideal of pure reason was as unaffected by material science as that of its opponents. The sceptical school of the Great Encyclopædists (which is still and will long remain the one half of the Catholic culture in Europe) was in no way shaken because certain of its adventitious conceptions, in no way connected with its general philosophy, were proved false. The profound effect of Voltaire was not lessened through his ridicule of fossils, and his conclusion that the imprint of fishbones upon Alpine rocks came from the dried herrings of mediæval pilgrims. These conceptions were proved false, but Voltaire's power did not depend upon their truth. Nor were the Encyclopædists' speculations upon some original, simple, incorrupt and admirable savage so essential to their doctrine that the full discovery of the real savage affected their influence.

No more, on the other side, on the side of those practising and affirming religion of the Catholic culture, did any material discoveries upset doctrines which were not connected with specific material instances, but were transcendental. It mattered nothing to the two great antagonists, Belief and Unbelief, in Catholic Europe whether man had existed politically on earth for five, ten, twenty, or fifty thousand years. Their quarrel was on another and infinitely higher plane. The vast progress of modern physical discovery has somewhat extended the powers of either camp, but has not changed the main issue, which was joined far earlier, from before the middle of the eighteenth century, and which turns on the great question, "Is Religion from God or from man?" No mere physical discovery can affect the Catholic culture as a whole, whether in its clerical or in its anti-clerical branches. The ruin of the Darwinian nonsense during the last twenty years has been largely effected by anti-clerical biologists : the greatest achievements in research—Pasteur's among others—have been the work of practising Catholics.

But with the Protestant culture of the north it was far otherwise. *That* had been based upon a book, and the literal interpretation of that book. It had, of course, its profound spiritual origin, an excessive and enthusiastic passion for lonely communion with God. But its rock of authority was the Book.

The fragments of Hebrew folklore which the Catholic Church affirms to be inspired, had always been used by that Church as examples, positive and negative, in support of her doctrines ; and particularly as mystical, often allegorical, prophetic figurings of one great event that was to come : the Incarnation. But, in the Protestant culture, these Old Testament stories were *lived*. They had become flesh and bone of their readers. The very characters therein took on a Divine air ; the cruelties, the obscenities, the puerilities, equally with the occasional sublime actions and sayings of those Old Testament characters, became in men's minds the attributes of demi-gods.

This absorption in the ancient relics of Hebrew Scripture produced a corresponding vivid attachment to the pictures aroused by their reading. The allegories became for men of the Protestant culture concrete and undoubted events, taken for granted as historical and, which is much more, made the basis of all daily life. Adam and Eve, for instance, were to Milton, and to all who read Milton, for one hundred and fifty years and more, a particular man and woman, of an aspect remembered from the frontispiece of the family Bible. They lived in a particular place not unlike the finer landscapes of England. They walked with God and with his Angels as one walks in a garden ; the humans and their majestic companions sauntered over real lawns, upon real feet, taking steps some two feet long—real steps. And the couple ate, not even a vague fruit, but a particular apple to their hurt. So it was right through. On such pictures, taken to be plain history and history inspiring all action, was the new culture of the seventeenth century built in the North.

When all this structure was blown to pieces in the nineteenth century by those discoveries of which this priest's at Torquay was the first, it did not follow that the tradition and momentum of the old superstition would disappear as easily. Far from that. The main effects of the old Bibliolatry are with us to-day in London, and in Berlin, in Scandinavia, in the United States ; though divergent and under various forms, the effects of Bibliolatry have clearly produced a something in common which still profoundly separates the Protestant from the Catholic culture.

The upsetting of the Bible authority, then, did not produce in the nations of Protestant culture a revolt against the Protestant rule of life. That is not what happened. But what did happen was a bewilderment, a chaos, a disintegration of all the solid things which had stood firm in the North from the first generation of the seventeenth century down to the first generation of the nineteenth. The Protestant culture did not separate into a clerical and an anti-clerical, a traditional and practising as against a mocking temper : it moved in the main as one. But it moved, eddying and changing continually, like a great cloud of dust following on the crash of a building. It continued, after the catastrophe, to whirl and change : so much so, that no one can tell at this moment, or could tell under the very different spirit of, say, twenty years ago, what form the ultimate settlement may take.

For there is no settlement yet. Even to-day, even in the (for the moment) popular mythology of Cave Men and Prehistory and the rest of it, there is nothing fixed. Characteristically enough, the guess-work is turned into Dogma, and faith reposes on concrete images. But the dogmas change every few years, and the images as well. All within the murk is still changing, and will continue to change, until the dust of the explosion has come slowly to earth and has stratified. When that happens there will be a new heresy. I wonder what it will be like?

Well, the man who first lit the match, the man who was the author of the explosion, was Dr. McEnery, Catholic priest, of Torquay.

He was not listened to. The truth seemed too fantastic. The great Cuvier had dealt with so many hoaxes of the kind (men having sent him, among other things, the bones of fossil elephants by way of pre-Adamite giants) that even in a rational society there would have been hesitation. In the provincial society of England, 1829, there was more than hesitation—there was contempt and silence. Man older than 4004 (or 4005) B.C. was a mad blasphemy. The idea was not to be tolerated.

It took a solid thirty or forty years before even educated people in this country could be made familiar with so simple an idea. Now—after less than a hundred years—not only has that idea soaked right through society to its lowest depths, but a new conservatism has taken root, and we find the same provincial people clinging tenaciously to-day to exploded nonsense like Darwin's Natural Selection, and the imaginary evidence of embryology.

On the whole it is a good thing, this ultra-conservative instinct. It has ridiculous sides to it, but it is a great deal better than the iconoclast spirit. It does harm when it is used to bolster up injustice or false doctrine, as in the case of men who still go on defending human cruelty and oppression on some muddle-headed plea called "survival of the fittest"—which simply means survival of that which survives ; or when they convince themselves of some impossible blind process of uncreative change without a Creator, and therefore conceive that they may at once abandon even such poor wrecks of moral discipline as have survived in them.

More interesting to me (I am sorry to say—for I have few companions in this, and it is a lonely interest) than the discovery of evidence to the great antiquity of man, is the absence of evidence which *ought* to be there in the nature of things, but which no one has yet come across. What I ardently desire is discovery showing, or even hinting at, the way in which man became what we call *civilised*.

As far as you can go back you see civilised man existing, and, side by side with him, barbaric man : I mean, " as far as you can go back " in any real record not only of writing, but of monument. Take · the whole period of surviving record, whatever it may be (no one really knows : but it is certainly more than five thousand years, and may be more than six thousand). You find at the origin of it men sculpturing, building with cut stone and bricks, and leaving record of their actions ; inhabiting cities ; possessed of laws—and all the rest of it. Then there is a halt. You come to the end of a blind alley. You come up against a wall and there is nothing beyond.

There is plenty of guess work, of course, passing for knowledge—but that is negligible. All you have in the way of real evidence is a few bones which are almost certainly older than the records of any civilisation, and quite numerous relics of barbaric culture, fish-hooks, and coarse weaving, and coarse pottery, and so on. Behind that you have—but after an impossible gulf—roughly-chipped stones, of which some small proportion may have been fashioned by an intelligent being, but of which most, in spite of the cocksureness of those who collect and describe them, are very doubtful indeed. No one really knows how far back these things go, for no one knows the rate at which earth may be or was laid down in floods, of what nature the catastrophes of the past may have been. But of transition from such doubtful fragments to the neolithic and from this to civilised man who carves splendour out of granite, and who measures earth and heaven, not a trace.

What is most remarkable, no one that I have ever read has properly tabulated the rough stone implements in a series.

Now that is what we want. We ought to have some large monograph, properly illustrated, showing in a graduated series such so-called "paleoliths" as are possibly of human handicraft ; then others less likely to be so, and so on down to the most doubtful. It is of no use to the ordinary educated man to be told by self-styled experts that this or that lumpish thing was (though it doesn't look it) of human handiwork ; he can judge that for himself : and as the expert is all out for making it human if he possibly can, he is to be discounted. What we want is, I say, a monograph giving specimens in a graded series : and then, side by side with these, a full description of the place and conditions where they were found.

When that is done we shall be able to judge for ourselves, and not to accept the priestcraft of the people who call themselves scientists ; we shall be able to make some rough judgment on the comparative age of such implements. If evident paleoliths are discovered under a depth of stratified stone (not gravel or earth) which argues some very long period of accumulation, I should conclude that man did make them in some very remote time, to which, perhaps, a minimum limit can be set ; but until we have them all graded and discussed, according to their grades, and with proof of the rate of stratification, we are at the mercy of men whose business it is to bring forward as many marvels as possible, as it has been the business of all who in all times desire to cut a figure before the people.

And, again, even if we had (which we have not) a proper analysis of this sort of evidence, there would still remain the unbridged gulf between the barbaric and the civilised man.

It stands to reason that civilisation cannot have been born complete. It must have arisen from simple origins ; of what sort were those origins ? The only reply so far is silence on the part of the wise, and loud, unsupported affirmation on the part of the popular writer. We have, for instance, no series in sculpture proceeding from the rude to the complete. There is a series from the archaic onwards, but the archaic is the work of a high culture. Nowhere in the world is there, so far, apparent, in any art, a set of vague beginnings gradually becoming more definite. The same is true of writing. You may show, indeed, the development of picture writing in the Valley of the Nile, but no one has yet shown the groping and the tentative origins of the thing—if tentative and groping origins there were. Sergi launched what was merely a guess, quite unconvincing, that certain marks upon Western rough monoliths were the origins of the alphabet ; the proof he adduced was quite insignificant. No one would invest £5 on the strength of it in a prospectus.

The truth is that we do not know where writing

came from, nor how it was developed. Nor do we know where building with cut stones and with bricks came from. Nor do we know where any of the origins of civilisation are to be found.

One despairing suggestion has been that its origins are now drowned under the sea. That is as likely a guess as any other. At any rate, we know nothing of the way in which the full life of man took its rise. It may have come catastrophically in a very short period of time. Under what influences, through what accidents or guidance, we cannot tell. All humanity remembers dimly a very good state of affairs a very long time ago—and beyond that mere memory and tradition we have nothing to go on.

So much for "prehistory"—I am weary of it and of its now discredited prophets. Speculation is the concealed material of their Mumbo-Jumbo ; assertion its ritual. Rather let me consider the known past, and, entering Torbay all alone under so glad a morning, let me consider that other, that real, that known affair, the landing of the Prince of Orange, the Patron of Belfast and of St. James's Square, and of other things less suitable to ears polite.

I should like to have seen that big Dutch fleet, with its few English renegades on board, come sweeping into Torbay. I should like to have seen the crowded boats passing to and fro, landing the Dutchmen and other foreign troops, and the great lords who were conspiring against their king, and the saturnine William himself. I should like to have seen that mercenary army of adventurers, hired to give the last blow to so great a victim as the wounded kingship of the English, formed in column, and the march up to Exeter : with the villagers timidly peeping from behind closely-shut windows at the strange faces, hearing alien speech, and wondering what the issue of the invasion would be.

There was a fine pageantry about all that miserable business which ended the age-long, but dying, tradition of monarchy in Britain, and put the rich in the saddle for good, without a master. From the moment when the huge armament bowled through the Straits of Dover under a south-east wind (forming such a crescent that the horns of it neared either shore) to that afternoon, two days later, when the high gilded poops of the Dutchmen stood out in line across Torbay, the whole evil thing was full of grandeur and of colour.

Whenever I recollect that business of the fall of the Stuarts, two things stand out in my mind : so much pageantry and so much comic stuff. For, to my thinking, there is something comic in the financing of the expedition with Dutch money, secured upon taxes promised *beforehand* as sure to be levied from the English (specifically on their tobacco), should it succeed. This way of making the victim pay for his own execution without his knowing it, and without consulting him, is full of the spirit of comedy. There are a hundred other comic details. Churchill leaning his handsome, villainous face over the dinner table of the inn and trying to persuade the unfortunate James to come out for a ride on that fine moonlight night ; Churchill well knowing how, on that fine moonlight night, the scouts of the enemy were waiting to carry off the King. And, again, the picture of the subsequent dinner at Andover ; James dining with his daughter's husband, the Prince of Denmark, and that great bagful of stupidity, repeating to everything that was said, " *Est-il possible !* " ; then he and his suite excusing themselves for a moment to attend to some business ; James, the King, wondering when they would return to the room. They never returned. That business on which they had excused themselves was treason, and the woman in town and her husband at Andover had betrayed.

What a Calvary James had to climb ! It is a pity that Anne should have done such a thing, for she seems to have been the best of all that gang—which is not saying much. I have always trusted Swift's judgment, who wrote of her : " The only good woman I ever met in my life." But there he exaggerated ; for he certainly profoundly admired at least two others, and he would not have admired them if he had not thought them good in a very evil world.

. . . .

From Torbay westward the bold man in the small boat makes direct for Portland Bill, cutting across the Bay, and looking for the bell buoy halfway, if it is too thick to see his direction. There is nothing to disturb him here, no strong current, very little inset, and he is pretty certain of making the Bill by his card, even in thick weather. He will do well to keep a little north of his course, so that he may have a choice of coming down the Bill on the strength of the flood, and of anchoring to wait for his tide, if that be necessary ; though it is true that anchoring ground has to be carefully picked in that corner by Chesil Cove.

But I am not bold ; and when I leave Torbay, I run to Lyme Regis.

The mouth of the Exe puzzles me with an unanswered question, which recurs in one river mouth after another all over the West. It is this : How were they used by antiquity ?

The trade of the ancients and of the earlier

Middle Ages, (and sometimes the later trade,) the pirate fleets, every form of seafaring, used these silted rivers from the Gold Coast to the Baltic. How did they do it ? Some say that even Salisbury was reached from the sea, and Winchester. Certainly Exeter was ; Arundel still can be by ships of some size. Bramber was so reached, and Rye, and, I suppose, in its day, Lewes. And the Stour formed a harbour, once at Canterbury, later at its mouth; and so on all along the coast east and west. The mouth of the Kus, in Morocco, at Larache, and that of the Sebu, at Rabat, tell the same story. All these places are to-day impossible or difficult.

The general answer given to this question is that rivers silt themselves up in the process of time, and that is the obvious, rational answer to give. These harbour mouths were once deep, but the river kept on bringing down mud and sand, checked at the mouth by the sea, and forming a bar.

Like nearly all merely rational answers to distant questions on which we have no direct evidence, this answer breaks down. The rivers have been running for centuries incalculable. They have had half an eternity in which to silt up their mouths ; and if this were the chief factor at work it must have reached its limits long before man sailed the sea. It cannot be the chief factor at work. I fancy the chief factor must be the heaving up and down of the earth. In places the level rises, and the river mouths become very difficult, and the lagoon becomes dry land. In places the level sinks, and harbours of which you never hear the use in antiquity come into play. The truth is, we know nothing about these things, or so little as only to give food for speculation, and for guesswork, which is the breeding-ground of false dogma, and of quarrel, and the true accelerator of the

human mind. I find that things affirmed carry a
curious kind of conviction—a disturbed, exasperated
kind, when they repose upon an apparently sufficient process of reason, proof ; whereas things
affirmed, but reposing upon no proof at all, are
accepted most kindly, and the faith in them lasts
much longer and is altogether better rooted :
indeed, sometimes (when the thing affirmed without
proof is true) it lasts from the moment of its first
affirmation throughout the story of all human life.
I suppose the reason of this is that things affirmed
without proof repose upon general experience, and
have, converging to support them from every side, a
great body of half-recognised experiment.

Thus, a religious doctrine is tested by the moral
experience of innumerable individuals, and also by
its effect upon society through generations, and also
by its consonance with a vast number of other
observed things, small and great.

There is here, to use a mathematical metaphor,
integration. Certitude comes from the integration
of an indefinitely great number of differentials.
It is in this way that we have certitude of a personality, of a voice, of a type. We see an elm tree
half a mile away, and say : " That is an elm tree,"
although if we could set down exactly what it is we
see, the indications would seem quite insufficient
for so certain a conclusion. What we see is but a
vague blotch, but we read into it, from an indefinitely
large number of slight indications, what we have
always known nearer by for an elm tree.

This kind of belief stands on the broadest base,
even when it deals with things not appreciable to
our senses (for instance, the ancient Western doctrine
of immortality). But the affirmations of the sort
called to-day " scientific," are balanced upon a point,

The apparent proof of them lies along a narrow chain, every link of which, behind the first physical appreciation of the senses, depends upon a number of postulates, each capable of breaking down under some new consideration.

For instance, our senses tell us, and we know, that if you mix two known substances in a certain fashion, and in a certain proportion, say two portions by weight of the one and four portions by weight of the other, they will disappear, and a third totally different thing will appear in their stead. That is what happens when you try any one of a thousand chemical experiments. It is what happens when an electric spark is passed through a certain mixture of oxygen and hydrogen under certain conditions. We know that with the same conditions, and the same proportionate weights, this astonishing thing takes place : the substitution of a third totally different thing for the two things which have disappeared : all that remains being the combined weight, which does not change. We also know that, under suitable conditions, the new third thing, totally different from the two original things it has supplanted, will disappear, and the two original things will reappear ; and we know that the combined weights of the first two, and the weight of the third thing which takes their place, are the same. All that is real knowledge, definite, proved and certain science, in the old and exact sense of the word *science*—which signifies a sort of knowledge depending upon proof so conclusive that the human reason cannot admit the possibility of the opposite.

We further know that when we repeat these conditions a dozen, or a myriad times, the same results appear, as in the case of any other natural sequence in the physical world ; as in the case of a stone falling from a height, or a sound following from a blow. On such knowledge we erect an hypothesis, we say that the mysterious substitution of a third totally different thing for the first two, but the maintenance of an equal weight throughout, can only *on the analogy of our other experience* be explained by the constitution of matter in certain ultimate particles which we call " atoms " ; for, as it seems to our very limited imaginations, if that be not the ultimate constitution of matter, the only other way in which the thing can take place, the only other way imaginable to us—that is, capable of being presented to our minds as a picture—is a transformation through the mere effect of number, a certain magic in number having some inherent power to affect the modes of what we call matter.

But as the former concept—that of the atom—is mechanical, and easy to picture, while the latter is highly mysterious, escapes measurement, and involves qualities which we do not to-day associate with any inherent power of number, we accept the first hypothesis. We assume—we do not prove— that matter consists thus of atoms.

Granted that hypothesis, we can give the measurement of the supposed atom, and investigate its qualities. But having begun with a hypothesis, each new stage of investigation depends on a further hypothesis : a second built on the first, a third on the second, and so on—till you get to the exceedingly hypothetical electron. Strictly speaking, pure science stops at the first phenomenon ascertainable by the senses—the change of two into a third and of the third back into the two. All the rest is but a scaffolding of *presumptions* built upon the *supposed* nature of that change. It has not attaching to it proof so conclusive that the possibility of an opposite cannot be imagined. It is not Science.

It is, further, true that with each stage in hypothesis the element of probability, however high, is less than it was in the last stage ; the tenth of ten successive guesses, each reposing on the last, is less secure than the ninth ; the ninth than the eighth.

But the academies do not grasp this evident truth ; they live by imaginaries, which they affirm to be things ; and that is why one of the wisest of the moderns launched that decisive phrase, " The bankruptcy of science " : that is the bankruptcy of the promises advanced by false modern Science.

The great Ferrero quarrels with that famous phrase. Yet he himself has written one more damning ; for he writes : " The men of the nineteenth century thought they knew everything, and they knew nothing."

.   .   .   .

The harbours of that coast between Torbay and Portland I do not sufficiently know. I have never entered Teignmouth, in spite of the lyrical invitation to its beauties, which is set like a gem in the " Channel Pilot." I have never attempted the shallow bar of Exmouth.

Bridport Haven I only entered once, with several companions in a crowded boat. Never was I more fascinated by any little haven, for it has the delightful qualities of a model.

I had been running for Portland Bill in a fairly fresh wind, which rose more than I liked. It was blowing from a little west of south so that she would just point at the smooth water which usually lies between the Race and the land. We were far outside, and had about ten miles to go, but the wind rose more and more, until it threatened us, and also backed a little southerly. We turned round and ran for Bridport, which was about seven miles away to the north of us, and a little east. It was near high water, so we had no fears for getting in, and we ran through the long, narrow bottle-neck of an entrance, more like a canal than a harbour, to find ourselves in a basin about the size of a large drawing-room, but with everything complete—a Lloyd's office, a harbour master, and a signal station, a hotel, and all on the scale of the place. It was above here, in Bridport town, that Monmouth, who had landed at Lyme (and I must say it did great credit to his shipmaster, for he came with three craft, if I remember right, and seems to have found room for all of them) met his first check. But the name Monmouth starts me off again—I cannot hold the mount when that hunt of history is up : and I don't want to.

The more you read of those expeditions—as of William's two years later—the more difficult you will find it to estimate what measure of support the invaders had. What may be called the legend—the sort of rodomontade you get in the clear, if obvious, rhetoric of Macaulay—may be left aside with contempt. It is not historical, and it is not intended to be historical ; it is pamphleteering for a prepared audience ; a flattery of ignorant complacency : written not to examine or to inform, but to sell. The picture of a whole England, ardently opposed to James, desiring nothing more than his dethronement, is as false as would be to-day a picture of an England ardently desiring prohibition. But there were elements present which made it worth while to risk the throw ; and (as we know), with the aid of a group of very wealthy men, and of plenty of hypocrisy and foreign subvention, the second invasion, the Dutch invasion, succeeded.

I think the real reason we find it difficult to-day to estimate the forces of that society, is that we have a false way of thinking in terms of exact measurement; a habit we have borrowed from the more advanced physical science of our time, but one not applicable to political factors. We think in terms of majorities, and ask ourselves how many men were on one side and how many men on the other.

Now things did not stand like that at all in 1686, or in 1688, and they hardly ever so stand in any national crisis. The bulk of men will accept an event, unless it be quite outrageously opposed to their daily habits. Further, the bulk of men are moved by tradition and custom and nearly always incline, very vaguely, to a continuance of what they have known. And at the same time, paradoxically, all men have an appetite for *something* new and are more or less adventurous for a change. In the main issue of the Revolution of 1688, we can be pretty clear on two large majorities, not dividing men into groups, but dividing the mind of each man within himself.

There was a very large majority in general sympathetic with the Protestant culture which had gradually triumphed, since the pivot-date of the Gunpowder Plot. What proportion of this was ardent, and in what degree, no one can establish ; but you may safely say that throughout England as a whole, there was, by the last quarter of the seventeenth century, not more than about one-seventh definitely Catholic in confession and open adherence, and hardly as many again indifferent, or slightly sympathetic with that one-seventh. But, on the other hand, the number of people who believed that James II. was attempting the impossible task of upsetting what had become the national religion,

cannot have been large. It is true that popular
illusion is capable of anything—witness " the
Russians in England ", during the War. But I see
no sign of that absurd accusation against James
having taken root in the masses. The number who
objected to his policy of toleration and to his proposal
that Catholics should have the same rights as their
fellow-subjects was large ; but it certainly was not,
and could not have been, an enthusiastic majority.
On the other hand, the number who objected to the
idea of their national king belonging to what was
to them an alien religion, was certainly very large
indeed : nearly three-quarters of England.

But then you get another cross category : the
number who desired to see the Stuart dynasty
extinguished was insignificant. Charles II. had
been immensely popular and deservedly so, and
James, the reigning king, represented legitimacy.
Had not the two princesses remained to carry on the
idea of the royal house—the symbol of it at least—
I think one can safely say that the nation would not
have tolerated a change ; as for those who desired
the reign of William, who were attached to his
character and who respected, let alone loved him as
a leader, there were none. Monmouth, if he had
had the money, if the moment of his attack had come
after the birth of the Prince of Wales, if he had
intrigued at length and with skill to get the full
support of the small wealthy group which was
conspiring against the King, would have had a
better chance of success than William.

I wish we had more details on the way in which
he recruited his little army. It seems to have been
mainly got together from the very poor miners of
the Mendips : men who could be hired for any
adventure : who had nothing to lose. They seem

to have been pretty well the only material available, and, of course, they were worthless as soldiers. They must have been quite untrained. Sedge Moor was not a battle.

．　　　　．　　　　．　　　　．

There is also in this coast an entry called Charmouth, where the Danish pirates of the Dark Ages fought hard against the King of Winchester, but I know it only as a slight mark caught far off from the sea.

What I have made over and over again in this way, in one boat or another, and often in the "Nona," is Lyme Regis.

What produced Lyme Regis? How came there to be a harbour there?

Men need harbours almost as much as they need the gods.

Men so much need harbours that in any long stretch of harbourless coast they will catch at any small advantage of reef, or projecting headland, and make shift with that. Thus, all down the line of eastern Italy, where for hundreds of miles the Adriatic meets nothing but one low even line of coast, they have caught at the sorry opportunity of Ancona. But this coast has plenty of harbours, small and large. A British or Roman road came down to Lyme Regis, but that could not have produced the harbour. It must have been the other way about. The road can only have come down here because there was a harbour here. Perhaps there was here something like what was for centuries at Hastings (but is now washed away), a crumbling piece of harder rock curling out to sea in an arm and giving shelter within, and perhaps it was upon this that the Cob was afterwards built.

The modern great havens, which we can artificially make, spoil us for the harbours of antiquity, and make them small in our eyes, but Lyme Regis was a port of entry all through history, and did not lose its position until almost within the memory of men now alive. How characteristic it is of the growth of our towns inland, and of the change in English life through that growth, that, when men and women hear of Lyme Regis to-day, they think not of the English seas, nor of armed men landing here, but of works of fiction by Miss Austen. Tennyson wrote admirably of the "Revenge," and believed himself a seer in the matter of the English waters and their command, but his interest in Lyme Regis was from Miss Austen. For my part, I am not ashamed to say that in my nineteenth year, when I capsized all by myself in a little open boat under Golden Cap, and with difficulty saved myself, though I was quite close to shore (it was in the month of December, dear friends, and poor weather for such gambols), I had not so much as heard of Jane Austen ; nevertheless from that moment Lyme Regis was vivid enough to me without her aid, and so it was when, three years ago, touching Lyme Regis again for the tenth or twentieth time, the "Nona" herself capsized.

'Twas a dark and stormy night, *camaradoes*, and the wind blew from the south-west, which is the stance it likes to take up when it proposes to drive at doing a devilry. I knew well that the tide running out during the darkness would leave us high and dry, and by lantern light I made every kind of contraption and fastening from the mast to the quay, so that she should lie even when she took the ground. But at four in the morning, with a noise like thunder, she fell over enormously to starboard upon the then dry bottom of the harbour and threw us all one on top of the other—we were three. That night we slept no more.

The English do well to build their boats deep, for only such boats can hold the sea, or rather I should say, they " did " well to build their boats deep in the days when they did so build them, before lines were ruined by racing. But there is this disadvantage about your deep boat : that it will not sit, but lies over. So did the " Nona " on that stormy night ; and damnably. You will tell me that when the tide rose she floated. Yes ; but not until very much water had trickled in through the dry seams, so that the pale and stormy dawn from over Dorset, and the distant grey of Chesil and the Bill saw us still bailing —and so much for Lyme Regis.

.   .   .   .

Thence eastward, coasting back home, any man who belongs to my county and to its harbours must face the passage of Portland Race and the difficult rounding of the Bill. So had I always done, whether coming or going, whether easting or westing, leaving aside all that long coast of Dorset hither of the Isle of Portland, and watching afar off the endless unbroken patch called the Chesil Beach quite empty of men.

What a gift of compensation it is that the horror of our great towns and the ease of our new communications has produced deserts in between !

No one knows those deserts as well as the man who sails along the sea, following the coasts of England. The foulness of the great towns is discharged by the trainload upon beaches of sand; but all in between, or nearly all, is left more lonely than ever it was before in our history. Those cliffs of Dorset coming down on to the sea are less known to travelling Englishmen than much of foreign land.

That Chesil Beach along which I have so often run is utterly bare and silent except for the noise of the sea.

There never was such loneliness ! One big house, built there I suppose for the sake of the isolation, inland, under the cliff, where some old landslide has oddly disfigured the face of the earth: then, for miles and miles, nothing. At the eastern end salt waste lagoons forbid human habitation, and between them and the sea comes the strange formation of huge rounded stones, falling very steep down into the water, so that you have many fathom deep within a stone's throw of the beach ; and at last, that forbidding Chesil Cove where a few houses of fishermen, huddled together, look out upon the most inhospitable mass of threatening waters I know.

There are few corners of the English seas which give the effect of a curse ; but this is one of them. The terrible Race of Portland lies three miles out, at the end of the Bill. The prison with its abominable memories stands above. The main traffic of the Channel lies far out. The gaunt and bare rocks of the Bill come down stark upon a lonely water, and that water heaves and turns unnaturally, even when there is little wind. For the roaring and the movement of that huge turmoil, the Race, send on their effect to the false shelter of Chesil Cove.

And it is a treacherous anchorage. Eastward, well in-shore, there is good holding ground, but it is only a patch, and one must be careful not to disturb the fishermen's snares. Just outside this, in deep water, there is nothing but the rough and tumble shingle of great stones, and the anchor drags on any burst of wind, even from off-shore : with a strong wind on shore you are done : and if such arise there is nothing for it but to up anchor and beat out into the teeth of it : for that lee-shore is deadly.

I have never been caught by the rising of the south-west wind in this desolate place of peril, but I have read the sailing directions about it, and I have often talked to men who have been so caught. There is nothing for it, I say, but to beat right out, unless it has come from a quarter far enough round south to enable one to scud down along the coast towards Devon, with enough sea room to spare. Chesil Cove is in the very eye of the great gales, and if a man should have taken up his insecure anchorage too near the shore, he is on it before he has got the first wind into his sails. An abominable spot !

The evil is recent. It is the work of the historic centuries. Portland Bill was once an island : and those strange tides which are now baulked and therefore twist and boil round its point, once ran normally through the strait between it and the mainland. But it has been joined to the main land these hundreds of years by a very narrow belt, high piled, of these great rounded stones, which the sea and the wind shovelled up westward until they closed the entrance.

It is a strange feeling to leave one's little ship at anchor in the dreadful cove, to land as best one can on that steep shore, risking the dinghy under the pounding of the sea, pulling it up over the screeching stones beyond the mark of the tide and then, in a few minutes' walk, to be on the great placid expanse of the new Portland harbour on the other side. It is like coming indoors out of evil weather, into firelight out of the dark ; for it is only this minute or two on foot from the outer beach to the inner water; but to sail it, you must run down the millrace of the tide along the Bill and risk the buffeting of the Race.

If you fail to hit the narrow belt of smooth water at the end of the Bill you are swept into the Race, and even if you just hit that smooth patch, you must calculate exactly, so as to catch the other tide up the eastern face under the old prison, and at last make Portland harbour after ten long miles—and as many hours, and as much peril as God sees fit to send you.

.   .   .   .

Portland harbour is one of the very, very rare successes of man in his coaxing of the sea.

I will not be sure, for I have not the knowledge, but, at any rate, I know of no other in my narrow experience except Cherbourg ; and Cherbourg is not thoroughly closed. Dover is a failure—they say it ought never to have been built. Newlyn in part dries out. Fishguard and Holyhead are open to certain winds. Boulogne is not finished, and, perhaps, never will be (I have been told, I do not know with how much truth, that the Germans were paying for the building of it to receive their great liners and that the War checked the effort). Casablanca is not finished yet, so we cannot judge it— and how many more are there ? I can recall no others of the great artificial harbours, unless we admit Genoa, with its noble mole, but, if I mistake not, it is not quite upon this scale. Of the artificial harbours which man has attempted in imitation of the few great natural harbours, how few have succeeded !

It would seem to be like man's attempt to resist time in the case of his own body, of which the poet has written

" There is no fortress of man's flesh so made
But subtle, treacherous Time comes creeping in.
Oh, long before his last assaults begin

The enemy's on ; the stronghold is betrayed ;
And the one lonely watchman, half-dismayed,
Beyond the covering dark he hears them come :
The distant hosts of Death that march with muffled drum."

And, indeed, it is very ridiculous the way in which
men try to withstand this influence of their enemy,
Time. They had far better accept the condition of
mortality and remember a truth which was plainly
painted in large black letters upon a large white
placard in Eden, which was restated by Dante,
and then repeated by Malherbe, that our only
peace lies in the doing of God's will ; which
includes going to pieces in the 'fifties, or 'sixties or
'seventies, like an old disreputable, sodden, broken-
down hulk too long adventured upon the sea.
Shakespeare (another of those poets) also said that
we ripe and ripe, and then we rot and rot. It is all
in the Providence of God. Yet will men talk like
women " of keeping their figure," and they will
wear stays, or hypocritically compromise by putting
whalebone into their clothes, or they will tie themselves up with bands like the infants of Italy, or
paint their faces . . . .
. . . . after the fashion of the warlike
Germans. But here it must be admitted in fairness
to the fierce Nordic stock of Mecklenburg and
Pomerania that since the little trouble of 1918 they
have issued an Army Order forbidding any officer
to paint his face until he has attained the rank of
major ; for they judge (does the present successor
of the Great High General Staff) that until a man
has become a major, the furrows in his heroic skin
are not deep enough to be worthy of filling in with
white lead or delicately disguising with cosmetics.
To return to harbours.
When Man became the master of Earth and sup-

planted Heaven—which was round about the middle
of the last century—he bethought him of making
great harbours where no harbour had been before,
and of supplementing the few secure inlets of the
sea. Cherbourg was the first of them, the French
being here, as usual, in the vanguard of challenge. It
was attempted even in the century before. There
were rocks and islands to afford a foundation, then
the great breakwater was flung like a bridge across
them with a pass to the left and to the right. But
though Cherbourg is secure enough, there can be
a memorable swell when the wind is in a northerly
point.

Plymouth was, I think, the next and serves its
purpose, but it does not wholly check the violence of
a southerly wind.

Did not this same harbour of Portland come third ?
At any rate, it is the one complete success. It has
caught an angle and the defences have been made
sure. It is deep, yet not too deep, and no gale
alarms it. What Nature built up in the Chesil
Beach protects it from the main gale, and the land
so curls round that no weight of wind and sea can
strike it from the north-eastern side ; and even
from the south-east the Shambles are a sort of
protection. Moreover, the entrances are not endan-
gered by the make of the tide, nor, I believe, do they
silt. The southern one was blocked during the
war by the sinking of a ship ; but even so, the great
harbour is an easy refuge and a wonderful good gift
for sailing men. But when people thought that, on
the model of this, they could continue indefinitely,
they were disappointed : yes, even in the tideless
Mediterranean. We shall see whether Tangiers,
standing outside and subject to the ceaseless strength
of ocean, will succeed or no. But for the rest, the

natural harbour still holds the field, and any one would rather have the roads of Corfu, or the inland water behind the Wight than anything man ever made.

I wonder sometimes whether the Roman Empire did not attempt the same sort of thing. If it did, all the traces have gone. There are great Roman roads which come down now right on to open shores : that one, for instance, which I spoke of running through Pembrokeshire and striking the sea just above that narrow torrent of a tideway between Ramsey Island and the mainland. I thought when I first came across this strange ending of a great road, I thought, fantastically enough, what a fine harbour this narrow passage would have made had men of old blocked it on its northern entry. Then you would have had a good quiet inlet, many fathom deep, looking into the sheltered water of St. Bride's Bay and quite secure. I half persuaded myself that the lords of the world, from whom we inherit all that we have and are, did so block that northern entry, and did so create a harbour. But it was a nightmare guess not fit for the waking brain, for if they had built a wall between the Welsh mainland and the island, surely some traces would have remained, and there is nothing whatsoever. Yet why does that great road end so astonishingly to-day, (and so many centuries past), upon an impossible coast, whence nothing could be shipped ? The Pedlar's Way through Norfolk, ending as abruptly on a coast some way from the harbour of Brancaster (itself now eaten away), may be explained by the disappearance of some former shelter engulfed by the sea, as Dunwich has been engulfed ; or worn down as the natural breakwaters of Hastings were worn down under the influence of the waves. But I must confess that St. David's Road, ending sharply

on that wild shore, puzzles me. The Lead Road
of the Mendips comes down to where there is no
harbour to-day. All the other Roman roads which
I can call to mind in the island, and which reach the
sea, reach it at a port, or at a ferry, or what was once
a port or a ferry. But this St. David's road remains
inexplicable.

It is a strange thing, beyond the average of chance,
that so very few deep land-locked harbours should
be of service to mankind. One hears it said sometimes that the number is small in any case. This
is not so. The number is not small, though ill-
distributed : it is exceedingly large. The whole
Dalmatian coast is made up of a mass of such
shelters. The Fjords of Scandinavia are a wealth
of the same, and the Arctic abounds in them. But
there seems a perverse arrangement whereby the
deep harbours and secure have nothing inland to
serve, while endless stretches of coastline are to be
found all over the world, with much for export, but
to which, in the same most exasperating manner,
harbours have been refused.

Africa is quite astonishing in this. There are not
four natural land-locked harbours, I believe, in the
whole line of coast from Alexandria round by Barbary and the West, up from the Cape to the head
of the Red Sea. The most that man can do is to
use the shelter of islands, or the curl of a headland,
or here and there a small and insufficient recess, or
the mouth of a river. The French have made their
small harbours in Northern Africa artificially, and
Alexandria is artificial. The few openings which
serve Morocco are very ill-provided, Rabat almost
dries out at low tide, so does Laraiche, that charming
little Spanish, cleanly, port, which I hope the coming
perils will spare.

All down the Adriatic coast of Italy, there is nothing between the thigh and the heel, since Ravenna dried away. Ancona is only a curl of headland, and Bari means very little. Brindisi is ideal, and Taranto must have been exactly what antiquity needed, shallower than, but as secure as, Cadiz. But for the rest, all the eastern shelf of Italy, and the heel of the boot, is without a base on the sea.

Unwisely, pedantically, but much more hypocritically, the less exhausted countries, who were for the moment the masters of the settlement, refused the Dalmatian coast to Italy after the war. I trust that the force of things and the new vigour of the Italian people and the now increasing embarrassments of what is Puritan and base in Europe, will, before I die, repair the error.

. . . .

And so for rounding the Bill once more—a thing by me always dreaded—for Portland Race is a terrible affair.

Portland Race should, by rights, be the most famous thing in all the seas of the world. I will tell you why. It is a dreadful, unexpected, enormous, unique business, set right upon the highway of all our travel : it is the marvel of our seas. And yet it has no fame. There is not a tired man writing with a pencil at top speed in the middle of the night to the shaking of machinery in Fleet Street, who will not use the word " Maelstrom " or " Charybdis." I have seen Charybdis—piffling little thing ; I have not seen the Maelstrom, but I have talked to men who told me they had seen it. But Portland Race could eat either of them and not know it had had breakfast.

I have nearly always been successful in catching

the smooth, narrow belt near the point : but I also once found that smooth belt fail me, and so have gone through the tail-end of Portland Race ; only the very tail-end. I had seen it from close by half a dozen times before in my life. I had very nearly got into it twice. But this time I did actually make knowledge of the "thing in itself"—and there is no mistaking it. It is one of the wonderful works of God.

Portland Bill stands right out into the Channel and challenges the Atlantic tide. It is a gatepost, with Alderney and the Hogue for gateposts on the other side. They make the gate of the narrow sea ; outside them you are really (in spite of names) in the air of the ocean, and look toward the Americas. Inside them is the domestic pond. Portland Bill thrusts out into the Channel and challenges the Atlantic sea. In my folly, for many years I used to call it " William," but I will do so no longer. For there is something awful about the snake-like descending point, and dreadful menace in the waters beyond. And here Portland Bill differs from his namesake of the land. It would be familiar to call a William of the land " Bill." But in the matter of Portland it is familiar to call the Bill " William." I will never call him William again.

I thought I had well known what the Race was before I first heard it bellowing years ago. I knew after the fashion of our shadowy nominal knowledge. I knew it in printed letters. I knew it on the chart. I knew it in the Channel Pilot. Then I came to it in the flesh, and I knew it by the senses, I saw it with my eyes, and I had heard it with my ears. I had heard it roaring like a herd, or park, or pride, of lions miles away. I had seen its abominable waste of white water on a calm day : shaving

it by a couple of hundred yards. But there is all
the difference in the world between that kind of
knowledge and knowledge from within !

He that shall go through even the tail-end of
Portland Race in a small boat and in calm weather
will know what he is talking about, and for so vast
an accession of real knowledge, even that pain is
worth while.

Portland Race lies in a great oval, sometimes
three, sometimes four or five miles out from Portland Bill, like a huge pendant hanging from the tip
of a demon's ear. It is greater or smaller, according
to whether the wind be off-shore or on, but it is
immense always, for it is two miles or more across.
It lumps, hops, seethes and bubbles, just like water
boiling over the fire, but the jumps are here in feet,
and the drops are tons.

There is no set of the sea in Portland Race : no
run and sway : no regular assault. It is a chaos of
pyramidical waters leaping up suddenly without
calculation, or rule of advance. It is not a charge,
but a scrimmage ; a wrestling bout ; but a wrestling
bout of a thousand against one. It purposely raises
a clamour to shake its adversary's soul, wherein it
most resembles a gigantic pack of fighting dogs, for
it snarls, howls, yells, and all this most terrifically.
Its purpose is to kill, and to kill with a savage pride.

And all these things you find out if you get mixed
up in it on a very small boat.

Perhaps the reason why Portland Race does not
take the beetling place it should in the literature of
England is that those who turn out the literature of
England by the acre to-day never go through it,
save in craft as big as towns—liners and the rest.
Even these have been taught respect. During the
War Portland Race sank a ship of 14,000 tons, loaded

with machinery, and if you were to make a list of all the things which Portland Race has swallowed up it would rival Orcus. Portland Race is the master terror of our world.

And here I can imagine any man who had sailed saying to me that there are many other races abominable in their various degrees. I have not been through Alderney Race since the 'nineties, but I suppose it is still going strong. The Wild Goose Race you have already heard of—a very considerable thing. The Skerries also—I mean the one off Anglesey—is worthy to be saluted. And even little St. Albans, though it is a toy compared with Portland, is a nuisance in any wind.

But the reason Portland deserves the master name, which it has never achieved, the reason I write so strongly of the ignorance of England toward this chief English thing, the reason that Portland Race makes me seriously consider whether literary gents be not, after all, the guardians of greatness, and whether their neglect be not, after all, the doom of the neglected, is that this incredible thing lies to everybody's hand, and yet has no place in the English mind. The Saxon and Danish pirates of the Dark Ages must have gone through it (and—please God—foundered). Every one making Dorset from France for 2,000 years must have risked it. To-day the straight course of innumerable ships out of Southampton, making for the Start and the Lizard to the ocean, leads them right past it—yet I know nothing of it in our Letters, unless it be one allusion of Mr. Hardy's to the ghosts which wander above it. But there is no ghost so full of beef as to wander above Portland Race !

It is, perhaps, in that word " Southampton " that I have struck the cause. Until Southampton

became the port for the Americas the Race lay off
the track. No man running down Channel from
the Thames need touch the Race : no man running
up. Even beating down or up Channel you are
free to go about before you touch the broken water ;
running, you need not go near it. And steam need
have nothing to do with it—except all that steam,
which, during the last thirty years, has begun to use
again more and more our one inland water of the
south inside the Isle of Wight.

There is a great deal more I had intended to write
about Portland Race. I had intended to talk about
the folly of the Bill challenging the sea, and how it
ought to be an island, as it was for centuries. I
had intended to say something of that canal between
Portland Roads and the West Bay, which ought to
have been dug long ago, and which some day people
will wish they had dug, when it is too late. I had
intended to give rules for getting round by the
narrow smooth. I had intended to curse the absurd
arrangement whereby the tide, instead of behaving
like a reasonable human tide, and running six hours
either way, runs southerly nine hours out of the
twelve from both sides of the Bay, leaving only three
for the dodge round. I had intended to add much
more.

But I cannot. Let me end with this piece of
advice.

Never trust any man unless he has gone round
Portland Bill in something under ten tons. Never
allow any man to occupy any position of import to
the State until he has gone round Portland Bill
under his own sail in something under ten tons.
But most of all, never believe any man—no, not even
if you see it printed on this page—who says that he
himself has done the thing.

After Portland Race, as you run down that coast, there comes only one other patch of sea (for you will avoid the Shambles), which is a nuisance, and that is St. Alban's Race. When you have just been through Portland you hardly notice St. Alban's, but if you are going westward, so that St. Alban's comes first, you notice it more than a little. For all the way down England, from the North Sea and the Straits onwards, you will have come across nothing of this kind. Everything to the east is more or less reasonable. If the sea rises, it is because there is a wind. If you are checked, it is through a known tide. But off St. Alban's Head you run into a piece of water which has no rules.

You are first suspicious of something odd by an inability to follow the rhythm of the seas. So far you have been going well, say, with a south wind, luffing regularly to every sea and paying off again in the hollows ; the regular beat of the successive ridges has become companionable—when all of a sudden a little sea from nowhere jumps up on your beam, and catches you a smack, and immediately you are in a tumble of water without rhyme or reason— nothing perilous, but intolerably inconsequential. You will suddenly find the helm pulling hard for no reason, and then as suddenly losing grip ; and with all this, there is no guessing the rate at which your stream will move. I have been half a night passing St. Alban's with a leading wind—light, it is true, but sufficient ; and that only just after the neaps, when the flood should be running slack. I have watched there in the darkness hour after hour the blacker line of cliffs against the blackness of the sky, and the shore, apparently immovable, refusing to slip by. What is worse, St. Alban's Race is a sentient thing. It knows all about you, and whether in its heart it only desires to play, or whether it has a wickeder mind, a mind it certainly has.

Some years ago I was running down this coast with many companions—too many for so small a craft. All was with us : an excellent wind, bright sun, and a clear air. I warned my companions about this mischievous patch (which is also haunted), and I said we would go right outside and cheat it. So we put the bow a point or two off the course we were making, so as to get right out into the open and leave the exasperation of St. Alban inshore in the place to which his bad temper belongs. But not a bit of it. Even as we were looking landward, and laughing to see the tumble of water between us and the cliff, which tumble we thought to have thus escaped, even as we thought we had passed it, *the thing ran at us.*

It came on in a long line of white, just like a lot of dogs running up to play. It was abominably conscious and alive. It had said : " Here is a boat which thinks that, because it has gone outside, it can escape me," so it galloped up in a rush, and swarmed all around us, and we were in for an hour of it before we got to the regular water beyond.

I know a man who so dislikes this patch of curse upon the sea that he boasts of passing it as of a feat, though, in truth, there is no feat in it at all, but only an annoyance. So much did he pride himself upon the passage of it once that, in coming into harbour, and being asked to write something in the visiting book of the inn, he put down his name, and the date, and this poem :

" I made my passage through St. Alban's Race
And came to anchor in this bloody place."

The person who owned the inn was very angry on seeing this poem, and asked that it might be rubbed out. This the man of whom I speak very humbly did, and substituted for the offensive couplet a long, long poem in the heroic style, all in rhyming decasyllabic couplets, and iambic at that, which poem is to be read there to this day.

You gentlemen of England—if gentlemen I may still call you—who travel about in mechanical ships as big as a street of houses, know nothing of these things.

But I will tell you one last thing about St. Alban's Race. I have said that it is haunted. Well, what do you think of this ? As I was passing there once, there came up to me, catching me up, at a pace far faster than the dear " Nona " could ever sail, such a fine, rich little boat, with canvas so new and so tight, and so white, and painted and enamelled, and gear well trammelled, and the brasswork shining like the sun, and the cordage new, and varnish upon all the combings, and on the tiller, and at her helm a man dressed as though for Cowes Week in *opéra bouffe*. She foamed, and was running past in a streak. The day was bright, well past its noon, and the shores of England stood clear all abeam. There was the Wight, with its brilliant chalk cliffs taking the sunlight, and there, very clear, the Hampshire coast, and right at hand, Purbeck : all as neat as a picture. But the man in the exhibition-shop-window boat hailed me, and shouted through a horn, pointing fiercely eastward, as he stood up and steered with his knee, " Are those the Needles ? "

Now what could such a portent mean ? What was the explanation of that mystery ? The sea brings all adventures, but what adventure was this ? Whence did this man come ? How could any man so lay a course from the Bill eastward without knowing what the Needles were, and without recognising them when he saw them ? It is true we were end on ; but they are the most conspicuous rocks, by their shape, in all the Channel, and they are as familiar as Piccadilly. Even a man who had never seen them must know by his chart where they lay, and by the obvious, unmistakable, glaring white point of the Island. To ask " Are those the Needles ? " was like asking " Is that the Eddystone ? " when one had been sailing with a good breeze southward from Plymouth, and perceived a tall tower standing up utterly alone in the midst of the seas, very far from land. This man could not have crossed the Atlantic (though men have done so in boats no larger), for she was spick and span. And even had he crossed the Atlantic, he would have a chart. Was he, perhaps, a western man, who had lived all his life as in Devon or Cornwall, and had set out thus in middle age to explore the strange eastern people beyond Portland Bill ?

There may be some few such remaining who wisely root themselves in their native place, and such a man might for so short a course take no chart—in which case he would have only himself to blame for running through the Shambles, and drowning if God so willed. At any rate, there he was, asking poignantly whether, indeed, those were the Needles.

For a moment I hesitated whether I should not tell him it was the Old Man of Hoy or the Giant's Causeway, but the spirit of truth entered into me, and I answered, " Yes."

He remains a problem, and to me, therefore, fascinating ; for there is nothing so holds the mind— my mind at least—as a problem connected with reality. I know that many men get an equal pleasure out of problems set them in fiction ; that is why a good detective story very properly com-

mands a large sale, especially among the intelligent :
that is why a good detective story is bought by men
as well as by women, whereas your ordinary best-
seller, so full of what they call "psychology," is fed
to the other sex, not mine. Bismarck also, intelligent among the Germans, delighted in the detective
stories of fiction ; but, for my part, though I take
pleasure in them also (especially when they are of
first-rate construction and diction, like "Trent's
Last Case," Mr. Bentley's book, which is, without
a doubt, the best detective story in English to-day),
yet it is a pale pursuit compared with problems
set in the midst of reality : it is all the difference
between dreaming and doing. Moreover, the
wretched writing-man can never forget that a story
written is at the author's pleasure. That author
knew the solution from the beginning—as is
proper to a creator—and as we read we know that
he can make the evidence fit any way he chose.
But when you are dealing with reality, the evidence
upon either side of the problem is not made to fit
any end. You have to reconcile as best you can
two opposite sets of equally certain things, which
seem the one set to contradict the other. If the
problem as to who that Needles man was, and where
he had come from, had involved great issues, racial
hatreds, the fate of a fortune, or the destiny of a
realm, it would have become an historical problem ;
and historical problems are the most fascinating
of all.

There come first in order those involving human
motive, and the known probabilities of human action.
Take three of them. The affair of the Diamond
Necklace, the Tichborne case, and the Dreyfus case.
In each of these the difficulty of finding the solution
lies in the discovery of motive, and in the estimate of

truth proceeding from a group of witnesses, or sometimes from only one witness, and in each of these
there is an opposing set of accounts, and of deposi-
tions contradictory the one to the other.

In the affair of the Diamond Necklace, you have
either to believe that a man, living in the heart of the
court life of Versailles, accepted a ludicrous signature
as that of the Queen ; or else you have to believe
that about twenty people, who had no connection
one with the other, and were separated by every
conceivable kind of social circumstance, place and
time, conspired to tell unshaken the same lie. If
you ask whether a man living in the heart of the rich
society of London would accept as normal the
signature " The Hon. Henry Hound, Esq." at the
end of a letter (he having known for many years the
said Henry Hound, let alone the fantastic nature of
such a signature) you would certainly say that the
thing was morally impossible. But what if you had
to decide between such a moral impossibility and the
necessity of believing that a railway porter at North
Berwick, a small farmer in County Clare, a *dilettante*
friend of the said Henry Hound, and Henry Hound
himself, and a chance taxi-man who had once driven
him, and a policeman who had noted the taxi go by,
and about a dozen others equally separate, did all
swear and remain unshaken under examination, and
after a long process of time, to testimonies which,
combined, made the conclusion inevitable that this
man, accustomed to all our social usages, and living
in the heart of our rich society, did regard such an
absurd signature as normal ?

The Tichborne case depends upon contradictions
in which I have little reading ; but, if I remember
right, the main contrast in it lay between two sets
of undoubted fact. On the one hand, a man's

mother recognised him ; his distinguished advocate
preferred ruin to the concealment of his own
passionate conviction of the man's identity—and,
after seeing all the evidence, and hearing everything in
confidence, deliberately broke the most sacred rules
of his lawyers' trade union, inviting certain disaster
in order to leave conviction to posterity. As against
a set of things like that you had the unaccountable
ignorance of a man of middle age upon habits and
words, and the rest, in which his youth must have
been steeped, and many other contradictory points
as well. There has been formed a comfortable
legend upon this particular problem : a legend
which affirms the certain justice of the verdict.

Personally, I mistrust such legends. The tendency of men to believe what it makes them happier
to believe is so strong that one should lean with
all one's weight against it in public as in personal
affairs. But that does not mean that the verdict was
not just : it only means that the accepted legend
has no authority in itself. During my boyhood the
opinion of men amply qualified to judge, men
eminent in the legal profession, men of the Tich-
bornes' social standing and religion, was as violently
divided as were later men of the same capacity for
judgment in the matter of the Dreyfus affair.

Though I was too young to remember the heat of
the quarrel, yet I always listened with interest to the
violent disputes I heard between my elders, especially
those which regularly took place in one of the Sussex
houses, the Squire of which had no doubt at all of
the claimant's right ; and my reason for such interest
in a matter to me remote is this : that the Tichborne
verdict is the first thing I remember. We were
living in a house in Westminster, and my nurse,
who was excited in the matter, as all folk then were,

rich and poor, took me into the press of people at Westminster Hall to hear the result. Of course, very early memories like this (I was but three years old) are falsified by the continual repetition of the subject by one's elders, but I am as certain as any one can be of such a memory, and I believe it is the earliest thing of which I have any clear memory left.

Upon a similar very early memory depends one of the longest links with history with which I am acquainted. Mademoiselle de Montgolfier, the daughter of the man who made the first balloons, lived as a life-long companion of my Irish grandmother in France, and died well after her ninetieth year, when I was a boy of ten or eleven. That woman as a child of four was present in Paris when the mob poured up the Faubourg of St. Antoine to the capture of the Bastille in 1789, and I, as a child of seven, eight and onwards, was brought to her time and again to hear her tell the story. I am now in my fifty-fifth year, and the stretch of time is already remarkable. Were I in extreme old age, and told a child of this incident, that child himself, living to a similar old age, would be able to say that he had spoken to one who had heard of the fall of the Bastille from an eye-witness ; and that would be as though some very old person to-day were to tell one that he had spoken to one who had known a page at Charles II.'s court, and had seen as a child the funeral of General Monk ; or again, it is as though some very old person to-day were to remember having met in childhood a person who had talked to one who had seen John Milton.

The Dreyfus case, after all these years, still rouses such passions that I tremble even to mention it. I have myself (so many years after!) been subject to mournful rebuke in public from the excellent pen of

Dean Inge, who has reproached me in well-knit prose for being the only man in England who did not take the side of the accused. He is wrong there ; for I could cite the names of half a dozen prominent Englishmen who had the right to judge through a knowledge of European affairs, and who remained in doubt of Dreyfus' innocence, notably Lord Russell of Killowen, the Lord Chief Justice, and Mr. Labouchere—and there were many others.

Here also the difficulty lay in weighing opposing sets of undisputable facts. The nearer men were to a position where they could fully judge all the technical details of that highly technical evidence, and the probable motives of the clashing witnesses, the more were they divided ; they remained divided to-day upon the issue after more than thirty years. On the one hand was present an overwhelming motive to secure the conviction of a man against whom there was strong *primâ facie* evidence. That motive was the desire to preserve the Intelligence Department of the French Army intact, though rival powers were bent on its destruction. On the other side was another motive : the overwhelming motive of freeing a man who was believed innocent, and the lesser, but still very strong, motive of defending the immunity of that small immensely wealthy, very powerful clique of international financiers, one member of which—the first and the last in our time—had been challenged by the authority of a modern State. Such men regard themselves, and are, in practice, usually treated, as though they were above the law.

I, for my part, pretend to no certain conclusion in the matter, for I doubt whether any man could do that who was not on the Bench in court, and physically confronted with the witnesses, and acquainted with all the documents, and able to weigh them all—even the use of the most technical terms in gunnery. But it is to be remembered that there was division upon that Bench itself, and that a minority of the five judges—two out of three—were (I am told) for acquittal.

Of my own intimate acquaintance who were on the spot and competent to judge, most were for the innocence of Dreyfus : but the rest, fully competent also, were and are, convinced of his guilt.

There are in England to-day two Englishmen whose wide knowledge of Europe and especially of Paris, and the French tongue and society, enable them to judge. They are both close friends of mine. One is for, the other against.

I believe that, when the passions have died down, the Dreyfus case will remain for history very much what the Diamond Necklace has remained, or the Tichborne case ; that is, there will be a popular legend, intellectually worth nothing ; and, for the historian, the task of criticising that legend, but hardly of solving the problem.

The historian will have one point to make in connection with it, and that a point of capital importance. It is to the Dreyfus case that we owe the four years of war, 1914–1918 : for it destroyed the French Intelligence Bureau and so permitted the German surprise on Mons and Charleroi.

Perhaps problems depending upon human psychology can never be finally determined. But there are others equally absorbing which involve no such heats, and no such moral doubts : only physical and mathematical oppositions.

It would be a worthy task to draw up a list of such essentially historical problems not involving guess-work upon human motives, but dealing with plain, physical facts ; problems which have remained unsolved, and which do not seem to be in the way of being solved either. Your academic writer shirks them nearly always ; he writes as though they had been solved, and as though he knew the solution ; so that his readers go on imagining they have been given an explanation which as a fact has been carefully avoided.

For instance, when you read of a fleet in antiquity " drawn up " upon a shore, how was it done ? The fleets of antiquity preferred to use, but did not depend upon, harbours ; they were able to use a beach. Their large armies—for instance, a Carthaginian army of 150,000 men—were landed in this fashion. Cæsar landed at Deal his small, but respectable force in this fashion, not through a harbour, but on a beach ; and civilian sailing and piracy all used the same method. The ship of antiquity could ride, and also be moored in harbour, but was also beached. It came up to a shelving shore *and was pulled up on to the land*. It was pulled up out of reach of the waves ; and it will be remembered how Cæsar got into trouble during his first expedition (and second !) because he had not allowed for an exceptionally high tide accompanied by a storm. He got his ships on shore all right, but he had not pulled them up far enough.

How was it done ? You cannot say it was done by capstans, because that could only apply to beaches already prepared. If you say it was done by hauling upon ropes over rollers the answer is not sufficient. How was the boat kept upright while this was going on, and what numbers would not be required to beach thus even a single ship of three or four hundred tons, and, having so beached it, by what means could one rapidly float it again ?

The ancients had some method which they took for granted, for they knew the difficulty of it, and which landsmen had seen practised a thousand times, and yet of which no description has come down to us in our fragmentary records of the past. The poets tells us that the ships stand upon the shore, and they leave it at that. They seem to tell us also that the boats were helped up stern foremost, but how on earth the thing could be done with a very large armament rapidly, and upon a beach unprepared, baffles us.

There is another problem I have never seen solved. How did Barbarians organise and commissariat the enormous bodies which came across the Alps for the plunder of Italy, and were as a rule destroyed by the Italian armies in antiquity. How did they get such a force as that of Radagasius across the Alps, or that of Brennus ? I choose the Alps in particular because it is an extreme case, but it is almost as difficult to understand how they moved across flat country. In the case of the Alps, you had narrow tracks for much more than a day's march, often for a week's march ; tracks from which it was impossible to deploy to right and left. There must, therefore, have been a very long column in file, a column of many, many miles. It is easy to calculate, in the case of Radagasius, that he could not possibly have extended over less than thirty miles, and probably his column covered a good deal more. Our academic writers seemed to think that a body of this sort moves as a matter of course, like an individual, or like a small body which can easily organise its movements : a dozen people out for a walk. But here you have numbers in respect of which any one with an elementary knowledge of military history, knows that high organisation alone could prevent disaster.

Ask a modern staff with every modern advantage, and even with a good modern road on which the columns could advance on a front of four, to move by a single road a quarter of a million human beings, half of them fighting men, from Augsburg to Milan. Consider the preparation such a march would mean. The exact forethought required, establishing the position of each column at the end of each day's march ; the calculation of provisions, the arrangement for the passing up and down of waggons or of pack animals, the strict discipline necessary to prevent bunching throughout the whole column; the confusion—these and a hundred other points. We all know that very good staff work, taking plenty of time, and with every modern advantage of map and transport, will do it in such and such a fashion. We also know that a few mistakes on the staff might easily so bungle the affair that only a dribble would get across in time, and the bulk would starve and die. Yet these huge Barbaric forces, in some un-described way, so traversed the mountains and debouched upon the plains of Italy, having evidently thought out some form of screen or advance guard —otherwise they would have been blocked on emerging from the pass—having some clearly elaborate system of commissariat, and so on. Not a word of all that has come down to us from antiquity. We do not know how it was done. What is more, we cannot see *how* it was done by men who had no writing, and only the vaguest notions of topography.

．　　　．　　　．　　　．

The harbour of Poole, for which we were making during that run along the Dorset coast when we were hailed by the Needle man, has a problem of the sort attaching to it.

You come round the Anvil Point, and there, if you are lucky, you catch another tide. There are many such points on the coast where you can carry the tide with you much longer than the due six hours or so, by coming into the midst of a fresh tide at the very end of the old one. The main stream seems to shoot past Anvil Point, towards the Island. If you come to Anvil Point and the corner of Dorset just at the very top of the flood and have the good fortune to get round and open Swanage Bay, you are out of this main stream just before the ebb begins, and another, younger flood takes you up past Old Harry and towards Poole.

Old Harry is an isolated chimney of chalk rock which still stands, expecting doom. He had a wife standing by him for centuries—a lesser (but no doubt nobler) pillar. She crashed some years ago and now he is alone. He cannot wish to remain so much longer, staring out to sea without companion-ship. I think he longs for his release.

Beyond Old Harry you come to that odd entry of Poole, the history of which is, I say, inexplicable to me. It was a main harbour for the Romans ; and when the Scandinavian pirates came down to destroy this outer province of Christendom, they used it as a known base. It was sailing out of Poole that a great fleet of their ships—ninety I am glad to say—coming to pillage this Roman Land, were piled up and destroyed in Swanage Bay ; and it was from Poole that they went up water to Wareham, and thence made their foray by land to Exeter.

Yet Poole, thus easy to the ancients, could never be entered without local knowledge. It is a trap, baited and set. As you look from overseas, there stands clear before you the entry to a great harbour. You see plainly a narrow gate, an obvious door into a wide sheet of sheltered water within. But if you steer for that entry, you strike. For, running down parallel with the coast for more than a mile, is a long, high, hidden sandbank, so that you must get into Poole to-day by making for the shore more than a mile below the entry to the harbour, and then running up a trench of which you can see nothing from the surface of the sea, but which you must keep to or wreck your ship. To-day that strange approach is amply buoyed with a bright light at the seaward end, and no one can miss it. But what did the ancients do, who had, it may be presumed, no charts—certainly the pirates had none —and who could not, save in some very special weather, have determined the exact point of entry by the lead? The savages from Norway may have depended upon captured pilots, or upon men who had purchased their knowledge of the fairway by disasters of their own in earlier pirate raids. But we hear nothing of all this in the records. We are simply told they came to Poole continually as though it were as simple a matter as going up Spithead.

Poole harbour has traps within as well as this grinning trap of an entry, and the worst of these traps is the patchiness of the holding ground. Unless you know where to drop anchor, you may be dragged in Poole, upwards, upon as fierce a tide as I know, with the flukes of your anchor dragging as easily through the soft mud almost as they would through water. But with all that, and although the "Nona" has caught fire there (the sea brings all adventures), Poole is a harbour that will always have good memories for me ; and perhaps the "Nona" will go there at last to die.

Now that I am upon the home seas steering eastward out of Poole after rounding that last great buoy of theirs (for I dare not try the Swatchway) I am concerned to defend the proposition that there is more exploration to be done in things familiar than in things unfamiliar.

With what hesitation do I not set down those words ! For they are paradox, and paradox is to my personal taste as detestable as advertisement. I will even confess to a little distate of too much metaphor—or, indeed, of any trick or hook for catching the attention of the reader. Why should I suppose him jaded when I have so many interesting things to say ?

But here paradox is unavoidable ; for it is clear that in the plain sense of the words the exploration of a place unknown must yield more matter than the exploration of a place familiar. What I mean is that where one knows a thousand things, each of those thousand leads on to another thousand, and so quickly makes you a million. Whereas where you know nothing, you go on from your first discovery to one or two more, and then to ten or a hundred all in a chain. So that the exploration of the known is like multiplication, and the exploration of the unknown is like addition. Or again, the survey of the known is like the sowing of a field with a manifold harvest ; whereas the surveying of the unknown is but the lengthening out of a trail.

And all this mass of words am I tempted to because I am entering the home seas, which I count from the Anvil to the South Foreland as being my garden or back-yard ; though it is true that my general estate extends much further afield. What is more, the home seas themselves expand a little during these last years of too much sailing along the coast of our Great Island, and I am not sure that Portland Bill is not now my gatepost, instead of the Anvil.   But all this matters not at all.

. . . .

The Bay between Poole and the Wight is so domestic and inward a thing that many would laugh to hear it called the sea at all.   But let them be as I was on that night and they will find it is the sea right enough, and that it can raise a fine hubbub, and that the salt water of it can tumble about with the best of them.

I take it that there is no trial more trying in the sailing of a little craft than taking her through blinding weather at night close in-shore—whether that weather be blinding through feather-white slants of snow or through violence of sudden rain.

Well outside you make your course and keep to it indifferently, for you have all the room you need ; but when you are running from a coast point to a coast point with the wind on shore through the darkness it is another matter.

The wind that night had backed to the east of south ; having so far favoured me, however, that it never backed round enough to make me go about. I was abominably short-handed, and on that particular occasion could only count upon myself, for reasons which I will not debate.   My course was for the North Channel under Hurst Castle, where there is a passage so narrow that even the " Nona " could hardly beat through it between the shingle bank and that odd spit of land on which Hurst Castle itself stands, and where Charles, the last true King of England, lay a prisoner after having lost his power. That channel has to be made with skill.   You must lie close to the land, but if you lie a thought too close you touch a hump of gravel which lies off

the point. Your business in shooting at that mark
on such a blinding night is to keep Hurst Light
just on your landward bow until you judge that
you are perhaps a mile off. Then you must pass
it over your bow just to the starboard side, and then,
when you are close up against it, so that it seems
you might strike almost, you must pay away again,
put the light to port, and skirt the land by half a
cable or less, and so you will round the long spit of
Hurst and find yourself inside the sheltered water
of the Solent ; all this if you have a leading wind.

At the setting out from Poole you must make a
course lying well outside Hengestbury, not going
too close inland, for there are shoals and, I think,
rocks. It is only when you have the mass of Hengestbury Head standing up like a sort of dull island
against the night and a mile or two north of your
beam that you can begin, or a little later, to make the
Hurst Light your mark ; and it was there on this
stormy night that my troubles began ; for both the
Needles far away a-weather and Hurst itself were
continually obscured by the most violent sheets of
rain, which came in gusts driven before the wind.

I would not go about into the open and try the
Needles channel itself for three reasons : First, that
it would have meant a long beat to windward ; next,
that in the Needles channel I should have had to
meet all the outward and inward shipping, which on
a night like this might have put me in some danger;
and, lastly, that I should have missed my tide and,
I think, met the ebb ; that is why I made for Hurst
and for the narrow passage between that light and
the Shingles Bank : a shifting mass of gravel that
shows its changing back like a whale above the seas.
Now that passage demands skill.

For the first five miles or so beyond Hengestbury

Head it was easy going, for after each heavy gust of
rain the light appeared again, and I had not veered
too much in the interval. (Whether there were an
inset to this bay I had forgotten, and I could not
leave the tiller to go below and read my directions.
But if there were it had not affected me, though we
were on the flood.)

As we came nearer to the light the difficulty
increased, because it was essential to keep in that
direction, and the recurrent blankets of rain blotted
out the mark for five minutes and more at a time.
Happily, however, the wind, though increasing,
went a little more southerly, and left me free to play
with the direction. She was a trifle over-canvassed,
and was leaning heavily over, stiff boat though she is,
and the beam-sea over that low freeboard of hers
took me on the face and body time and again with
little packets of salt water and spray.

It was important to get through the North Passage
with the flood, for the ebb runs furiously through that
trench, and I had known half a dozen times the
necessity of dropping anchor outside in a seaway if
one failed to get through in time, and of waiting
through six hours of darkness, during which the
wind could not stem the tide.

That night, however, I had good fortune, for there
was no rain during the last mile of my approach.
I took the " Nona " quite close to the Shingles, and
then round through the racing channel into the
calmer water beyond.

It was as well ; for all that ground of big round
stones is bad for holding an anchor. The good
holding ground in this part is round the back of
Hurst Spit, in what they call the Roads ; and if
with your anchor on that bottom the wind rises and
it drags then, whether from the north or from the

south, you are done ; for you will either come up
against Hampshire or break up at your leisure upon
the Shingles, which shifts with every gale, and has
upon it in the least sea a boiling of white water all
around.

In the Solent I carried the flood with me and, at
the same time, the wind diminished and all rain
ceased, so that when day broke, which it did before
I had come near Little Yarmouth (the stream was
then just turning) the first dull light appeared in a
watery but open grey sky to the eastward, over the
hills of my own county far away.

There was a great number of craft about, for it
was the season of the year, and their riding lights
swung and twinkled like a dance of stars. They
were so beautiful that I forgave the rich their spick-
ness and their spanness, and their great yachts kept
like toys. Yet neatness is a virtue of a kind : though
the "Nona" will have none of it, but keeps as plain
(and dirty) as a fishing boat, to which sort of ship she
is first cousin, but no relation at all to the R.Y.S.

This character of smartness in certain externals
is one of the things which separates modern nations
most sharply one from another. It is based, of
course, upon states of mind, and these in their
turn, ultimately, upon religions ; but there are cross
categories.

If you dig down to the fundamental, the real
difference is not so much that one mood goes in
everywhere for smartness, and the other allows all
things to get dirty and slipshod, as that one mood
wants smartness in one kind of thing, and the other
wants it in another kind of thing ; one mood
wants accuracy and the satisfaction of proportion in
one set of things, and another wants it in another
set of things. The difference to the eye is very

striking. I fancy it is the difference which the average casual and rapid observer notes most strongly in travel. Every one has remarked it in the contrast between Belfast and Dublin, between an English ship and a French one, between a Basque village or road, and a Castilian or Galician one over the boundary : between the Swiss-German railway management and the Italian. I am told, by those familiar with those countries, that there is a similar sharp change when you pass over the border of Finland from Russia.

It is exceedingly difficult in so subtle a matter of human motive to ferret out the root, though obviously that root must lie in the mind, and we have to seek for some mental need which is being satisfied. It is no good, for instance, saying that the Italian railway looks more slipshod than the German-Swiss railway because the Italian is lazy, and the German-Swiss is industrious. We all know that both are industrious, and that of the two the Italian is, on the whole, the harder worker. It would not be true to say that Englishmen aboard ship were men of more energy than Frenchmen aboard ship. The whole point of a Frenchman is the intensity of his energy—indeed, its excess—which is what accounts for most of the achievements of the French, and also for all their disasters. What one has to do in examining the thing is to find out what it is which makes the Englishman, say, or the Dutchman or the Prussian uncomfortable in circumstances which he feels to be dirty and slipshod, so that he cannot rest until they have been put right, while the other sort of man is equally uncomfortable in another set of slack circumstances, and cannot rest until they are put right.

What are the two categories ?

I say again it is exceedingly difficult to judge, and still more difficult to put into words, but they seem to me in my travels something of this kind. The one set of people feel their whole community to be dependent upon a *gentry*, a class possessed of more than the average of wealth in their society. When people take such a standard, an appetite spreads throughout the whole of the community to reduce all, as far as possible, to the conditions under which a wealthy person would live. While in the other set of people you have a conception that the community must be taken as a whole. Their centre of gravity is necessarily much lower than a gentry : it is lower even than a middle class. It is the standard of the people. Thus, in the one sort of community certain forms of decoration in a room, such as having a carpet and curtains, will seem essential. If that standard cannot be maintained, then one must expect degradation and dirt—as in our lodging houses of London. But in the other sort of community they aim at the cleanliness of a very poor room, of which the floor is bare boards. They wash and scrub the bare boards, as in every cottage of Normandy.

Yet that difference in social ideals is not really the heart of the difference. The heart of the difference lies surely in the relative values which people put upon different human activities. In the one community people will take it for granted that a certain smartness of externals is essential to what they call efficiency : in the other the actual working of the instrument towards its end is alone considered. The impression produced upon the citizen of the one type when he sees untidy accessories, even where these are of no service at all to the end the instrument has to serve, is that such untidiness connotes inefficiency throughout. But the other kind of man disassociates those two ideas, and is contemptuous of any one who confuses such different things. In Picardy they keep out cows with chance thorns, in England with a £3 gate. Both keep out cows.

I have had sharp personal experience of the matter in one definite instance, and that is a battery of field artillery. In the ideas of the English service, a French field battery is extremely slack. The harness is dull, often old, and pieced together, sometimes shamefully tied up with string. The uniforms are not over-clean. There is nothing too smart about the pieces themselves, even when they are prepared for a review. The conclusion is immediately arrived at that these foreigners ought not to have guns at all, seeing they do not know how to treat them. It is the same connotation of ideas as makes one think that a man without a collar is poor, though he may be a millionaire who has just taken it off to ease his neck. Now the other commentary is worth remarking, for I have heard it from the lips of many men, and it shows the difference of mood. The smartness of the English batteries I have always heard vastly admired by the French gunners, *but never in connection with gunnery*. They regard it as an adjunct, as a sort of ornament which a wealthy nation possessed (as England normally is in peace time) of but a small armed force can afford. They think it rather like wearing a top hat, or like a woman wearing jewels ; something having no relation whatsoever to the function of a gun and its gunners, which is to deliver projectiles accurately and rapidly rather than to look pretty.

In other words, the French gunner looks at an English battery very much as you or I would look at a good poet who had been something of a dandy. It would never occur to us that his clothes were a function of his poetry, and, on the whole, we would more likely connect the idea of good verse with slackness in clothes than with neatness in clothes.

Still, neatness is a virtue, and an excess of polish, even at sea, must be forgiven.

What is less forgivable in the rich is their contempt for the usage of the sea, and their forgetfulness of its brotherhood. I minded me as I ran down that water under the dawn, of how, when I was still young, I picked up a buoy in Cowes Roads after a long night outside, and in desperate fatigue I made fast to it and slept. I had not slept three hours when I was woken by a man so rich that he must have stolen it. He came up, rowed in a boat— I had almost written "of pure gold," anyhow, all glittering with wealth, and rowed by many serfs in white raiment shining like the sun. He hollared and he swore like Mrs. McKinley in the song, and his face was purple with passion ; all because I had picked up a buoy which he had bought and paid for. Now this is not the custom of the sea. One may pick up a buoy at need, though one must let go when they ask you. As for this man, his monstrous great ship soon steamed away down westward, and I sincerely hope that he struck that honest reef, the reef called Calvados, in a fog, making for Deauville, and was drowned.

But of all the picking up of buoys and moorings, the most astonishing cast I ever made was in Orford River. There was a tearing wind up-stream, and I was bowling along in front of it with a tall great noisy comber of foam at the bows, and straining my eyes for something to round up to, as it was at Orford that I had planned to lie for the night. There

was a crowd of men upon the shore. They shouted
to me and pointed, and I took their cries to be an
invitation, for there, sure enough, was a little buoy
of a fine red colour. My companion put up the
helm, but not so abruptly as to lose all way, and,
when I came near to the buoy I picked it up and
made sure that she would swing round head to wind
when she felt the strain of the moorings. Far from
it : there was no strain. The little buoy came up as
light as a cork, and, as the poet has it, " the waves
still broke about the bows and the ship sailed on."
The people on the shore were behaving with frenzy,
and even at that distance I gathered that they were
threatening us. The more readily, therefore, did I
beg my companion to put her right before it, and go
up-stream into the night as fast as we could. And
so we hung on till the darkness fell, when we
brought up outside Aldborough. Then it was we
learned what we had done ; for the buoy was a
marking buoy for a race, laid down with the most
loving precision, and showing to an inch where the
winner should pass. Nor have I since dared to land
at Orford.

. . . .

There is no piece of inland water in the world so
crowded, so too well known, as this three-spoked
lake of the Solent, Spithead and Southampton Water.
There is none upon which so many thousands for a
lifetime past have spent their leisure, and none
which is thought to be more exhausted in all that
can be known of it. But those who think so,
neglect the dimension of time. For, though you
should know every entry and every sounding, the
first hour in every flood when your craft can safely
go over the banks, the dredged channel under
the Hampshire coast, and Lymington River, and

Cowes Roads and Ryde Sands, and Beaulieu and Buckler's Hard, where I am told they launched great men of war, and Portsmouth Harbour right up to Fareham, and the Hamble to its bridge, and all the yard and wharfs of the Test and the Itchen, yet you do not possess that piece of water unless you see moving upon it the fulness of its past. You must see the last tragedy of the Civil Wars: the craft that might have taken Charles away from Southampton to freedom, and his young son cruising with the loyal fleet (which had declared for the King against the oligarchy), cruising just outside the Wight, but unable to save the King at Carisbrooke. You must see that which I shall always regret that I am twenty years too young to have seen—the great ships under full sail making out through Spithead in line for the open water. You must see the pirate boats of a thousand years ago stranded on the Bramble, because they did not know the water, and Alfred's men capturing them so, and taking them off to Chichester to be hanged : a proper end for all Vikings. And you must see the great fleet of Roman transports coming in by an August night with a comet in the sky, for the recovery of Britain seceded and turned into a separate realm ; the German mercenaries landing and pouring up the Winchester road, and meeting their fellow-Germans in battle before London, and the Emperor Theodosius riding up Ludgate Hill in triumph after the usurper's death.

Because of its size and of its security, because of its nearness to Europe, because of its many harbours, and one great harbour, this patch of water has been packed with history as no other in Britain, except London River ; and now in our time the great London Dock Strike, more than thirty years ago, has brought Southampton Water back to the mass of modern traffic, and made it the great port of entry from the West.

For it was the great London Dock Strike of '89 did that, of which you may say, as of all the industrial battles of our time, that the victors lost.

Well do I remember the fevers of that struggle ! I was but nineteen years of age ; it was my delight to follow the intense passions of the time ; and those passions were real. It was before the socialist creed had been captured for sham battle at Westminster. The leaders *did* desire, and *did* think they could achieve an England in which the poor should be poor no longer, and in which there should be sustenance and happiness for all. They *did* still believe the amazing proposition that what they called " the community "—that is, in practice, the politicians—could own all we have and handle it with a superhuman justice. Great God ! They believed it !

I well remember that I was myself near to believing it, but I had the excuse of youth. They had also another excuse : not intellectual, indeed, but moral ; for, intellectually, the socialist has not a leg to stand on, seeing that his theory is but a piece of arithmetic, and its application, coincidently with honour and freedom, a contradiction in terms. Morally, I say, those men, those socialists of '89 were justified by the imbecility of their opponents.

Nor has that imbecility grown less. The argu ments for the capitalist scheme have to-day, after half a lifetime, the same bewildering fatuity they had then. In the interval the power of combined capital, the control exercised over us by a few exceedingly unworthy men, has multiplied I know not how many fold ; but the valueless defence of such a condition goes on. One might imagine, to hear them, that the defenders of capitalism honestly believed their ephemeral and empoisoned chaos to have been present amongst us from the beginning of time, and to be normal to the human race.

It is no little irony to remember that those who have to state the most contemptible of such arguments in the Press are themselves men commonly indifferent, or even hostile, to the interests they are paid to serve. It is not your sudden millionaire out of the gutter who writes in the paper he owns ; he could not write ten lines if he tried. It is not your monopolist in ships, who, bleeding his country dry during her life-and-death struggle in the Great War, sets out to prove that his vile wealth is of Divine origin. It is not the great bankers, getting their usury out of nothingness, who could put forward that apologetic which is necessary for the continuance of the affair—even for its doubtful and uncertain continuance to-day. No ; it is a scribbling proletariat, insecure and exigent, which regularly turns out column by daily column to explain how right and just it is that he should himself remain insecure and exigent. It is as though the torture were applied to some poor prisoner to compel him to proclaim the beauty of torture.

That old socialist fervour of the great Dock Strike of '89 and its time is dead : I regret it, for there was something very noble in its folly. A good half of it or more was made up of the love of men, and of a passionate hunger and thirst for justice. There was also in it that Apocalyptic, that Messianic, expectation of a new Heaven and a new earth, and of its near approach, which is out of place in men of European blood, for it is not native to them, but it moves them all the same with the flame of its

enthusiasm. In those days one paper at least, and
that a paper of power in the London Press, supported the Revolt of the poor. No one has such
enthusiasm to-day.

It was a time when men who have since been
caught into the net of professional politics, and have
lost their souls, went down to speak fiercely at street
corners, and to light in the hearts of broken men the
flame of human dignity.

I have seen in those days a young man, the heir
to a great fortune (later a minister of sorts) standing
under the flaring naphtha lamps of a muddy London
evening, calling out the new gospel and the promised
land. I remember the eager, stupid, upturned faces
of the men and women, who had come there from
bestial depths of the slums to hear him ; to go back
into those depths, and there to remain. They lie in
those depths to-day. It is not such a creed that will
save them. I remember the great mobs that
followed John Burns, and how I myself would go
miles through the East End to hear him ; and I
remember that great whirlpool of men in Trafalgar
Square on the most critical day when he and others
accepted imprisonment. There is nothing now for
which men would act so ; no one now has a creed ;
therefore, I call that time of my youth a better time.

Of all that enthusiasm and conviction nothing
came ; the mill turned noisily enough, but it ground
no corn. Those fevered exaltations were transformed within a few years to a contemptible shrieking
and raving called " imperialism," and that also went
its way, and worked itself out to its ignoble end. . . .
We survive to-day to hear a perpetual flattering of
America, a perpetual grumbling against the workers,
their sullenness, and, overseas, the increasing peril
of control over the alien races once so easily governed.

The vulgarians who invented this music-hall cry of empire now suffer the vacillation and the increasing peril into which their own base bullyings have led them. They must live a little time longer and dree their weird, and learn what happens to those forms of pride which have not even the merit of dignity.

Of those years, one thing remains : the dock strike made Southampton.

I see the monstrous ships of the Atlantic passage pass up and down the dredged channel to Southampton Water, and, as I look at them earning their millions for the few masters of such machines, I say to myself : " This was the fruit—here is the only fruit—of those nightly enthusiasms by the London Docks, and of the cry for freedom, and of the passionate belief that within a few years after 1889 the poverty of London would have passed into an evil memory."

.   .   .   .

I carried on between the forts at Spithead under the new day, with the wind steady from just west of south until I was relieved at the helm, and hour by hour we made for the Looe.

Now, with the Looe stream, which is the gateway to the Sussex seas, I knew not whether I should take the coast in its order between the Owers and the Forelands, or carry on day and night to the straits. For I have cruised up and down that garden wall of my own land so much that it stands in my mind as a perpetual come and go, sometimes far out into the salt beyond sight of England, sometimes a run in before too much wind, sometimes a beating up for Beachy, sometimes just missing, and at others just making, any one of the impossible entries of my harbours.

For the county of Sussex—and Kent, too, for

that matter—up to Folkestone, and beyond has had tricks played with it by the Creator of the sea and land. There has been done to it what is often done to a human life—that is, the granting of an insufficient opportunity ; opportunity enough to compel the use of a function, not enough opportunity for the fulness of that use. All the harbours are such that they can be made, but only on sufferance ; Chichester Harbour, which is also Bosham, Littlehampton, Shoreham, Newhaven, Folkestone in its day, are not to be approached at low tide save for the work of man, and Pevensey is dead, and what was once the shelter of Hastings has been worn down by the seas, the chalk reef which came out like an arm to keep off the south-west weather ; nor is the breakwater they have made there sufficient. Newhaven is dredged, indeed, and they have pushed out a great pier of stone into the sea to stop the eastward making of the bank at its mouth, and Folkestone has a roadstead made for it though it is incomplete and open, but in their nature all these harbours are to be used by the favour of the tide, and that is why it is so awkward to be caught in a gale outside while Arundel River, or the Bramber River, is still ebbing out over Littlehampton or Shoreham Bar ; for both those bars show out at a low spring tide. Sussex in this is less favoured than the Caux Country of Normandy, which is her opposite number. For Trouville and Dieppe, of course, and Fécamp, and even St. Valry, a boat like mine can get into at any time. This is for two reasons, first, because the Norman streams do not come from the country beyond the chalk hills as do our Sussex rivers, but are mere brooks, so that there is no weight of water to bring the clay silt down to through the harbour mouths ; next, because they are not open to the south-west wind and to the eastward drift.

The Sussex rivers left to themselves get a bar piled up in front of their mouths by the south-west wind and the in-shore tide, so that a bank of gravel grows up eastwardly continually in front of them. Thus the mouth of Shoreham river, the Adur, travelled eastward for three miles and more between the Conquest and the civil wars ; until at last it came out into the sea right up near Hove. But later a great storm burst through the bank and made the present entry, half-way down.

Exactly the same thing happened with the Ouse. Its bank of shingle crept out eastward until, in the Middle Ages, the entry was at Seaford, and that is why Seaford was called " Sea " Ford, and that is why the French would attack Sea Ford, and that is why when they so attacked " This Pelham did repel 'em back aboard," as you may read in Lewes Church. After that a storm broke through the shingle bank, making a new entry right down to the westward, and so brought into being what is still called the " New Haven."

.   .   .   .

I have just said that the Looe Stream is the gate into the Sussex sea ; and so it is, unless you go outside those rocks called Owers, which is a long way round : for the Owers run miles out to sea.

The Looe stream runs like a river in the midst of the sea between the long-concealed flats and little rocks just under water at low tide of Selsea Bill and the reefs of the Owers outside. There is nearly three fathom in it at low spring tides, and the entry is marked by a couple of buoys just as one might mark the entry to a harbour : also, as with the entry to a harbour, you had best take the Looe Stream on the flood. So did we on that morning after the storm make our way against the ebb until we had Selsea Bill close before us, and we caught the flood through the Looe by the afternoon.

There I saw, upon the left, the pole and basket of the Mixen, that sea mark which is my Sussex gate post. And from that point, taking a course just south of east, I carried on for Beachy all through the night. The wind held, strangely unchanged, and no more rain fell. It was one of the longest spells of similar weather, exactly suited for my little boat under all plain sail, that I had known. For when the dull morning broke (and it was hazy) she still carried the same wind in her sails.

Indeed, it was so thick that I was a little anxious to catch the chalk precipice against the east and know where I was. There is a little inset making into the bight of Sussex once one is beyond the Owers, and I might have been carried—especially with some little leeway—inside the point.

When I did see land it was not Beachy at first, but, a good way off on the port bow, a murky gleam, from the Seven Sisters : but then, quickly after, I saw dimly on a grim sky the sharp, perpendicular line of the Head and the stump of the lighthouse at its foot. My course had been well kept : I was heading well outside.

. . . . .

There is little to tell of that run, for it was uneventful. We had that day, somewhere about the Royal Sovereign Shoals, a dropping of the wind and its rising again from off-shore, north of west, but nothing heavy in it, serving us well for our course up-Channel, the weather still too thick to see much of the land between Beachy and Dungeness. It was in full darkness that we made and passed that light and, with the next day, still carried on to Dover.

I have a grudge against that great harbour of Dover : mainly, I suppose, because I have had bad luck in it, but also because it seems to me so wasted an effort of human energy. It has founded one of our new peerages, and while it was being made there was any amount of political talk about it, and also about the electoral conditions of its town. Those who know assure me that it was of vast service in the war, but I have read recently, I know not on what authority, that the Navy has abandoned it. It must always have been a difficult place to enter, with its two narrow gates and the violent tide across them. There is nearly always a lump outside, where the sea shows its annoyance at having this obstacle thrust into it ; and trying to get in with a small boat like mine and in a light wind is a trial. There is peril of missing the entry in the rush of the tide, unless one comes close up to the breakwater heads. If one does this, one never knows but that some great death-ship, on its way to Calais or Ostend, will not leap out suddenly upon one as one opens the harbour. Moreover, there are all manner of regulations which I do not understand, as to where you may drop anchor, and as to where you may not, and once, when I left the boat for some weeks in secure care, I found her on my return completely covered with the soot of His Majesty's coal.

We put in that day for water and to provision. We stayed but a little while, coming in by the southern and going out by the eastern gate, and passing as we did so that sad wreck of munitions wherein lay, I believe, the bodies of men entombed.

My companion took the helm up past the Fore-

land in a rather fresher breeze than we had yet had,
and with more north in it, and I looked back along
our wake and thought how here our time has
managed to change too thoroughly what was the
most famous sight of western Europe, the entry into
England.

Although the old harbour (which lay between the
hills—where the gasworks are to-day) had long ago
gone dry, yet the marks of it and much human
ingenuity added, maintained the port at Dover ;
and through that port went the prodigious traffic
which bound this province of Christendom to the
rest. Here, throughout the intense activity of the
Middle Ages, passed and repassed the blood of the
State, and the life running outwards from the heart
of Europe at Rome. During all that time, on to
days I can myself remember, this main majestic entry
into England presented something of the same
aspect to the traveller coming in from the sea. There
was the town in its cleft ; the masts in the little
harbour ; the castle on its height. Now, to my eye,
the huge new haven, with its miles of wall, has spoilt
and changed all this.

But, alas, something worse, more dreadful and
more definite has come by way of change. Something which cannot be undone and which has
subtly stolen their meaning not only from old
Dover, but from the great keels of the fleet and its
guns.

You may see the memorial of it marked upon the
turf : the memorial of the place where the first man
(and he a Frenchman), having flown the Channel,
landed upon the sacred island, without leave of the
sea.

That was a date for you, if you like ! That was
a year to remember ! In history perhaps, many a

generation hence, it will be made a dividing point between the old and the new relations of the peoples of Europe.

. . . .

It is in the irony of Providence that the more man comes to control the material world about him, the more does, he lose control over the effects of his action ; and it is when he is remaking the world most speedily that he knows least whither he is driving.

It is absorbing to watch change coming upon a whole civilisation. The thirty years of active manhood, the forty years of consecutive experience and memory which a man of my age can remember, the years 1884–1894–1924, form, perhaps, the best period for watching such things that we Europeans of the West have had since the Renaissance.

That may sound extravagant. The very great change introduced by the use of coal, and the machinery dependent upon coal, one hundred and fifty years ago, produced, I suppose, greater outward effects ; but the spiritual fruits of the change were not ripe till our day.

The characteristic of our time is the crisis in the *philosophy* of western Christendom : the thing began with Voltaire, but it has come to a head somewhat suddenly, following long after the material change.

For the great characteristic of the mental change between, say, 1885 and the present day, is the final segregation of Catholic philosophy from an opponent mood. That is the formula now applying to all the Occident, to all the one group of human beings who are variously called the Spaniards, the French, the Italians, the English, the more southern Germans of the Rhine and the Danube ; the Dutch, the Scandinavians, the Irish and the Scotch.

It is this group of human beings which conducts

the world and will probably continue to conduct it ; for it has the best physical stock, the greatest energy, the greatest intelligence, and the strongest and most continuous will : and its colonies can never replace it. It has always been at the head of humanity, even before it acquired, through its conversion to Catholicism fifteen hundred years ago, those vast new powers which have since distinguished it. Before Western Europe had opportunities for conducting the world as a whole, it was still manifestly the greatest thing in the world, and when its soldierly adventurers and seamen and its growing mastery over physical things gave it opportunity it took a place from which I do not think it can be dislodged.

Most modern men assume a shifting of the headship of the world from our regions to some other ; as to Asia or to the New World. But as they base their calculation upon mere measurement they are sure to be wrong. They make their estimate of human affairs on the analogy of Physical Science : counting only what can be exactly calculated and noting only the growth or decline of numbers, in men, in goods, in speed.

But Human Affairs are moved from deeper springs altogether. A spirit moves them. It is by the acceptation, the denial, the renewal of Philosophies that this society of immortal mortals is marked, changed, or restored.

The Catholic philosophy is, I say, to-day, at last clean separate from its opponent. Its opponent is losing all trace of Catholic dogma. That is the special mark of our time.

It is important to emphasise this position; unless we understand it, the future which is upon us will not be understood.

In the sixteenth century the unity of western
Christendom made shipwreck. But there did not
then arise (as would seem to have been the necessary sequence when one reads the great men of the
Renaissance, Erasmus, or any of the lesser ones) an
immediate separation between the Catholic exposition of the world, the Catholic revelation, and a new
scepticism. The process was much slower than that.
It covered nearly four hundred years, and it went, as
is a habit of human change, through very tortuous
channels before it settled into its final form—which
has now arrived.

First came a curious process of irrational selection in dogma. Nearly all those who were
reacting against the authority of Catholic truth preferred to select a bundle of Catholic dogmas, and
even of Catholic disciplines, out of the total and to
reject the remainder.

Most of those in revolt, for instance, accepted the
Incarnation and the Trinity ; nearly all accepted
the personal immortality of the soul. The general
Catholic disciplines of society, such as property,
indissoluble monogamous marriage and the rest, were
still taken for granted.

For more than a century the growing division
appeared as a contrast between Catholic tradition
and what was called " Protestantism " in its various
forms, the latter presenting bodies of doctrine
chosen out of Catholicism, but less than the total of
Catholic doctrine and discipline. The new selections
produced, of course, a harvest of social results more
tangible and concrete than the abstract differences
in dogma and formula, and there arose a Protestant
culture of the north side by side with the remaining
Catholic culture of the south. The geographical
division was purely accidental. Nothing could be

more Catholic than the Irish of Donegal, nor more Protestant than the Hugenots of Nimes, and the living centre of Protestantism was rather in southern France than in any other one region of the west.

But to this there succeeded another phase which, again, was not as logical, as it should have been : a respectable development called "rationalism," which arose in France and gradually permeated Europe. Its highest moment of expression was the middle of the eighteenth century, its greatest pen that of Voltaire, and perhaps its clearest intelligence that of Diderot.

This short-lived but attractive philosophy reduced its main dogmas, or postulates, to as small a number as possible, and proposed that nothing should be accepted save upon the criteria admissible by all sane men : particularly the criteria of the senses and common experience. It still tended to preserve a certain small but fundamental proportion of Catholic dogma ; but it did so on the plea that such dogma was (as it imagined) universal to the human race, or at least to all sane men. Most of its adherents—not all of them—postulated one, personal, creative God, the sustainer of the universe. Of the Catholic discipline they accepted property as a moral right, and its twin institution of indissoluble monogamous marriage as a necessary thing in society, though they were perfectly ready to discuss these and any other disciplines.

Undoubtedly the underlying conception common to the rationalists was this, that there is a certain knowledge of reality to be obtained through the reason dealing with the senses and experience common to all men, and only what can be so obtained is to be affirmed as true. What could not be so obtained is to be rejected as doubtful or false.

But while this was their underlying conception, they could not shake off a considerable body of their Catholic past.

This rationalism rejected the miraculous in every form, and even the unusual. It began to substitute the document for tradition in history, it proceeded to a strict and most successful progressive examination of the physical world, discovering more and more of its sequences. This imprinted on all the rationalists did (not *thought*) a very special stamp, the stamp of *proved certitude*. They carried the feeling of scientific certitude, which physical research had given them, into the field of ideas. They came to imagine their metaphysical dogmas to be not transcendental but demonstrable by experiment, or, at least, by the common sense of mankind. Here was a curious and, perhaps, unique incident in human history : a faith which did not know it was a faith. The rationalists had not any doubts at all, because everything exterior to their faith seemed to them insignificant save in so far as it combated their faith.

For instance, if you take Gibbon (who was the principal English writer among them, and who was the chief English pupil of Voltaire) you will see that most transcendental truths affirmed by Catholicism—such as the divinity of Our Lord, the affirmation of miracle, the admission of tradition in history, side by side with the document, etc.—were to him ideas ridiculous in themselves, and in themselves therefore of no value. But though direct Catholic statement inspired him with a strong aversion, yet he revelled in, he took for granted, that very civilisation, Europe, which the Catholic Church had made. He had no conception whither rationalism was leading.

These people were certain ; they stood upon a

rock ; and from the nature of their certitude they took it for granted that all the world would come to the same certitude by a mere process of evidence. They took it for granted that there was in all men a certain line of reason which only had to be turned upon any mass of affirmation in order to distinguish at once what was false in it from what was true, reckoning amongst the false whatever was affirmed without such proof behind it (of document or experiment), as they required.

They made no doubt that all this was final, that they themselves had reached finality, that the world was rapidly reaching it, and that nothing could disturb such a progress save some hardly imaginable reversion to Catholicism.

They were quite wrong. Before they had so much as convinced the bulk of educated Europe, three further developments were upon them, one of which has survived, and has become the modern opponent of the Catholic Church. These three developments were first a sceptical attack upon the postulates of the rationalists themselves : a questioning whether humanity and its common experience had ever grasped reality. That nonsense was German; it was Kant's muddlement of the great and clear Descartes.

Next they had to meet a development rather English than German, which noted with great practical common sense the irrational flaw in the rationalists' position. This flaw was the statement that a thing affirmed without the proof of common experience could not be true. It does not at all follow that because a statement lacks material proof, therefore it is untrue ; it does not at all follow that because a thing is most unusual therefore it has not been.

For instance, witnesses were brought forward to state that a man had lifted himself off the ground without material force to aid him, and had so remained suspended in an ecstasy. The thing was most unlikely ; it was opposed to the common experience of mankind. Therefore, said the rationalists, it is false. They were attacked by those who replied : " Your ' therefore ' is ill-chosen ; it is itself a mere affirmation without proof. The thing *may* have happened." Hence mere suspense of judgment and what was called " agnosticism " in England.

This second phase also was destined to a very brief life ; but it contained two permanent elements of truth. These were, first that it denied the necessary truth of the rationalists' postulates save only the postulate of the evidence of the senses (it denied the necessity of common experience being the only experience). Secondly, it affirmed (what was obviously true), that a mass of things credited to be real were not susceptible of proof through the evidence of the senses, or the common sense of mankind.

This spirit advanced to the denial not of a personal God, but of the rationalists' belief in a personal God ; and it attached to the Power or Powers behind the Universe the comic term " Great Unknowable."

The third development attacking the rationalists now occupies all the western mind outside the Catholic Church. It came not from the head, but from the heart. It is an affirmation that truths may be recognised emotionally, and are not to be rejected because the intellect is either incapable of analysing them or of discovering any foundation for them. One might take as the germ of this movement a common-place sentence of Pascal's which has become, because it is obvious and superficial, far more famous than his deeper sayings : the saying that "the heart has its reasons of which the head knows nothing." This emotional protest against rationalism appealed to the vivid response awakened in the human heart by the life of nature. Such a trend could only end in Pantheism : and Pantheist the modern world, outside the Catholic body, has become.

The reason, for instance, that the poet Wordsworth attained so ill-proportioned a popularity in the latter part of the nineteenth century in England was his Pantheism. He is the exponent of that mood. Not the most vivid—for he is vivid only in a few flashes, and usually dull and thoroughly bad. Not the most intelligent, for he made no pretence at an intelligent exposition of the mood. But because he was so thoroughly steeped in Pantheism : because every line of his betrays a taken-for-granted and, as it were, necessary Pantheism.

In France and Italy this same reaction took the form of accepting the Universe as blind but moral ; the Pantheist movement of the anti-clerical factions deified what were taken to be the common moral emotions of mankind speaking particularly of " Truth " and " Justice " as though there were real beings in a Universe where the personal power and virtues of a Creator were denied. Throughout the more cultivated Europe a certain number of special marks of the thing increased, notably the insistence upon landscape, upon our fellowship with the rest of animated creation, and side by side with these a disdain or negligence or despair upon the sharp points of Divine Will, of personal immortality, of possible doom.

There was formed at last in our own time, as the

crystallisation of all this boiling, a philosophy, a set
of judgments accepted vaguely, but finally, by all
that is not Catholic in the Occident, and this I will
call " Sceptical Pantheism." Over against it stands
the defined, exact and traditional revelation maintained by the Catholics intact. This Revelation is
as separate from that other mood as is the firm
strand from sea water, or waking from dreams.

Here many men reading me (if indeed many
men shall read me, for whatever number of men
may read this hotchpotch of a book, most of them,
I think, will skip these musing passages—seeing
that their subjects are the only ones of real import)
will reply :

" In face of this great, new, general, modern
spirit, which you call Sceptical Pantheism, and which
I admit to be the chief moral phenomenon of our
time, the Catholic Church is negligible. I accept
your statement that there is a great general modern
spirit or mood full of this feeling for nature and
of brotherhood with all animated creatures and a
substitution of emotional materialism for dogma. I
may or may not accept your particular title ' Sceptical
Pantheism,' but I know what you mean. We are
all agreed that the spirit is there ; and in face of it
the Catholic position no longer has weight : it no
longer counts. It is a mere surviving habit with
most of its so-called adherents (who at heart are
themselves shaken in their adherence). It is ignorance on the part of a few sincere ones ; a bitter
refusal to accept evidence on the part of a larger
number of less sincere ones : a deliberate shutting
of the eyes. Catholicism is in process of dissolution
and has become politically negligible."

That is the reply which I think most educated
men in England would give to the proposition I

have just advanced : the proposition that the modern
world is now divided into two sharply defined camps
(of which Catholicism is one) standing each over
against the other.

Now these objectors are provincial, both the better
informed and the less. They should appreciate the
modern world more exactly. They could arrive
at such an appreciation by a wise use of travel, and
of even their own contemporary society ; by getting
to know many kinds of men intimately in France,
Italy, Germany, Spain and Belgium, and by reading
the words written upon the Catholic side—a thing
which, for the most part, they wholly neglect to do.

Indeed, I have noticed that the finest and most
conclusive pieces of Catholic apologetics are, in
England and America, hidden away in little publica-
tions read by no one but Catholics ; and by few,
even of these.

If those who make the objection I have just
recited would use travel wisely, or even read contemporary Catholic writing in their own country, they
would appreciate that what I have said is true if
one regards Western Europe as a whole. Outside
England every one is aware of the Catholic Church ;
two great armies face each other, and the issue is
doubtful. All instructed Europe sees a great duel
set between the Catholic Church and its opponent.
All instructed Europe sees that this duel is taking the
form of anti-Catholic laws and of proposals of laws
upon the one side, and upon the other of growing
Catholic social power.

Those who, in England, once followed Calvin,
who then at second hand followed Diderot and
Voltaire, who then at second or third hand followed
the French romantics, would to-day do well to follow
this great modern quarrel, as it is joined up on the

old battle-ground of European debate : the arena which lies between the Pyrenees, and the Channel between the Rhine and the Atlantic : Gaul.

They will find that you can hardly take up a random French newspaper in a French café without coming upon the great quarrel. They will find that the statues in the towns express it ; the names of the streets ; the titles as well as the tendencies of the novels.

In Italy, though in a different form, it is the same thing. In Spain it is manifest ; in Belgium it is the centre of interest. Throughout the Occident the struggle is engaged.

The forces on either side use every weapon to hand. Those opposed to the Catholic Church use, when they are in political power, the bludgeon of a universal and enforced anti-Catholic popular education, against which the Catholics use the force of personal intelligence and individual argument, as also a sort of perpetual wrestling against their opponents through the claim of freedom. Where it is the other way about, and the Catholic tradition has at least the sympathy of those in political power, you have not indeed (as you may have later) strong insistence on the Catholic side—as defined, as direct, and as violent as the present anti-Catholic action— you have not, for instance, an insistence upon the compulsory public teaching of Catholicism in the popular schools, as you have anti-Catholic public teaching under the anti-Catholic governments ; but you have the continued support of essentially Catholic things. The new dictatorship in Italy, for example, when it had cleared out the Parliamentary nastiness, took for one of its first principles the restoration of the crucifix to the schools, and insisted upon the official world hearing Mass.

Having thus stated the great quarrel, I ought, perhaps, like a good modern, to begin prophesying, and state what its development will be. But I deny the capacity of our popular prophets. I do not know the future. But that these two comparatively simple elements, the Faith and anti-Faith, stand before us to-day should, I think, be clear to all sufficiently experienced observers.

There is upon the one side (everywhere except in England) a now large, a believing and a coherent Catholic body : there is upon the other side the mood of which I have spoken—the mood in which it is even thought worse to be cruel to an animal than to a man ; the mood in which the existence and nature of the human soul are contentedly or discontentedly left aside as undiscoverable ; the mood in which the most fundamental institutions of society may be questioned or denied ; the mood in which the fixity of marriage is universally abandoned, and in which property has no longer a reasoned moral right. Indeed, in poor support of property (outside the Catholic Philosophy) to-day only two rotten struts remain : first, the assertion that possession by a few in the midst of a free community is natural because it has always existed. That is mere ignorance of history. Secondly, the asinine pretence that the few who possess have a right to possession through their greater virtue and intelligence—as for instance a millionaire eating uneatable things to the noise of an intolerable band in any one of our cosmopolitan hotels. . . .

I marvel that those who possess on such a tenure should not perceive the frailty of their tenure. They are, it is true, now fallen into a permanent state of panic, but they still have a vague conception that the present arrangement is in some ways secure.

It is not secure. It has no moral basis or custom behind it. The stability of a society depends upon an acceptation of its laws. If their enforcement is thought right, and the institutions which they defend are accepted by the conscience of men, the laws and society stand ; if not, both fall.

But who to-day defends the right of our handful of rich men to govern as they do, and to control the State ? How many even grant them a moral right to property ? They are themselves the negation of property. They boldly proclaim that the over-reaching of others, the catching up of other men's fortunes into their grasp by tricks, is the only talent they can exercise, and, indeed, the only one which they revere in their fellows. They have ruined that middle class, lacking which the institutions of the State, and particularly ownership, lose their foundation. Nevertheless, our society, of which these millionaires are to-day the masters, will not endure ; for no one thinks of them as lords : all despise them, and the greater part of men have ceased to envy them, and have begun to hate. The rule they exercise through demagogy, and particularly through their purchase of the Press, and (less important) through their purchase of the politicians, cannot endure. So much is certain ; nor is it prophecy to affirm it any more than it is prophecy to affirm the consequences of a natural law. Yet does it not seem probable that when this ephemeral phase is over, normal freedom will return.

The mass of men in an industrial civilisation is now caught in a machine from which they cannot escape, and subservience to which has become at last their nature. Every day there dies some number of those men and women who could still remember an England of he countrysides and of personal loyalties. Soon, very soon, there will be none left but those who, all their lives, have known nothing but the universal wage system of our towns.

It is this which makes the coming of compulsory labour in our great industrial cities probable enough. Any one can see that there are only three possible solutions to the present insecurity of all public service. The best solution would be the production of a contented populace through the better distribution of property. Such a populace would, though workers, be interested in the stability and security of a society in which they were also partners ; but that solution will not be reached, or even approached, because it is against the mentality of time ; because it seems fantastic. The next solution is the servitude of all under a tyranny of public officials. It involves confiscation of property now owned by a few, and the organisation of the industrial world despotically under a group of politicians. It is called Socialism.

That will not come either, although it is the ideal still favoured by some few belated Utopians. It will not come because the rich are too powerful and the politicians too corrupt. If it did come, it would mean a complete breakdown of society—but that is by the way.

The third solution is compulsory labour legally conducted, as it is virtually conducted to-day, for the advantage of the owners ; and *that* solution seems to be approaching.

When the general services of the community are interrupted by a strike—the necessary service of communication by rail, for example, or the necessary service of the modern Post Office—the clamour for compulsory labour at once arises. It sounds reasonable. It is consonant to the mind of the whole community ; and whether it is called arbitration or fixed contract, or disciplinary power of trades unions, compulsory labour is the underlying idea. It is close upon us.

But though the chance of servitude is a thing of the highest moment, I cannot help watching with amusement a small concomitant of the great process. I confess rather ashamedly to too great an interest in a subsidiary point, and that is, watching the euphemisms under which the process is covered.

For when men return to an old institution which they have discarded, and the proper name for which has grown odious (as we are returning to the enslavement of labour), they are particularly anxious to avoid that name, and spend much of their energy in discovering some way of getting the old thing under a new title—thus no one will call compulsory labour slavery, nor will even the words "compulsory" or "compulsion" appear on the surface. There will be some other term, and I for one shall follow with curiosity and delight the evolution of that term.

Just for the moment the odds are in favour of the term "loyalty"—it has a fine chivalric ring and makes an admirable mask : so men who continue to work for the profit of their masters during a strike are called "loyal." To insist upon one's right to sell one's labour at one's own price, instead of being ruled by some corrupt trade union leader who has been bought by the masters, is to be "disloyal" to one's union, or even to one's "leader."

There is quite a chance that the words "loyal" and "loyalty" will capture the position, and that a few generations hence we may have placards on the wall : "Notice : A disloyal employé of the Meat Trust is at large," with a description of him following ; and then we shall have "loyalty" courts for

trying and punishing people who rebel against
compulsory labour.

Another word which is still in the running is the
word " constitutional " ; it has a grander sound than
" loyal," but it is less tender. Men acting as free
men are nearly always striking " unconstitutionally,"
breaking the terms secretly purchased by the capital-
ists from a "leader." "Loyal " has also a better chance
than " constitutional," because it is a shorter word ;
but perhaps the two will be used side by side. The
legal indictment against a runaway slave, a couple of
centuries hence, will be, perhaps, that his act was
" unconstitutional," while the conventional term will,
perhaps, be " disloyal "—or there may be some new
term. But two things are probable—not certain :
(1) that compulsory labour will come ; (2) that it
will be given some name not even remotely connected
with the idea of slavery or compulsion.

Probable, not certain ; for who can tell, in the
millioned complexity of affairs, what new factor
may not arise ? A man may go round on a mule
calling himself a prophet, and change the whole
world to-morrow.

Yet men prophesy to-day, when all is mist and
fog. They prophesy as never did they prophesy
before : with an assurance and a conviction born
of physical science misapplied.

This passion for prophesying has several sources
which converge to produce such modern folly. I
think the strongest motive is mere relief to the nerves.
Men find that, by prophesying that a thing will take
place which they desire to take place, they are
themselves soothed.

One could make shoals of books by merely cutting
such pronouncements out of the European papers
during the last ten years, cuttings in which it would

be manifest that the writer was in a reckless mood, indifferent to the probability of his assertion.

Another motive is the motive of reputation ; for if the prophet brings it off, he can point to his success and be sure of a following, whereas if he does not bring it off, he can rely upon that atrophy of the memory which the universal reading of the daily Press has brought about. Another cause, as I have said, is the influence of physical science, that influence which affects the whole of modern life, and nearly always for ill. Physical science has proceeded from discovery to discovery in our time, until men are prepared for any marvel. It is true that side by side with this advance in the control of physical things there has gone a corresponding decline in the critical faculty, in the powers of reason : and a still more rapid decline in morals. But the main fact is familiar to the whole world, and is, superficially, the most astonishing thing of to-day. Our time has advanced in its knowledge of inanimate nature and in its control thereof as no other past time advanced.

Now this process was everywhere accompanied by, and tested by, prophecy. The seeker after some new " law " (as a sequence of physical phenomena is rather oddly called) would experiment until sequence was discovered, and, when it was discovered, he could confidently presume upon its completion; as, for instance, in the series of atomic weights. He could say, " You will find that this series will follow upon such and such a course," and when he was proved right he had achieved his end. The whole method of the progress was of this nature. It was like a man plotting down points upon a curve until he had aligned a sufficient number to give him the general formula, after which he could confidently say, " You will find, when the curve is fully described, such and such other points to lie along it." Or it was like a man re-establishing a Roman road. He says : " I find a section of it here pointing right to a neighbouring port, and a little way on another section still pointing the same, and I am confident that I shall find some place-name or parish boundary or other relic confirming that Roman road throughout." He is pretty certain to be right.

On the parallel of physical science, this habit of prophecy as the confirmation of judgment spread to things, in which, by their nature, mechanical judgment is impossible.

Another negative source was ignorance, and especially ignorance of the past. Our moderns have more and more lost the knowledge of the past. They have been taught to despise it ; they think of it first as of something foreign and odd ; later, if they study, as something very different from what it was. They, therefore, miss the lessons of the past, and especially the chief lesson, which is that the developments of society follow no mechanical process ; that their way is not the way of an arrow, but of a serpent. Ignorant of this, men fall into the simple error of taking the tangent to the curve, of prolonging the actions of causes immediately before their eyes, and of conceiving the future in terms of the present, as children do. Hence these confident assertions that in so many years such and such a country will have grown to such and such a population : that such and such a language will have become dominant—and so forth.

But it is to be noted that this process is not often applied to evils, for men do not like to face an evil future.

I notice in this political or social prophecy one

very strange omission : they never by any chance allow for that cause which is the major cause of change in human affairs : I mean religion.

Thirteen hundred years ago, the great fact before all men's eyes was the Roman Empire of the East. The commander of the armies, a half-divine being seated in Constantinople, was the centre of the world, and the acknowledged head of all that counted from the Atlantic to the Persian borders, and from the Northern Barbarism to the desert. Pressure menaced from the Persian hills and from the Tigris, and there was pressure from savage hordes in the mountains, and in the plains beyond to the north. Had men then been in the habit of prophesying after our foolish modern fashion they would have told you this or that, but all in terms of the Empire, or the German and Slav Barbarians, or the Persians ; and while they so thought in terms of the only things they knew, there had already arisen, in a place remote and utterly insignificant, among tribes of a few hundreds without power, culture or tradition, under conditions utterly negligible, the flaming spirit of Islam.

To our own modern world there must come either some vast religious reaction, or some vast religious novelty, or both. It is inevitable ; for men live by religion. Yet no one speaking of the future takes it for one moment into account. I know of but one book, a book of singular genius, in which the thing appears, though tentatively ; and that is in Jefferies' fine vision called "After London." But even Jefferies did not make of it the main source of change. In his day men had already begun to lose the significance of religion in human affairs.

The great light of the Forelands on the weather

side, the Goodwin lights on the lee, stood like the lamps of a street in the fall of that darkness as, with the tide beneath us, we ran up for London River. But, the wind coming from more northerly, we had to choose between beating up and standing out.

We did the last, though the wind was falling, because that lane of water is full of the world's shipping, and it was plainer to keep a course. By midnight the breeze had died down to a light air, and, somewhat later, the sky now very clear, we bore up on the other tack, the starboard tack, and went round till we had the dying air right abeam, and so came under brilliant stars within the point of Thanet land and dropped anchor and slept.

But early the next morning we woke to see the sun rising up undimmed over the wide North Sea, cut sharply by the calm horizon. It promised a warm and kindly day. . . .

. . . . .

I could wish that this book, already so long as to have become intolerable to the reader, the writer, the printer, and all others concerned in its production, already so heavy as to have become a business to the publisher, the carman, and the railway people (if, indeed, they transport it, but I have known of books transported in bulk on shipboard, and sinking to the glory of God, before they reached their destination, and that to the great advantage of our miserable world, which is abominably overcrowded with books); I could wish that this book, already so prolix, so otiose, so weary of its way that no poor gabbler in an inn ever more offended his audience than I will mine ; I could wish that this book, which may be called the Great Sea Serpent of books, or again, The Cromwell Road of Books, or once again, The Pambiblicon, or endless Compendium, or again,

The Long Arctic Night—what you will—I could wish that this book were longer still, I say, in order that I might drag you to perdition with the tedium of a million memories north of the Forelands, north of the Goodwins, north of Long Nose : memories of the Muddy Rivers of the Trinobantes, whose descendants inhabit rather than cultivate the Essex clay : memories of sandbanks rising out of the misty seas like whales, and of the platters of Harwich, and of the King's ship called *The Serpent*, and of Orford River, and of the Onion, and of Lowestoft, Yarmouth, and the exceedingly difficult labyrinth of the Wash, and of the awful great tide at King's Lynn.

But I renounce—not so much for your sakes as for my own, nor do I even speak of that Thames River which sailors called London River, and of the getting across it slantwise in spite of the great ships and the way in which time has silted up that harbour.

There are many curious things to be noted about the opening of London River. There is the double tide, so that a man making Long Nose from the Channel finds a new tide taking him up towards London. There is the way in which the best of all the channels into the river is the one least used, because it would make ships go out of their way. Ships come into the Thames either from the north or from the south, so they save time, which is money, by skirting either coast, but the main mid channel only the Dutchmen use when they have occasion to come up London River ; I approve them. Then there is the way in which undoubtedly all this has silted up and risen since the time of the ancients. It is not only the stuff brought down by the river which has piled up these banks ; there is also, I am sure, a lifting of the land. Nothing else could account for Thanet ceas-

ing to be an island, or for Richborough standing now
high and dry. The surface of the earth moves
slowly up and down over centuries, and no one shall
persuade me that Pevensey has run dry, Rye has been
drained, Lympne has run far inland, Dover inlet
has been closed, and the Wensum turned from a
great sea passage to a ditch by any action other than
the lifting of the land. The last thing to be said
about Thames mouth is this, that it was never shut
for traffic since the beginning of recorded time.
. . . until. . . . Men always traded up and down
it with a swarm of shipping since men first left
memorial of their doings, *until* the fourth of August,
1914.

It is not the least arresting of those many portents
accompanying the Great War that in its first week,
for the first time in human history, the Port of
London was paralysed.

. . . . . .

And so back to the Forelands, and the run between
the Kentish corner and the Goodwin Sands, with a
few kind words to St. Augustine, and Julius Cæsar,
and the men that murdered St. Thomas, and so grew
tails, and such others as have landed at this turn of
the coast ; but none for Hengist and Horsa, who
never lived at all, and yet have done all manner of
harm. So through the Downs into the Channel
again and back on my way to the sea of Sussex, and
to the shores which may be drowned and swamped
for a while by alien townsmen, but will keep their
own counsel and in due time will rise again.

. . . . . .

We brought up as night fell under the shelter of
Folkestone breakwater. It had fallen almost calm
as we slid into the oily place under the darkness,
and there was a long exasperating swell, not regular,

but coming in stupidly from the south-east, whence no wind blew, and washing back from the stones of the pier. A drizzling rain also was falling, and, in general, my companion and I paid for the splendour of those last days round the corner of Kent and across the Thames. It was too early to sleep and, as I had had the helm the night before, I had slept also during the day. I sat looking at my main chart, though I knew every inch (oh ! come ! say rather milli-metres) of the coast I was to follow ; and I pondered upon that shore line of Kent and Sussex, and upon places which I had passed far off on my way eastward, and which I would now see from closer by as I stood down Channel on my westward journey home.

How well (too well ? . . . No) does a man get to know a bit of coast like this, between Selsea and the Downs, after half a life of lazy passages along it, and (to be just) sometimes of wicked winds. It becomes as familiar as a street ; not only the aspect of the shore—changeable as that is—not only lights and buoys, and the hours for the turn of tides and all the rest of it, but the very sea itself in spite of its innumerable diversity.

But one effect of this familiarity is odd and un-expected. I know not whether others have felt it— I have felt it profoundly (especially in the last few years), and that is, the way in which the sameness of the sea, the reiteration at sea of similar emotions, of similar heights and bearing marks of the coast, the unity of scene, of time, of action, the eternity of the sea, throw into relief the catastrophic change, the cataract of change, inland : the revolution which has transformed modern England ; so that, of all the States I know, none has become so intimately different from its own immediate past, within the

memory of men elderly, but not yet old, as England :
yes, even South England : the refuge.

To many I know this is a cause of rejoicing.
Worse things have given way to better in their eyes.
To others it is a despair ; they are of that tempera-
ment which can only repose in fixed sanctities.
For my part, it is to me a regret. Because the
change is unhappy, and happiness is the end of
man.

The older England I knew (the spirit of which has
almost disappeared) was a happier place ; happier
not only in the immediate elements of personal
happiness, but in the more distant elements of corporate happiness, such as national pride and security.
Yet some find the change to be good : so they do.

At any rate, in this mixture of good and evil, the
thing that we should note—the thing the historian
will note with amazement—is the profundity and the
rapidity of the change.

There stand the same marks, the same headlands,
which I knew as a boy ; the sight to landward is
very little changed. There are the same three forts
of Spithead, through which I used to set out from
the sheltered water. There is the same odd entry,
somewhat shoal and difficult, to the branches of
Chichester Harbour and Bosham, that famous
hamlet in the story of England. There is the low
shelf of Selsea Bill and the mark on the Mixen, and
the two buoys of the Looe stream and the Owers
Light winking outside—as I remember it winking
when I watched it, a little boy, from the height
of the Downs. The entry to Littlehampton is the
same, and to Shoreham. The breakwater at Newhaven, though it still seems new to me, is already old.
Beachy Head Light, which used to be on the summit
of the cliff, has been shifted to the beach below.

The breakwater at Hastings has failed, but Fairlight gives you the same marks ; and the entry to Rye is what it always was, a caution to camels who have passed with honours through the eyes of needles. Dungeness slowly crawling out to sea still seems the same. The only material change in all that passage is the dangerous failure called Dover Harbour, against which the rushing tide of the Straits tumbles angrily, finding interference after so many æons of freedom : so that just outside Dover in almost any weather you are tossed by a confused and irritated sea. But all the rest, the Foreland Lights and the Goodwins, are what I have always known. Up and down that stretch of water there is somewhat more building on the land, slightly changing the aspect of the distant shore. There is the curious long group of huts on Shoreham beach, Seaford sending up red brick on to the green of the heights above it, and Bexhill to-day where once was loneliness. But take it all in all, it is the same scene, after nearly forty years of sailing on that sea and watching that land with Highdown still for the best sea-mark, and with the clump of Chanctonbury—yes, even the stump of Halnacker Mill, though it is now all ruins. The marks are the same. I might turn boy again and set sailing and not find the sea-things other than I had known them.

But on land—in the heart of man—what a transformation ! There went into it the England of the 'seventies—an England aristocratic, free, with ease of movement within and acting externally, at will, upon all nations. An England with a sense of increasing wealth and of increasing knowledge, and an England English. Of all the men and women you met, most had been born in the villages, or little market towns, which are the roots

of England. It was one society : that of to-day is
another, almost foreign to the first.

Of all this revolutionary change, covering the
short space of half a lifetime, two effects are most
prominent : the fall of Parliament from great
honour to contempt, and the change in the Press.
Of these the change in the Press is the most obvious,
and perhaps the most remarkable.

The Press of England has passed, as a whole, in
that space of time from one social condition to
another totally new. There are still dignified exceptions, but they are survivals and abnormal. The
general spirit of the Press has utterly changed. It
is as great a change as a man might experience who,
having been brought up, let us say, as an English
public school boy and university man, should so
sink as to pass his middle age up-country in a strange
colony far overseas, as a labourer among labourers.

At the beginning of the period, England had a
Press—daily, weekly, monthly and quarterly—
especially designed for, and consonant to, an aristocracy : not designed for, and consonant to, lords
and ladies ; but designed for, and consonant to, a
highly cultivated governing class whose power was
unquestioned, and which then directed the whole
community. The intellectual life of the nation was
concentrated in that class : it included men of all
births, but having in common the same cultivation
of spirit, the same manner of talking, the same
sufficient knowledge of the European past, the same
less, but still sufficient knowledge, of contemporary
Europe : and, what was most important, the same
philosophy and social outlook.

This class (the gentry, or whatever you like to call
it) had its own Press, the great daily papers, the
weekly reviews, the serious monthly and quarterly

reviews. Side by side with that Press there was a frankly popular Press, which had no sort of power, and which was intended to amuse the non-political mass below. It was represented in two or three very vulgar Sunday newspapers full of police court cases, and murders, and the rest ; and weekly papers with tittle-tattle about the superiors of the class which read them ; but it was the Press of the educated class which represented, mirrored, and to some extent influenced the general action of England.

In that Press you had, for its daily papers, information more rapidly acquired, better balanced, more detailed, and more extensive by far than was to be found in the Press of any other country. Everything of importance was known to the governing class of England through that Press, and was known at once ; and, on the whole, was known in something like the right proportion. The weeklies, monthlies, and quarterlies were powerful organs of intellectual expression, and set also a literary standard. You saw in them the names of Tennyson or Browning, of Huxley and the Duke of Argyll, of Lord Salisbury, of Arnold. There was about the whole atmosphere of this Press something of that tone of equality, ease and sure touch which is the mark of a governing class in any aristocratic State.

To-day, you have a Press in which the less vital of these characteristics remain ; the essential have wholly disappeared. Information is still rapidly acquired (though the English Press here has no longer any advantage over the Continental, such as it used to have a generation ago), but the type of information is wholly different ; and as for that quality vital to truth, the sense of proportion, it has vanished. The knowledge of Europe has fallen to a level negligible or contemptible. All the most weighty things are either hidden for private purposes, or (this is much the most common fault) unappreciated. While the Italian, French, and German papers are giving with full detail and with right balance the aspects of our contemporary civilisation ; while men like Ferrero or Maurras are perpetually before the eyes of the Continent, we have here men who are no more than the servants of wealthy, half-educated, or uneducated millionaires, their owners : men who write to order any nonsense about Europe which those owners desire to publish. Therefore the great movements abroad, reacting upon the national life of this country, are misunderstood and invariably take opinion by surprise. I will give two examples which will be fresh in the memory of all.

No newspaper here either foresaw or, when it arrived, made comprehensible the Italian movement which led to the resurrection of the country by Mussolini. Compare such astonishing ignorance with the state of affairs in England a lifetime ago, when Italy was first rising to her modern position. *Then* the English papers closely followed all the ferment in Italy. It was to their columns that foreign statesmen turned for the facts and news on the progress of Savoy. To-day no Continental statesman looks at our Press, save now and then to protest against some childish blunder. Again, even as I write, there is taking place in London a highly important conference between the bankers and politicians, the object of which, on the one side, is to diminish French power and, on the other, to maintain it. I turn to the *Temps*, or to the *Corriere*, and I find in the first paper very full and detailed accounts of the debates of the committees with an adequate educated judgment upon the results attained. In the second paper, I find a good, balanced judgment upon the situation with a leaning towards the English interest regarded as nearly identical with the Italian. But I defy any one to make out from *The Times* what is really going on at that conference ! You will read plenty of abuse of the French ; plenty of self-praise and acres of generalities. But you will not find yourself informed—although the great business is going on here in London right under our eyes.

I thought it the part of a contemporary to follow the affair as closely as I could. I soon found it necessary to give up looking at the English papers, and to buy the papers of the Continent in order to instruct myself. The method had the disadvantage of delay, but had the advantage of giving me real information. The few papers which still keep up the façade of culture in their form, though certainly not in their contents, are, again, of less importance than the new popular Press which makes no pretence to culture in any form, which is owned by impossible adventurers, such as no one a generation ago would have had in his house, even had they then existed ; and it is this popular Press now which is the main instrument in the moulding of opinion.

The revolution is complete. It is as complete as though the education of the country were to pass from the hands of the classicists and the mathematicians to those of Big Business, and boys were to be taught advertisement and salesmanship instead of the humanities. And this our passing from one mode of public expression, and control by suggestion, to another utterly different and far baser system, has come silently and has worked its effect unnoticed. It is only by contrasting *then* with *now* that we notice it.

We are arrived in England to-day at a condition

in which the popular newspaper gives its owner a power in the State comparable only to the power of finance and far superior to the nominal power of those poor play actors, embarrassed, furtive, who still bear titles of authority : Secretaries of State for this or that. And yet, by the very nature of the organism, this new instrument of power, the mob Press, must be ill-informed, unreal, and—what is not without its importance—morally vile.

Less obvious than the complete change in the Press, in its functions and character, perhaps less pronounced and less advanced, yet certainly of great moment, is the fall of the House of Commons and of Parliament in general from authority and dignity to well-deserved contempt.

But for this evil there is more hope of remedy than there is for the evil of the Press. When any organ of government reaches a certain degree of decay, some other automatically takes its place, and if the substitution is made promptly enough, the State may bridge over the passage without disaster.

Such substitution lies ready to our hand. We have only to increase the power of the Crown, and that would indeed give truth to the boast too often repeated that the continuity of names is valuable to society. The monarchy is still there in name, and the giving of true power to it is therefore still possible.

The decline of Parliamentary authority and dignity has been wholly a rot from within. The people of England did not desire it ; they desired nothing better than to continue their old respect for that aristocratic institution at Westminster round which every activity of the nation had centred. The damage was done by permitting personal corruption to go unpunished. When once the habit arose of condoning the use of public position for private enrichment—and that secret—it was impossible for the strength of the institution to survive. The temptation of the politician to enrich himself at the expense of the public good (to take bribes, to sell monopolies and contracts and policies), is so very strong that, unless it is met by as strong a check of discipline, it is bound to run riot, and it has done so. It has come on in a flood, especially during the last twenty years, taking every conceivable form, but all those forms proceeding from the immunity of the evil-doers. Men possessed of political power create public monopolies which they handle for their own enrichment : they take bribes, they give out contracts as against payment. They will assign a valuable State right to some company and then, resigning office, take up a highly salaried post in that company. The traffic in honours for the private advantage of those who bestow them is the least of these cancers which are eating away the body of Parliament. The habitual practice of blackmail in the course of personal intrigue for power (it is mutual between the politicians and the newspaper owners), is the worst. But all are excessive in degree, and between them they have done their work. It is now impossible to restore to politics, which are now professional politics, the old prestige. It is gone.

In the presence of these experiences, the commonplaces of Parliamentary life with which all Parliamentarians are thoroughly familiar, and which at last the public are learning, the attitude of the politicians themselves is one of tolerance : the attitude of the public is a weary and disdainful indifference.

This attitude of tolerance on the part of the politicians, this policy they have chosen of excusing and pardoning corruption, seems to me more worthy

of discussion than anything else in public life to-day ;
it is the centre of the whole affair.

Corruption in some degree you must have under
any form of government. Half the art of government is the devising of methods for the repression,
rather than the destruction, of corruption. So long
as men love notoriety and wealth, so long as notoriety
and wealth can be conferred by the possession of
political power, and so long as political power domi-
nates the Courts of Justice—that is, for ever—so
long you will have corruption present among those
who govern, except under a strong King. It stands
to reason that the appetite for wealth or notoriety or
both will incite men in political power to obtain
them, and as that power gives them in a large
measure control of the Courts of Justice and full
control of the police and of prosecution, they can be
rendered in the main immune from the consequences of their actions. I should not think it
remarkable to learn that in any country, at any time,
there was very great corruption among the public
men. What I should think remarkable, what I
should think a phenomenon worthy of special study
(because it would be exceptional and would necessarily produce exceptional results), would be to hear
that the corruption was not punished, and that those
who were caught and exposed in flagrant acts of
corruption were actually promoted. That is what
we have here to-day in England.

It is with the toleration of Parliamentary corruption as it is with disease in the human body. Hardly
anybody goes through life without some bad illness.
Most people have some one or other specific weakness which develops into a long illness ending in
death, and all human beings whatsoever are liable
to disease, even those few who do not for the

moment suffer from it. But everywhere you see the human race fighting disease, and trying to avoid its consequences. Now if you found a man who took his disease as a habit, and tended rather to accentuate it and foster it, you would think his action abnormal. You would say: "'Certain strange consequences will follow upon this." And you would be right.

I have found the modern toleration of bribery and blackmail in politics to be defended with very different arguments, but I fancy that the underlying motive of the defence, the real basis of it in a Parliamentarian's mind, is patriotism combined with a certain new scale of moral values which has come in with the century. I fancy all those who have in my hearing defended this later-day toleration of corruption, really had at the back of their heads a conviction that such degradation of public life did the country no great harm, being no more than a sort of permanent necessary evil. They think that the lessening of the security of the State, which would come from exposing and punishing the culprits, is a much greater evil than letting them go their way. It is something of the attitude which most people take towards a family scandal. They say : " These things will happen, anyhow ; and we shall lower the family by any public discussion of them." So say the more reputable at Westminster.

There are then, as I see it, two elements in the now admitted and universal toleration of bribery and blackmail among politicians. The first element is the noble element of patriotism which judges that of two evils you must choose the least, and that the evil of a certain minimum, necessary, amount of political vice is far less than the evil of shaking authority and order in society and at the same time weakening the country in the face of its rivals.

The second element is the judgment that the levying of and submitting to blackmail, and the offering
and taking of bribes among Parliamentarians, is only
one out of hundreds of moral evils in the State, and
is one of the least.

If these be the real foundations of the tolerance
of these evils, the artificial arguments advanced are
many and varied. I remember one political dinner-
table in Surrey where we thrashed out the whole
business at some length. Everybody present was
connected with public life directly or indirectly,
and no one, so far as I know, was himself or herself
guilty. Yet, out of twenty, only three of us, of whom
I was one, maintained the necessity of checking the
evil. All the others, the remaining men and, of
course, *all* the women, relied upon this argument :
that what you wanted in the conduct of the State was
ability, sound judgment of the elements in any
problem to be dealt with, and a good forecast of the
immediate future. If you had these, they said, the
country prospered ; lacking these, any disaster might
come. If you got these qualities in those who
governed, it did not matter whether they were also
given to peculation, or to odd tricks of spying and
threatening, or to selling policies and monopolies
or to taking bribes.

I think that answer would have been sound if
you could have proved that there was some necessary
connection between good judgment, resolute will,
patriotism, and all the rest of it, and the particular
vices in question. For instance, a man defending
the luxury and worldliness of a religious hierarchy
might very well say : " These are moral evils, no
doubt ; but you will hardly get men able to conduct
a great organisation who shall at the same time
be indifferent to pomp and pleasure." But I

would contend that in the case of Parliamentary life
the connection does not apply. The kind of man
who advances by taking or giving bribes, especially
the man who advances by taking bribes, the kind of
man who spends his energy in ferreting out the
secret actions of rivals and then threatening them
with exposure if they continue to compete with him,
is not the kind of man who will normally have good
judgment. Such men are, as a rule, of a very base
sort intellectually, and the vices from which they
suffer are the vices of small, uncertain and despicable
minds. If I wanted a man to manage a great
business with foresight, strong will, and a good
understanding of the elements of the problems
before him, I might choose him in spite of a record
for cruelty or pride—two very detestable vices. But
I should be unwise to choose him if he had a record
for petty peculation and perpetual intrigue among
his fellows. Men suffering from these vices do
very well in the lower ranks of the secret police,
but they are unfitted for high position. Indeed, we
have had experience in the last few years, and very
rude experience, of what happens when you give
such men even a small part of the governing power
in the State. It was such men who judged, for
instance, that the Jewish Communist revolution in
Hungary would succeed. It was such men who
supported the Greek adventure against Turkey, and
it was such men who capitulated to Ireland.

Another argument I have heard advanced is this :
that corruption on a far larger scale was vigorous
during all the lifetime in which England was rising
to its modern position of a Great Power.

From Walpole to the younger Pitt, from the
South Sea Bubble to the Act of Union, public life
was conducted universally upon a system of bribes

No one can deny that these were the years during which the modern greatness of England was founded ; therefore (it is advanced) there is something quite out of proportion in fussing about a modern Chancellor of the Exchequer taking a few thousand shares across the breakfast-table, or a modern Postmaster-General signing a contract in favour of some private company and then taking a highly-paid post with that company as his reward. For, if a very much more extended system of bribery did the country no harm in its formative period, we have nothing to fear from little individual peccadilloes in the way of taking a few thousands here and there, as is the habit of our public men to-day.

I fully agree that if the bribery were of the same quality in both cases, this argument would be sound. But the whole point of the affair is that the bribery is of a different kind.

The corruption of the eighteenth century was the purchase by those who controlled honours (and in a large measure the public purse) of votes in support of their policy ; at the same time it was the open grasping of lucrative sinecures and large salaries by those in power.

An eighteenth century aristocrat would give his dependent a lucrative sinecure, or a position in which he was free to accumulate great sums ; he and his would vote themselves an exaggerated salary ; he would vote out of the taxes great sums to his colleagues, and he would take many private opportunities for enriching himself, as the natural action of a man possessed of the power to do so through a public post.

But your eighteenth century aristocrats who gave the tone to all that system, the big squires of the time, and the great merchants whom they digested into their body, were neither influenced in policy, nor lowered in dignity by what they did. They did not profess to be acting otherwise, they did not put themselves into an absurd position, nor live in panic of exposure. A man would take money or honours as the wages of voting for the Government, but members of the Government themselves would not habitually take money in order to advantage company promoters who desired to fleece the public. There were occasional examples of this sort of thing, but it was not normal. You cannot imagine Walpole, for instance, or the younger Pitt, at either end of the period, taking money from a chance financial adventurer who should have come to him to get a new duty put on, or an old duty taken off, or a new kind of monopoly invented, whereby to fill his pockets.

I cannot imagine a man going to the younger Pitt, and saying : " My brother who is your colleague in the Government and I have a project for fitting sailing ships with such and such a device. If you will help us to make it a law that all British ships shall carry this device and purchase it from us, we will give you a share in the proceeds." Our modern politicians act in this fashion ; and, what is perhaps worse for the authority of Government, they do so in a fashion which makes them ridiculous : they loudly protest their innocence on the eve of exposure, and live always in some trepidation, and in a sort of incessant wrestling match with those who could make their lives intolerable by public insistence on their little habits.

Here is, I think, the core of the whole matter. Those patriots who rightly think they serve the country by strengthening the authority of even nominal governors, but who are persuaded that the

toleration of political vice strengthens such authority, make in this second postulate of theirs a very
obvious error. It is an error which they would not
make, I think, if they lived the life of their fellow-
citizens and knew the average Englishmen better
than they do.

All politicians live a life apart from the general
mass of the less wealthy, less privileged classes,
though they themselves are so largely drawn from
these strata. It is astonishing when one hears them
talking among themselves to discover how remote
they are from the general interests of the public,
and how seriously they take their own sham divisions
and sham battles, and with what strange simplicity
they believe that these sham battles are of vast
moment to the electorate. The public as a whole
is now fully acquainted with the nastiness and
degradation of public life. It certainly does not
appreciate the ultimate consequences of these, but
at any rate it is no longer under any illusions.
Indeed, my experience is that the ordinary member
of the public, the average man in the liberal professions and in commerce, rather exaggerates the evil
than otherwise, although he does not recognise its
danger. He is ready to believe that pretty well any
politician may be found taking money, and he does
not distinguish as he should between the two
sharply different types of Parliamentarians : those
with a dirty record of their own, and those with a
clean record who permit and support the dirt in
the midst of which they live. For it must be
admitted that public life is full of men who would
never dream of themselves doing such actions as
have come to mark their profession as a whole ; but
these men do not on that account stand excused.
They support the nastiness in the midst of which

they live ; they refuse to correct it ; they even, as a rule, join those who would prevent its exposure. They are accessories to all those acts which they not only personally despise and are disgusted with, but which in private they denounce. For they could put an end to the system if they preferred justice to their own little careers and the general good of England to their personal ease or notoriety.

Sometimes they try to salve their consciences by substituting a general for a particular condemnation —the oldest device known to governing man for shirking the duties of government.

I remember an excellent comedy of this sort in which I myself took part. The Admiralty had given an order for the making of an important part of a man-of-war to a small company (what is called a " one-man " company) run for the profit of a friend of the Prime Minister of the day.

There was nothing excessive about that bit of favouritism. It was natural that a politician should help a friend : some one must have the order, and there was no great harm done to the State. But the next step was of real importance.

It turned out that the part supplied was defective. Those who supplied it might plead that they did not know the defect to exist, nor indeed would it be to their advantage to have allowed such a defect. It was probably an accident, though it did point to the work having been given to people inadequate to its gravity. The part was sent back to be put right. Instead of being put right, as it should have been, an operation was performed with the effect of concealing the defect, instead of remedying it. The part was sent back in such a condition that, had the flaw not been discovered, the great man-of-war itself and its crew might have perished. This was obviously a very serious matter indeed. If there is one thing the politicians must not be allowed to play tricks with, it is the Navy.

Now, the Parliamentarians appointed to look into public accounts issued a fine bombastic denunciation of the awful business, and used such words as would have satisfied Jeremiah. *But they were very careful not to mention a single name.*

That seemed to me something of a defect. I was in Parliament at the time, and I set out to find out who were the actual human beings responsible for this crime. Unless one got on to them and punished them, one might as well have done nothing in the matter. If things of this sort can be done with impunity, they will certainly be done again.

I found the greatest difficulty in getting any single one of those six hundred odd men in the Commons to act with me in the matter. I did not, of course, approach more than a few, because there were not more than a few who would even consider the public good ; but by one of those few I was told that it was not usual to act in this fashion ; that such action was regarded as " personal " ; that the thing was now some months concluded and ought to be buried ; that it was difficult to arrive at the ultimate responsibility in these affairs—and so on. They all applied to a principal unit of the British Navy, to an English man-of-war and a thousand English lives, the principle that the politician was more important than ship or crew, and that their own parliamentary skins were more important than the country.

The individual private Member of Parliament has no power of action in Parliament except the chance of the ballot or the putting down of a question. I put down my question. It was answered in the most pathetic manner by the politician directly responsible, who called Heaven to witness that I had traduced by my question an old and valued friend of his own whom he loved as a brother. That the fault was that of "a subordinate." The House murmured its sympathy. I pointed out that I had traduced no one, that I had only asked for the names of the responsible people and for their prosecution. Whereupon, as another journalistic phrase goes, "the matter was allowed to drop." But I need hardly add that the person nominally responsible was promoted to a public honour, and that no "subordinate" appeared.

It was only a small episode, though it would not have seemed small to the officers or crew if their ship had struck in the middle of the night owing to a defect in the steering gear—still, honestly, it was a small matter as politics go. There are hosts of much graver instances, but it was a characteristic one.

The argument that this now universal taint covering public life is tolerable because the same thing goes on in every country where there is a Parliament, and therefore does not weaken us in the face of our rivals, has two bad flaws in it.

The first is a neglect of the fact that the cancer called Parliament is no longer universal. Some of our rivals are already rid of it : all are disgusted with it ; most will probably have cut it out within a generation.

The second is that nowhere is Parliament bound up with the nation as it is in England.

The French parliamentary system is at least as corrupt as the English : from the little I know of it, I should say it was worse. The American, I understand, is not so bad ; but it is still sufficiently corrupt to excite the perpetual vigilance of the

American electorate and Press, which are as ruthless in exposing such evils as we are resolute in concealing them. Of the Polish and German systems, which have just come into existence, I know nothing. The Italian was contemptible, and the Spanish a joke. They have both been happily kicked into the street, and I trust we shall hear of them no more.

But the parliamentary corruption of other countries is attached to an institution which in those countries is subsidiary to the national life. No one in France, for instance, regards the Parliament as a necessary, or even a properly working, part of the national existence ; it is a modern experiment, very unpopular, and standing in some dread of far more permanent and deep-rooted institutions, such as the University, the Army, the Church, and the landed system, with which it has to work as best it may. The politicians in Paris can and do work great harm in all departments, but they do not form the traditional organ of government, rooted in the country, as the Commons do here. They live under perpetual protest.

In the United States, as everybody knows, the central representative Assembly is altogether subordinate. The Senate is far more powerful, and far more respected. The President is high above both. He has monarchic powers superior to anything of the kind in Europe—superior by far to those exercised by the King of Prussia in the days when that individual was also military head of the Reich.

But in England Parliament is the great national institution. It is bound up with the whole life of the country. A disease attacking it is a national disease. The lawyers' guild, which is in England far, far more powerful than in any other country, is inextricably bound up with Parliament. There can

in England never be any question of the armed
forces acting apart from Parliament ; nor can there
be apparently (and unfortunately) as yet a kingly
power, like that of the President of the United
States. A King of England would to-day find
ample popular support against Parliament ; but
how is he to move ?

Therein lies the gravity of the situation. Parliament will not reform itself, and yet there is no power
external to Parliament capable of reforming it.
Though the nation were in the last extremity of
peril, we have not to hand some force external to
Parliament capable of pushing aside its maleficent
impotence and taking over the reins. Indeed, when
certain politicians were secretly trying to make peace
behind the back of the Allies during the crisis of
the Great War, no one moved—except a few humble
seamen, who stopped one important voyage of their
own accord. Should we live to see an invasion of
this country, or a shameful capitulation, I fear that
the disaster and the shame would still be presided
over by the politician. During the Great War we
owed half a dozen insanities to the fact that with us a
politician can order the movements of armies, in
spite of the soldiers, and affect—though he can
hardly direct—the foreign policy of the country, in
spite of its competent permanent officials. It is true
that the millionaire newspaper owner, especially if he
be devoid of instruction, and therefore of all responsibility, has more to do with the framing of a policy
than has the politician, and it is true that the great
and weighty financial interests are much more
powerful. But Parliament is the door through
which everything must pass—or, to change the
metaphor, it is the instrument which alone can be
used for direct effect ; and its decline is on that

account of very grave moment to the future of the country. It is therefore a despairing thing to say that the decline cannot be checked, that the disease must run its course ; yet I fear there is nothing else to say. It is manifestly too late to set things right. There came one moment after another in which a remedy could have been applied ; but each opportunity was refused, and I do not see how any sufficient one can arise in the future.

To have checked the rot at the very beginning, as, for instance, during the telephone scandal, would have been easy enough (already, a few years before, Mundella had been thrown out of public life for what was then thought a monstrous lapse, but what would now be thought hardly an irregularity). It was even possible to turn the current as late as the Marconi scandal. One virile decision in that crisis might still have saved Parliament. But I do not see, nor do I think any one else can tell me, how it can be saved now.

The test is very simple. On the day when a Cabinet Minister is heavily fined or imprisoned for irregular action in connection with money the tide will have turned. Does any one believe that such a day will come ? I for my part certainly do not. Therefore the decay will continue. The system, already deep-rooted and established, will become a matter of course, and there will happen in the long run to the House of Commons what has happened to every institution which gets past praying for ; but, meanwhile, what of us who have no other instrument ? What of the nation ?

One point of view was presented to me by a wise old gentleman who had spent about thirty years (doing nothing) in the House of Commons and then wangled a peerage (for nothing) out of his colleagues;

for he desired to live on under the same roof and to spend the last of his days amusing himself—remaining an indulgent spectator of what was still, to him, a slightly interesting affair.

It was on the evening of a day when I had been trying hard to dig one of the more noisome of the politicians out of the earth in which he had taken refuge after a particularly unpleasant affair. The old fellow had watched the process with an active amusement, and I think he was grateful to me for having provided him with an entertaining day. He had been watching from the gallery, but that evening, as I dined with him, he warned me against wasting too much energy in such a pastime.

I assured him that it was no pastime—that I took it very seriously indeed.

" I know you do," he answered, " and that is just what I am warning you against. The country is carried on not by these fellows," jerking his thumb towards the door, " but by the general activity of its people : that people is sound and will come well out of any ordeal."

The war proved him right.

" What the mass of the people do not do for themselves," he said, " is done by a rather too large but very conscientious body of permanent officials, underpaid, industrious, and exceedingly competent. The politicians are only the scum on the top ; they have very little to do with the happiness or the unhappiness of the nation, and not much to do with its strength. Even the points of policy are, as a rule, decided outside their circle in the weightier financial world. It is a waste of energy to draw that covert too long."

There is a great deal to be said for the old boy's attitude. But I could not help asking him what

Mr. Gladstone would have done if he had been faced with a Chancellor of the Exchequer taking shares over the breakfast-table ; for he remembered Mr. Gladstone well, and had for him that odd half-worship which so many men who knew that powerful, short, oratorical genius of a better past were smitten with. I said, " In Mr. Gladstone's time the Secretaries of State had more privacy than our modern politicians, and their actions interfered less with the general life of England than they do to-day : with the permanent officials far less ; yet you know as well as I do what Mr. Gladstone would have done if he had found a member of his Government taking shares from a company promoter over the breakfast-table."

The old man answered to this that the standard was altogether higher in his own youth than it was now, and that though he could not deny that Cabinet Ministers' present habit of taking money was a weakness to the country, yet he thought it a small weakness. He added a thing which I have since discovered to be profoundly true, " At any rate, it cannot be remedied, and so you are wasting your time."

In all the discussions—far too many !—in which I have engaged upon this subject I only found one really enthusiastic defender of the system, and that was a wealthy young Anglo-American who either just had taken, or was just about to take, up a place in public life. To him our present way of going on had a sort of special excellence peculiar to this country and worthy of Bacchic praise. He spoke like a man who has come into a promised land, and he was moved to indignation by my criticisms against certain recent events. He applauded a Cabinet Minister who had just given a valuable monopoly to a company promoter and then resigned and accepted a permanent highly salaried post in that company : for he repudiated any connection between the selling of the monopoly and the immediate subsequent acceptation of the salary. He was indignant that such a connection should be dreamt of. They were separate acts.

First the politician, in his capacity of public servant, honestly weighing all the pros and cons decides that a company promoter is the right man to have a great public monopoly—worth millions. He gives him that monopoly. There the matter ends.

Then begins quite another set of actions. The politician as a private individual accepts a highly salaried post in the pay of the said company promoter and lives on the profits of the monopoly.

Only insane suspicion could connect the two acts.

It was a startling theory to hear : it was also completely new to me. But it had this advantage : it made him a contented supporter of that which others either laughed at cynically or held their tongues about.

I shall be interested to see, as I grow older, whether this type of defence develops, and whether we shall find the taking of bribes and the levying of blackmail a matter, not for commonplace acceptance, but for indignant praise. I do not think that we shall have much of that argument. It is exotic. No man of our blood is really comfortable in the presence of financial corruption. He may tolerate it : he may practise it ; but it does not fit in with his conscience, still less excite his enthusiasm.

However, one never knows. There are very vile commercial transactions which certainly excite admiration to-day as surely as they would have excited in our fathers the determination to hang the culprit. Laxity in the relations between men and women which our fathers would at least have condemned is to-day not so much condoned as defended and made into a sort of religion. Direct treason in time of war merits a few months in the second division. So it is on the cards that I shall live to hear men say in awestruck tones, " What a fellow Binks is ! The Prime Minister's agent offered him £10,000 to clear out—but he got £100,000 in solid cash before he had done with him ! He frightened the old fool to death by showing he knew all about Chapel Street."

After all, I have heard much the same tone of religious veneration in those describing some Stock Exchange swindle of our day, and a fortune made in a few weeks by the deception of the multitude and the ruin of a thousand families.

So there is still hope.

The authority and prestige of Parliament have sunk like water in a river lock, sogging away rapidly before our eyes.

The process should normally have been more rapid, and the ultimate crisis to which it should surely lead was due to come long before this.

It would have been much better for the country if it *had* so come. The Marconi scandal was an excellent opportunity for an explosion and a thorough clearing of the air. The far worse Dope scandal, taking place when the nation was fighting for its life, was perhaps the last chance offered. If half a dozen of the politicians and company promoters compromised in the Dope scandal had been openly tried and sent to penal servitude during the war, we should have been the better for it to-day. Instead of that the whole thing was hushed up, and the loot remained in the hands of the looters : an example followed by I know not how many others in the short seven years which have elapsed since that worst of abominations was condoned.

Perhaps the strongest break that was put upon the pace downhill, the strongest force restraining a final collapse, and thereby condemning the country to the gradual and certain extinction of parliamentary authority, lay in the momentum of the old Parliamentary prestige.

To an older generation, of whom some few survive, the idea of a seat in Parliament was connected with honour and a social position worthy of ambition. That generation carried on an admixture of the old tradition which only slowly died, and while it lasted supported the collapsing fabric with which it was intertwined.

Such men, before the present nastiness began, had already acquired a habit of the House of Commons, they lived in the thoughts and customs of an older and much better time, and lent to the diseased institution of their age the memories of its health during their own early youth and manhood.

Some very few still survive to lend the corruption of professional politicians a remnant of moral support. When they are gone we shall have the problem to face in full as we have not yet had to face it.

Of those men who had thus obtained a habit of the House of Commons as it were, and who for long lent it a fictitious value which it had long ceased to possess, I would particularly recall—for I followed his public action closely and often discussed it with him—Sir Charles Dilke.

He belonged, of course, to an older time, when politics were still respectable and even dignified, and, having begun to take root in them much earlier in life, he felt acutely the wastage of his powers—for he could never have office. But he was treated by

the Chair as a sort of Elder Statesman, and I shall
always remember the solidity and detail of his
experience in foreign affairs. He was one of the
very few men of my own time (overlapping from an
older time) who knew what he was talking about
when he discussed the Continent, and who followed
the change which was taking place over all Western
Europe ; and he could value the degree and the
quality of it in each country, or at least in the
Germanies, in France, in Italy and in Belgium. Spain
he discussed less, and I do not know what his measure
of acquaintance was with Spanish affairs. I always
count his evidence as valuable in the interesting
discussion upon the origin of Gambetta. He knew
Gambetta well, and did not despise him. He said
that he was a Jew, and that, therefore, he was quite
alien to the French temper. That, of course, was
also the thesis of many of Gambetta's enemies (for
Liberals always seem to think that they are saying
something unpleasant about a man when they say
that he is of Jewish race), but it was not the testimony
of most of his friends. Two of Gambetta's friends I
knew well enough : one was a relative of mine, the
other was that very great man, Deroulede. I do not
think Deroulede was a very accurate observer, but
at any rate he testified to the intensely national
quality of Gambetta, and swore that there was
nothing Oriental about him at all. My own relative,
who was of a more cynical temper, said that he was
certain of the same thing from careful observation. Gambetta seems to have been a man who
commanded real and profound affection, but his
legend will be distorted, for it is one of the curses
of the modern political chaos that those who by
accident or by their desire enter its whirlpool of
personal competition and consequent advertisement

must inevitably be betrayed by fate. Not one of
them can appear as he is, and not one of them will
ever be taken by posterity to have anything of greatness about him, however great he may be, unless he
can exercise some talent outside the wretched parliamentary business into which he has been caught up.

There is in that life such an admixture of violence,
cunning and bombast, quite apart from the money-
taint, that a man's name becomes a mere label for
hatred and ridicule in places where the struggle is
taken seriously as it is in France or in Ireland. It
becomes a mere label for play-acting and make-
believe in a country such as ours, where politics are
not taken seriously.

No English parliamentarian could suffer the
legacy of hatred, virulent contempt and documented,
detailed, evidenced accusation which will prevent
the name of Gambetta from taking an honourable
place in history. But on the other hand, no English
politician, since the 'nineties, will cut any figure for
posterity unless he can do something outside his
profession. There is nothing to prevent the Postmaster-General, or the Leader of the Opposition, or
any other of the circus, from writing a good poem,
or painting a good picture ; but, unless he does
something of the sort, his name will only be one
of a hundred names, half-comic and all-wearisome.
For the trade has lost its dignity. It is found out.

I have delayed on this subject too long. It is
public property, and filth at that, and people are
tired of it, for in their heart of hearts they know that
nothing more can be done, that public life in its
parliamentary form is past saving.

It is possible that I exaggerate the effect of the
evil ; it is possible that some novel remedy
besides the obvious one of increasing the power

of the Crown may set things right. It has certainly done so in the past, the break up of one institution apparently necessary to society has discovered the importance of other forces which have saved society by bringing up new forces unsuspected. It is possible. Perhaps it is probable. It is to be hoped. And that is all one can say.

.   .   .   .

Such thoughts are suitable for a drizzling calm, and for wet canvas hanging useless and dead in a hopeless dawn upon a sea without life. But with the coming of a little wind, a little north-easterly wind in the growing light ; with its blowing away of the misty rain, and its bringing a heartening into the morning, I prefer to turn to better things, to the realities : to the English water and to the English land.

The mist scudded off from the Folkestone waters, the light not only brightened, but grew coloured, until at last there was a fine, flaming dawn over the Kentish chalk and the Bastion cliffs of the Kentish salient, and very soon she was running to it prettily, her wet canvas holding the wind well, and, if anything, pressing her a little too hard. My companion came on deck with the morning, woken by the new life in the hull, and by the run of the sea along the sides. As yet the water was smooth, for the wind was a trifle off shore, and would so remain until we had come into the hollow bend of the flat coast, the last of which runs almost due south, and which ends in the shingle of Dungeness. Also we were still on the ebb and the wind followed the stream.

After the sun had risen the breeze grew stronger, and even violent ; but as I greatly desired to round the Ness before the tide should catch me and raise a sea, I would not take in a reef. So I held on, though with the more southerly course we were setting, and with the wind still rising, it was not over safe ; for that wind was now coming almost due aft, her boom was right out, and I feared a gybe. To take every advantage of any slight northing of the wind that might come, I ran closer into the coast at a still greater risk of gybe, of course, if the wind should hold where it did when we came to the sharp turn of the Ness. We were now running for it very hard indeed, and the "Nona," splendidly as she lifts when properly trimmed, was burying a little owing to too great press of mainsail, and with head sails doing no work to support her bows. A slight sea had risen, although the tide was still with us and with the wind, and once or twice she took it green as she plunged forward.

Then it was, as I held the "Nona" with difficulty thus, right in front of a wind that was now much too strong for her canvas, that I understood what had long puzzled me, and that is, why the ancients, down to the end of the dark ages in the Mediterranean, and to, perhaps, the fourteenth century in the North, continued to step the masts of their square rig so far aft. It was to prevent burying ; to give the bow its chance of lifting to the sea. For this rig sailed at its best with the wind aft, and when their boats were running so with the great square sail driving them into the seas, had their mast been stepped forward, they would have buried dangerously.

And why do you think men were so long in adopting the fore and aft to larger boats ?

But I cannot delay to consider such things of the past, for I am at the edge of Dungeness, and with my heart in my mouth lest at any moment she should gybe over.

I handed the helm to my companion, who had

a better eye than I had, and a firmer hold, and he, with great skill, did just save the gybe. We had not the luck to hold the tide, we caught the turn of it and the early flood nearly two miles from Dungeness Point, and, as you may imagine, it raised a short and buffeting sea, which made our task the more perilous. My companion handled her beautifully, until I told him he could go as near as he liked to the end of the Ness, because the land shelves down here so steeply as to give one deep water right up against the shore. We were, perhaps, five minutes in the worst of the ordeal just opposite the lighthouse before we could put the helm a trifle over and get the wind fairly on our quarter and breathe again. It seemed about half an hour, for the strength of the tide, even against that wind, made us forge very slowly past the land, and it was astonishing to see the white foam racing by while the shingle, a stone's throw away, barely crept past us; but save the gybe he did, as I said, and there came that placid moment when she would take a turn a little west of south, and then fairly west of south, and the roar of the wind was at her quarter and I had no excuse for an excessive nervousness. But she was pressing too hard altogether, so now we threw her round (as I ought to have done long before), took in two reefs, and then were able to set an easy and comfortable line for the doubtful harbour of Rye which neither of us had yet made. We feared we might touch at the entry, but we had at least the comfort of a wind off the land, yet far round enough to take us in without beating, and we were on a rising tide.

I have often thought that a boat running snug, and properly reefed to suit the wind, is a model of the virtue which the theologians call temperance, and which has nothing to do with the historical dread of wine bred in those who have themselves suffered from, or have seen in their families, the disease called dipsomania. For temperance does not mean doing things half-heartedly, still less does it mean doing or not doing things extremely. It means suiting your implements to your motive power, and not carrying on at a risk. It is not unconnected with dignity, and there is something profound about it ; I will call it the contralto among the virtues, and leave it at that.

We sped on (the stream against us, very slight now that we were inside the Ness); we saw before us the broomstick, or whatever you like to call it, which marks (or does not mark) the entry into Rye Haven, and the last bare remnant of what was once the crowded fairway, a market for the nations—the harbour of Rye.

The little town stood up inland, neat and beautiful, red and grey, a pyramid thrown up towards its squat steeple ; for under that keen north-easterly air all was clear and well cut. The pilot book gave us no comfort, it only told us that the deep changes with every gale, and, as for the lead, there was no use for it, the shore would come too steep ; what we had to do was to look out for the outer buoy, and round it, hoping that as we turned we should neither touch nor get into irons, but still have the wind easterly enough to round to take us in.

On the plan I had by me the fair-way was marked dangerously near the point from which the wind was coming, but I trusted to luck, and still kept her to her course.

Any man making Rye Haven must first resign himself to the will of God, and consider, especially if the boat is running and a little over-canvassed, that death is but a mighty transition ; that it is all sand hereabouts, with no cruel rocks to tear the

tender body with their horrid fangs ; that nothing
is worth calculating in life, because things happen
by fate anyhow, or by chance, but certainly not by
our direction ; and that if, or when, she strikes, it
will not be his fault.   There is no man living that
can ever tell you the deep into Rye harbour, for it
shifts with every wind, and at the best it is of the
narrowest.   As for me, I have made it four times
in my life, each time I have touched and never have
I struck, and how the thing was done no one knows.
Nevertheless, they still build ships in Rye, and the
tradition of the sea is all about it, though what used
to be the old haven is now a field.

I remember sitting up to a very late and clear
sunset of a Whit Monday, gazing, under the sharp
north-east breeze (the " Nona " moored at last to the
wooden quay), at the pyramid of red roofs, and the
highly successful walls and battlements of Rye, and
considering within my mind many things.

First I considered within my own dear mind how
marvellously this place had been preserved, seeing
what modern England is, and what modern travel is.
It is, of course, a Stage Scenery town, such as I
have heard that Rothenburg is in Germany, and,
therefore, there is an interest in preserving it ; but
I never heard that any such pains were taken to
prevent its destruction by increase or rebuilding, or
by any of those courses which bring death to beauty,
such as a good train service, clubs, large and tortur-
ing hotels.   Rye manages to live on.   I suppose
there is a spell.   At any moment it may be broken,
and the flood will pour in.

Being what it is, you cannot begin thinking about
Rye without finding yourself dragged on to consider
preciosity, and from that to the business of letters
is but half a step.

Here at Rye did I meet and speak with Henry
James, who was in the very heart of letters. Here
also did I meet his brother, William James, whose
business in life it was to write about philosophy, but
whose conversation when I met him turned principally upon the subtle diplomatic genius of the King
of England then reigning ; upon the stability of
English institutions ; the excellence of the English
police, and the singular faculty shown by our
institutions of permitting differences without conflict. Also the piercing wit of the paper, *Punch*, and
the profound wisdom of *The Times*. I had just come
back with a companion from foreign parts ; I had
been sleeping rough, and I was in no condition to
take part in polite conversation, so I did all the
listening, and, as I listened, I still considered how
literary was Rye. And so now, years after, looking
at Rye from my boat, was I led on to consider the
trade or business of letters.

When a writing man approaches that subject,
he feels—at least I feel—like a man before a jumbled
heap of material of all kinds—one of those refuse
heaps in which you may pick up stray bits of
machinery, or salve a little fuel, or find what you
will. Or again, it is like being in one of those
shops—there are few of them left, alas !—where an
old half-wit has collected all manner of things, so
that one knows not whether to begin by the
furniture, or the glass, or the pictures, or the
second-hand telescopes, or the books. For there
is an indefinite number of ways of considering
letters.

To those who have had to pursue letters as a trade
(and to this I have been condemned all my life since
my twenty-fifth year) it certainly is the hardest and
the most capricious, and, indeed, the most abomin-

able of trades, for the simple reason that it was never
meant to be a trade.

A man is no more meant to live by writing than he
is meant to live by conversation, or by dressing, or
by walking about and seeing the world. For there
is no relation between the function of letters and the
economic effect of letters ; there is no relation between the goodness and the badness of the work, or
the usefulness of the work, or the magnitude of the
work, and the sums paid for the work. It would not
be natural that there should be such a relation, and,
in fact, there is none.

This truth is missed by people who say that good
writing has no market. That is not the point.
Good writing sometimes has a market, and very bad
writing sometimes has a market. Useful writing
sometimes has a market, and writing of no use
whatsoever, even as recreation, sometimes has a
market. Writing important truths sometimes has
a market. Writing the most ridiculous errors and
false judgments sometimes has a market. The
point is that the market has nothing to do with the
qualities attached to writing. It never had and it
never will. There is no injustice about it, any more
than there is an injustice in the survival of beauty
or ugliness in human beings, or the early death of
the beautiful or the ugly. There is no more
injustice about it than there is in a dry year hurting
a root crop, and a wet harvest hurting a corn crop.
The relationship between the excellence or the usefulness of a piece of literature, and the number of those
who will buy it in a particular form, is not a causal
relationship, it is a purely capricious one ; and I, for
my part, have never complained of the absence of
a market, nor flattered myself upon the presence
of one when a market turned up, though I have

certainly been astonished at the way the market
would behave.

For some few months thousands upon thousands
—at one moment sixty thousand a week—of the
articles I wrote upon the war were demanded by
the public. Some months later the same articles,
of the same value, or lack of value, were no longer
demanded. There was no particular reason, the
articles were clear, and based upon such insufficient
knowledge as I shared with all my fellow-citizens.
I had no private information save upon the point of
numbers, and that was the very point upon which
the public grew most easily fatigued, and were at
last most sceptical.

Mr. Hutchinson, for whose work I personally
have (though I am afraid my judgment is not worth
much in these things) a great liking, wrote among
other books a book called "Once Aboard the
Lugger." It was exceedingly amusing, fresh, and,
as I should have said, well worth anybody's buying.
I do not know how many copies he sold of it, but I
should imagine nothing very astonishing. A little
while after he wrote a book called "If Winter
Comes," and it sold by the stack, and by the ton.
One could see it piled up man-high upon the
counters of shops in America, and it sold, and it sold,
and it sold.

Mr. Wells wrote a book which is most remarkable, and will probably make a mark in English
literature. It was called "The Time Machine."
When Henley (I think it was) was bringing it out
by instalments, the appearance of each was, for me
at least, and for very many others, the chief event
of the month. I do not know how many copies he
sold, but there again I will swear nothing comparable to the numbers he has sold of later books

which certainly will not stand out in English literature. That one which I hear has sold most largely has always seemed to me to be a mere repetition of what his audience already thought they knew, and of a philosophy which they already held : I mean his "Outline of History." It was mainly a repetition of the popular mythology of to-day, of antiquated scientific jargon, full of the popular errors, but it was clean, well-proportioned and vivacious, showing a rare economy in the use and placing of words. It was also (and that is high minor praise for any book purporting to deal with history) astonishingly accurate in details. The names were properly spelt ; south was never written for north, nor east for west ; the dates were all right. Any one who has attempted the writing of history will not belittle such a feat : I, least of all, because I am constitutionally inaccurate in such things, and I will write left for right and north for south as a matter of course, and the word " Tyre " for the word " Acre," and so on. At any rate, the book, with all its good and bad qualities, is obviously not of the first class, and equally obviously is not destined to endure, while " The Time Machine " is quite certainly of the first class, and is quite likely to endure. But I believe that the huge ephemeral demand for the " Outline of History " created no special, certainly no very great, demand for the more permanent " The Time Machine." In general, I am assured by publishers, that when there is a sudden boom in a writer's work, they hardly ever manage to float on that boom a resale of earlier works ; while if these earlier works are unknown, it is almost impossible to give them a popular fame on the strength of the later works. Witness the late Mr. Hudson's " Crystal Age." I came across it as a young man in a book shop in the Euston Road on a winter evening. I took it up and began reading it, and I read it so long that the bookseller told me I must buy it, which I did. Now, towards the end of Mr. Hudson's life, he became deservedly famous as a writer upon the things of the natural world, and especially upon animals. But what made him famous was not his subject, though he was both accurate and learned ; it was his manner of writing. One would have expected, therefore, that the " Crystal Age " would, upon his fame tardily arising, have a quiet and equal fame. It did not. I say that there are no laws governing these movements. They are capricious and incalculable.

Sometimes one hears that a great demand for a book, or for a set of newspaper articles, is due to something touching a common feeling in a particular fashion, something which great bodies of men necessarily feel together. There is a sense, of course, in which that is a mere truism, for it is clear that obscure stuff, or stuff dealing with matters that could not interest great numbers, will never sell. Why should it ? But if the statement is intended to mean (as it usually is) that whatever sells in great numbers does so through this quality of a common appeal, that anything having this quality will always sell in great numbers, and that this quality is in some way a rare thing discoverable only in " best sellers," then the statement is manifestly false. A great deal of matter which possesses this appeal—enormously the greater part of such matter—remains unknown, and that which is best known is often rather weak in such an appeal. There are a great many factors entering into the result of a great popular demand which people forget because they are irrational: fashion is one, routine is another, inertia is a third.

I know one man whose name, for the honour I bear it (he is now dead), I would not publish, since what I am about to say of his work is not flattering. He wrote a great number of stories, all of them with exactly the same plot and exactly the same characters. There was a beautiful chocolate-box girl, there was a villain, there was a hero who became rich after being poor, there were parents who objected to the match, and there was a racehorse. Had he departed from the formula, he would not have sold. As it was, he sold by the million. He was not only as modest a man as you could find, but exceedingly generous. He put on no airs; he made no error as to the nature of his success; he is already forgotten. Nothing shall persuade me that any one of many thousand men could not have written exactly the same ; but a certain vast public got used to that particular insipid food, and wanted it unchanged, just as you and I get used to a particular kind of breakfast, and eat it every day of our lives.

Of course, there is a different set of factors operating in different phases of society. The popular best-seller of to-day depends upon the existence of our great towns with their machine-made citizens, all working blindly in little grooves, lacking any common direction—a dust of individuals. He depends also on that new-fangled, mechanical, and, let us hope ephemeral, institution called " popular education." If you tell millions of boys and girls (nearly all the citizens of the State), at the age when they receive unquestioning any dogmatic teaching, that their ancestors were repulsive savages, first actually bestial, later exceedingly vile, and that these ancestors passed through certain stages, and were "Cavemen," and men of the " Stone Age," and of the " Bronze Age," and so forth ; then, obviously, writers using such terms, and taking for granted such a mythology, will fit in with the popular market. The demand for books, or of writing in any form, is created by minds already moulded, and any kind of writing which tends to break the mould is resented and left on one side. In older phases of society, judgment upon writing was passed by a few well-trained and leisured people, who handed down their judgments to a larger class, but still a small class compared with the whole State; and it is clear that in such a condition of society—which was that of England from the last third of the eighteenth century to the last third of the nineteenth—there would be no best sellers in our modern sense, and that there would be a nearer approach between the demand for a book and its excellence. But there also the mould had to be considered. Macaulay's false rhetoric sold well, because it agreed with the religion of his day. No historical work telling the truth about James II. would have sold in his day, nor for that matter would any such matter sell in ours.

For religion is here, as elsewhere, at the root of effect. Robert Louis Stevenson was an excellent writer, but his popularity reposed not upon his excellence alone, but also upon the consonance of his religion with that of his readers. A man who was perpetually telling you that it was your duty to be cheerful, that you must take pleasure in God's creation, that you had a " task of happiness " would cut no ice with the Irish, or with the Italians, or, in general, with the Catholic culture of Europe, but he rings true in the ears of the Protestant culture. Conversely, what the French powerfully call the " bitter taste of reality " has very little chance with the crowd of the North. It is a spur and a relish to the crowd of the South. You could not sell Barrie in Arles nor Baudelaire in Pudsey.

The truth remains that the relation, or the lack of relation, between the economic result of a literary effort, and its success as a piece of craft, is of very much less importance than the consideration of the Canon, the attempt to achieve a standard. To get a Canon is the first requirement of letters. For though it is said that time will test literature for us in any case, this is not universally true; and, even in so far as it is true, it is better to have the good things to our hand than to wait for time to establish them. Such a Canon requires not only intelligent analysis, but a common philosophy into which our rules must fit. It is, therefore, with great difficulty arrived at, or perhaps not to be arrived at at all, in a period of confusion like ours. But the attempt to arrive at it never loses interest—no, not even to-day.

One of the things which always seems to me best worth saying in connection with letters is that prose should be distinguished, not only from verse, but also from rhetoric ; and that prose in itself, mere lucid, economic, unornamented prose, is the foundation of good letters.

If the national prose is sound, the rest of national expression will come of itself. But this matter of prose has to-day been nearly forgotten. For most of us perhaps the phrase " good prose," or " fine prose," really means rhetoric. It means a passage in which the soul is stirred by a choice of rhythm and sound, and a mystical connotation of words in some passage not definitely reduced to versification. Thus, all the great passages from the Jacobean translation of the Hebrew scriptures, which are familiar as examples to our generation, are essentially rhetoric ; so are the excerpts quoted from Bunyan, such as the fine closing passage of the "Pilgrim's Progress"; so is every single passage quoted from Carlyle ; so are even those quoted from Newman and (I am sorry to say) those quoted from the greatest of our modern prose writers, Huxley.

But prose is rightly to be distinguished from anything of that kind. The excellence of prose lies in its adaptation to the function of intelligent expression or of narration. It is a statement ; the end of it is not the exciting of emotion but the clear presentation, whether of a record (in fiction or fact) or of an idea, which the writer desires to communicate to his fellows.

He that succeeds in presenting the idea lucidly, so that no modification or subsidiary idea confuses the process ; he that succeeds in presenting as vividly to the reader an image of particular fact, or of imagined fiction, vividly arisen in his own mind, is a writer of good prose ; and the better he succeeds in this faculty of mere exposition, the more he excels in the supreme character of lucidity, the better his prose. Prose which is redundant is worse than prose which is economic in the use of words, simply because economic prose is the better statement. Exactitude of word and idea makes better prose than the use of many synonyms and of vague terms, simply because it ministers to lucidity. A mass of adjectives or adverbs is usually (not always) ill in prose, because usually (not always) the idea which the writer has to express does not involve all these modifications ; they only slip from his pen through laziness or through having heard them before. It is obviously better prose to say " I was tired out," than to say " I was wholly tired out," unless for any particular reason you wish to express complete exhaustion. It is obviously better prose to say "The sky," than "The blue sky," unless for any particular reason you are concerned in your description with the colour of the sky.

But the worst enemy of prose to-day is the snobbishness of rules and forms, the mumbo-jumbo of hieratic prescription. The influence of these is a very good example of that excellent rule laid down by St. Thomas Aquinas that all evil exists in mistaking, or misusing, the means for the end. This plague of pedantry does not rage quite as severely as it did when I was young, but it is still pretty severe. You are told that it is good prose, for instance, to have as few adjectives as possible. That is nonsense. It is good prose to have as many adjectives as you need, and *no more*. You are told, as a sort of eleventh commandment, never to split an infinitive ; the rule is that of an excellent master of English, the late Professor Ker, who adds, " except when euphony demands it." I would go further; I would say that when the spoken language has arrived, as ours has to-day, at the universal use of the split infinitive, the written language may follow at some little distance behind. We are told that prose must never be emphatic, or excited, or this, or that, or the other. All that is nonsense. Prose must be emphatic when special emphasis is to be expressed, excited when excitement is to be expressed, and so forth. But certainly the character of good prose is the subordination of everything in it to the end, which is expression of what you have to say ; and that is the distinction between good prose and rhetoric and verse. For in rhetoric and in verse the end is the emotion you desire, non-rationally, to excite ; but in prose the end is rational, presentation, narration or statement of thesis : nothing more.

Judged by such standards, the two best prose

writers in English are, I think, Dean Inge and Mr. Gosse ; for they, each of them, write on subjects where they have much to say, with the use of no words other than those needed for such expression, and they put those words invariably in the right order. Cecil Chesterton is dead.

I had almost written that there is no such thing as " great " prose, in the sense in which there is " great " rhetoric or " great " verse. The very best prose may be dull if the subject expressed is dull to the reader. You will get no better prose, for instance, than Newman's " Arians of the Fourth Century." It is not dull to me, because I happen to be interested in that bit of history, but it would be fiercely dull to any reader who was not. Nevertheless it is first-rate prose. Newman having to write about a particular thing upon which he had made himself immensely learned; having to tell a certain number of facts, and to express a certain number of ideas, does so with the best choice of words in the best order—and that is prose.

The very fact that any sound definition of prose involves many negatives and only one positive (to wit, the positive need for lucid expression) makes it true that good prose is a common art. Excellence in prose is not common to all : far from it ; but the faculties whereby excellence is reached are common to all. A man who is a first-rate walker, who carries his body with an exact poise, who can walk far without fatigue, and at a good pace, is a rare man ; but we can all walk, and we all approach in various degrees, the standard that man has reached. So it is with prose. Those who think that good prose must have something odd about it—a few archaic words, little eighteenth-century tricks here and there, subjunctives popped in, like currants into a cake—these resemble men who in walking every now and then in high spirits do a little dance for fun. They are free to do so ; we are not displeased. We cannot help noticing them (which is, perhaps, their object), and no one is the worse for the *gambado*. But in so far as they indulge in the fantasy, they are not walking ; and if they do it the least bit too much, they are playing the fool. A wise man said to me once, " Don't go and get your words from the artist colourman's." Would that I had remembered his words in youth as I now humbly acknowledge them in age.

But the rhetorician wisely indulges in extravagance, and as for the poet, he may use what words he likes, and go to any extreme, or to any excess, so long only as he hits the mark. For it is with poetry as with love and with singing in tune. It is with poetry as with the sense of reality. It is with poetry as with the toothache. Either you have it, or you have it not.

There is no getting near Poetry; and though there are degrees in it, the boundary between its being and its not being is as sharp as a razor : on the one side is It, and on the other is nothingness. By which I do not mean to say that poetry is only found in certain violent stabs of emotion such as Shakespeare and Keats can launch, for it often inhabits page upon page, as throughout (I will maintain) all the Fourth Book of " Paradise Lost," and countless other great achievements of the past in every tongue. But I mean that in a long flight or a short one, immediate or continuous—poetry is poetry, and not to be mistaken for anything else. Charles Kingsley (I ought to have dragged this in at Appledore, and not have waited for Rye) said to a woman, " Madam, there is poetry and there is verse ; and verse is divided into two kinds—good verse and bad

verse. What you have here shown me is not poetry,
it is verse. It is not good verse, it is bad verse."

. . . . .

But, really, if I go on in this endless way of
discussing the difficult trade of letters, I shall never
get her nose round for the sea again. I had almost
forgot I was sailing. What! Of two such occupations, the benediction of dealing with the sea and
the degradation of scribbling, can you forget the
better for the worse? I can. I am of a fallen race.
I follow downwards.

But I am aboard the "Nona" again, and must put
her out down channel. This will I now do, and
sail out of Rye by the first of the ebb under too
strong a north-east wind at two o'clock in the
morning with the waning moon just rising, the sky
clear, two reefs in my mainsail, the second jib and
a reef in my foresail, knowing well that I must
watch all night, and that I shall get no sleep till
morning. For it is one of the glories of sailing that
you are under the authority of the heavens, and must
submit to the whole world of water and of air, of
which you are a part, not making laws to yourself
capriciously, but acting as servant or brother of
universal things.

It would be no bad thing if some one (I am not
competent) were to draw up a list of advices for the
brutish man who is too poor to sail a big boat, or is
not such a fool as to desire one: I mean a list of
advices for a man who sails such a boat as the
"Nona": say, boats from seven tons to twenty.

The first article in such a list would be this:
Cruising is not racing.

But on this one could write a whole volume, with
digressions upon the general evils and corruptions
of these our latter times when the Beast has most

certainly been let loose out of the Pit, and is going
about the world breathing smoke out of seven
mouths, and stamping 666, with his Hoof, on the
foreheads of all his Elect.

For no one can doubt that the practice of sailing,
which renews in us all the past of our blood, has
been abominably corrupted by racing. I do not
know whence the evil came, but I suppose it came
like most evils, from a love of money. The love
of money made men admire the possessors of it, and
so they came to think of sailing as they do of riding
horses, or of any other sport—as something to be
tested by what the rich man could do. And clearly,
when it came to making machines for going fast
through the water by the aid of the wind alone, the
rich man had his advantage. Then I suppose there
came in also that craze for measurable things which
has done us all so much harm in the last lifetime and
a half. When I say of the "Nona" : "She is a good
boat," when I stroke her and she purrs, there is
nothing here measurable. When I say of that really
abominable boat, [*name censored*] (well worthy of
her name)—that I had rather she had been sunk at
birth than continue to sail the seas, you cannot apply
a single measurable test to prove that the solid,
noble "Nona" is good and the flimsy, whimsy [*name
censored*] is bad ; but in racing you can. Boat A gets
in front of Boat B. Any fool can test that, and to-day
was made for fools.

Well, then, whatever the root of the evil, evil it is,
and it has corrupted our way of living in happy little
boats. Remember, and write it down : "*Cruising
is not racing.*" If your boat is a home and a companion, and at the same time a genius that takes you
from place to place and, what is much more, a good
angel, revealing unexpected things, and a comforter

and an introducer to the Infinite Verities—and my
boat is all these things—then you must put away
from yourself altogether the idea of racing, as much
as, when you consider a wife, you must put away the
intellectual woman and the wax-work—both of
whom may have their place for all I know. The
cruiser, the strong little, deep little boat, is all I
have called it. It is a complete satisfaction for man ;
but if you let in racing you are letting in the
serpent.

Here you will say, " Have you then never raced ? "
Never, sweetheart, except to get away from danger,
which I loathe. I have never raced another boat
in my life, although I have been on other men's
boats when they were racing, and admired their
special talent, just as I would admire the talent of a
man who successfully climbed the greasy pole. You
must expect of your boat—your companion boat—a
rational behaviour. You must say to yourself that
when she is doing seven knots, she is doing well,
and when she is doing nine, she is excited, and will
be the better for a night's rest.

When you are on a long passage, even with steady
weather, you had better bank on three to four knots
and no more. For what with beating, fishing
perhaps, the falling of wind, over-reefing in terror,
and the rest of it, you will not do more. I have
always thought to myself, knocking up and down the
coasts of dear England, that if I did a hundred miles
in my twenty-four hours, I was doing very well
indeed.

Once I spent a whole day drifting with the tide
from the two Etaples lights to the Dune, and very
nearly all the way back, but even that did not persuade me to a motor, for, of all things abominable to
God and His Saints, I know of nothing more abomin-

able than machinery and petrol and the rest on board a little cruising boat.

I would rather die of thirst, ten miles off the headlands in a brazen calm, having lost my dinghy in the previous storm, than have on board what is monstrously called to-day an "auxiliary." The name is worthy of the thing. By auxiliaries the Roman army perished. Further, it is a nasty foreign sort of term. Call it the machine and tell the truth. I am told by those who use the abomination that it is ashamed of itself, and often will not start, as though to say, "You came out to sail the seas, and I am reluctant to cheat wind, weather and tide in your favour." I will not deny that mechanism is valuable to those who conduct huge hordes, the rich and the poor, from Europe to the New World, but in a little cruising boat I will have none of it. It would be foolish to be rid of it in armament, for there it does give one's country a great advantage, but in a little cruising boat it is as much out of place as is electric light where one should use candles, or as are motor cars in the hunting of wild beasts. But I must return to things more practical.

My next rule would be : *Get everything ship-shape and, so far as you can, keep it shipshape.*

That is, see that the falls are clear, that everything is properly stowed away; that you know where everything is to be got at in any emergency; that you have to look for nothing; that you make the most of every space—and the rest of it.

All this I say knowing full well that I myself am incapable of it; but I am giving advice, I am not practising. I am expending myself for the good of others, and what I myself do is no affair of yours. The best-known and the most tragic tag descended to us from antiquity is, "*Video meliora proboque*

deteriora sequor." Some would say that they are
not only the most tragic words the great Pagans
bequeathed to us—the Pagans upon whom we all
repose—but would add that they are also the most
ironic ; for if you stop a little after the *proboque*,
and add in another voice the following two words,
you will appreciate the sardonic accent.

My own boat has usually come into port more like
the disturbed nest of a dormouse than like the spick
and span arrangement which I advise. Half the
blocks will be jammed, the anchor will be caught
under the bows, and as like as not, the fluke of it
hooked over one of the whiskers. The falls will be
all tangled up together. The warping ropes will be
mixed up with the anchor chain in the fo'c'sle,
so that there is no getting at the one, or paying out
the other. She will perhaps be coming in under
three reefs with hardly enough wind to move her,
because it has been blowing a few hours ago, and
I have been too lazy to shake them out. Her jib
will be slack, her cabin light broken where I have
put my heel through it. A hundred other little
familiar touches will make whatever landsman is
passing his time gazing out to sea from the pier-head
recognise from far off the " Nona," as the Arabs
recognised the great ship of Richard the Lion-
hearted, saying, " There comes the red sail of the
Frankish king." There never was such a boat as
the "Nona" for coming in hugger-mugger. But do as
I preach, not as I practise. Have everything in its
place and a place for everything, so that, in a flash,
you can shorten sail, let go the anchor, get to your
warping ropes, or do any of those many things
required by sailing men. Even Plato was moved to
discover the way in which the horrible Phœnicians
used space aboard their ships, and had everything in

order, though Heaven knows he could have had little sympathy with the sailing of the seas. Indeed, very few men who have written in the sentimental and rhetorical fashion (of which he was a master) have had also a call for the outside. But even he, I say, admired the order of shipboard. So be it with you.

Go into all the least details, think of how any object you have aboard will be treated by the weather. Use no ornament which the salt air can spoil, and put not one ounce aboard beyond what you need.

My third rule is this : *Keep tight decks.*

I speak with feeling here, for most of my life the rain and the salt sea have come through upon my face as I slept, as coffee does through those abominable new contraptions which they call " filters," and which they put above your cup instead of boiling the coffee honestly apart as our fathers did. Most of my life, half the days at least that I have sailed the sea, water both salt and fresh, and always tasting of varnish and of tar, has trickled through also upon my provisions, notably upon bread, which it quite astonishingly spoils. Therefore I say from experience, keep tight decks. It is very simple. You have but to go along the seams carefully on a hot, windless day, with a spike or a screw driver and a mallet, prodding in shredded rope, and treating it afterwards with any one of the compositions they sell.

My fourth rule (I am giving them in no order of importance) is : *Have an anchor heavy enough for your craft.*

It is a temptation to have too light a one for the easier handling. It is always a mistake. An anchor drags mainly through lack of head. Holding-ground always makes a difference but, with little craft, lack of head is the trouble. You must pay the price of heavy work for the sake of security, and it is

better to have an old-fashioned anchor than the
stockless anchors they sell now. These are all very
well for large boats, but I do not believe in them for
small ones. Be at the pains of getting your anchor
up properly, and unstocking it, and also when you
let it down, of mousing the catch. Nothing will get
you into more trouble than not being able to let go
your anchor quickly, when there is necessity ; and,
in that connection also, mind you keep your chain
clear. It is a good plan to tie small but conspicuous
shreds of bunting or coloured string at every two or
three fathoms of the chain in the first part of it ; thus
you will know how much you have let out, for
although it is always better to let out too much than
too little, it is annoying to have a great length of
chain dragging about in shoal water, and the noise
of it moving may confuse you into believing that
you are dragging. I spent an abominable night
once off a shingle bank in heaving water, where the
tide ran strong, from having let out too much chain
in the dark. The metal lay all along the bottom
like the great sea serpent, and the movement of the
boat sent a violent wrangling of iron up the chain
all night long, so that I was perpetually running
upon deck, between poor intervals of sleep, to judge
by the distant light whether she were dragging or no.
And I had good occasion for anxiety, seeing that not
far upon my lee the shoal came right up out of the
sea, with the water breaking upon it. You might
think that however much chain you had let out,
your boat would lie to the end of it ; but it is not
so. If you have a great deal too much chain let out
in shoal water, the weight of it holds the boat like a
kind of second anchor, and it grumbles and shifts
and moves all the time.

Now the putting on of these little markings is of

value, also, to prevent you letting out too little chain.
The rule of thumb is : Three times as much chain as
there is depth of water. This, in my youth (and for my
youth I must be forgiven), I neglected in the port of
Harwich, thinking it was nearer high tide than it
was, so the little ship got adrift, and was rescued,
or, as the man preferred to call it, " salvaged " by
a barge called the *Lily*. The barge had no right
to be called the *Lily*, for it was foully dirty, and as
black as soot. The owner of the *Lily* claimed
one-third of the value of my boat, " Because,"
said he, " it was salvaged below London Bridge."
He attached to this formula a magical importance.
I offered him £2. He wanted much more. I
appealed for help to a ship that was lying in
that harbour, and they sent off a boat's crew for
me to convince the man. He took the offer I made
him, but said that he had been bullied. I do not
think he had. I think £2 is a fair price to pay for
the trouble a man may have been at to put a boat
out, and tie a rope on to a drifting craft of that size.
But still he complained that he had " salvaged her
below London Bridge," and had a right to one-third
of her value. But there again, what was the value
of any boat in which I had already sailed ?

My fifth rule would be : *Don't keep too close to
the wind; let her sail; keep her full.*

This attempt to be always pointing up is one of
the curses brought in by racing. Your own hearty
middle-class boat can never point close to the wind.
If she can, it is a bad sign, for she will be putting on
airs. Be content if she will lie and sail at an angle
of 45 degrees from the direction in which the wind
is blowing. If she cannot do that she is a bad boat,
but if she can do that, she is well enough. Now
this is called " within four points of the wind," being

one-eighth of the thirty-two points that make up the whole round of the compass. There are all sorts of smart craft which will point much closer than that, and there are particular kinds of rigs, used honestly and not for racing at all, which will keep much closer, I am told. Certainly the London barge seems to keep closer, that marvellous rig, that perfection of rigs for its purpose; and the Norfolk Wherries, shooting up the rivers, seem to keep quite miraculously close, though I think in this their great momentum and the flood of the water helps them. But as for you, sailing ordinarily upon the sea, be quite content if she does her duty with the wind halfway between beam and bow. It is here as it is with most things in life, be content with the sound average, keeping the limits which God has set all around. Do not wish for too long a life, for too large a fortune, or for too much honour. Eat your peck of dirt before you die; take the rough with the smooth; consider that it is all in a day's work; expect rain and fine. In general, write out a list of all the Commandment-proverbs and learn that list by heart. Then break them.

They that sail too close to the wind have great difficulty in bringing their boat round, especially in a seaway, and there is nearly always some of their canvas (if it is an honest boat, and not one of your millionaires' models) not doing all it should when you lie too close. In connection with this, I would add (without making it a separate rule): *Take care never to pin the boat—that is, never get your mainsheet too taut;* give the boom plenty of angle. Let your mainsail take the full wind. If you look at the pictures of the old boats in the time when men were men, you will see that they sailed with easy sails bellying, and were not concerned to look smart with stiff board-like sails. Of course, in the racing machines, you get more speed by these tricks, but it is no way to treat a good boat of stock and sound ancestry. It is driving her and playing tricks with her. Be content to feel the power of the wind.

There are times when all these rules admit of exception. For instance, you find that you can just make a difficult channel in the last of the flow or the ebb, before it turns against you ; and that you can only do it by lying very close indeed. Then you must coax your she-companion (by whom I here mean your boat), and even spill the wind out of her sails a little, so as to work her up and through, and you may then get in your mainsheet as close as you dare, and haul everything tight—too tight—headsail sheets and halyards as well, for you are attempting a feat. But I am all against doing such things as a habit ; and if again you ask me why, I cannot tell you, and I will not argue. But while I am on this let me add that a great deal of your ability to lie close depends upon the proper set of your jib. The halyard always slacks a little after a bit of a run, or perhaps your traveller is not really right out to the end of the sprit. See to all that; for it is by your jib that you fetch a reach ; and, talking of jibs, I come to my sixth rule, which is this :

Do not from laziness fail to change jibs often ; also, carry three jibs aboard. The jib is the most sensitive part of your canvas on a small fore and aft craft. Too much canvas there will press you, too little will make the helm gripe, and in either case she will not be sailing her best. Changing jibs is a bother, but it is a task which must not be shirked. Many a man has got his boat out of hand by failing to set the second jib, or even the storm jib, when it was coming on to blow. Note carefully also which of your jibs goes best with such and such a reefing of your mainsail. The temptation is to carry too large a jib, and, therefore, to carry too weak a weather helm. It is better to have your canvas balanced. She will behave better in every way. The "Nona," when she is under two reefs, carries her second jib pleasantly and with a smile, and yet how often (I must confess it) have I carried my first jib when I should have changed jibs; and that from indolence.

My seventh rule may seem a strange one, but I am sure that it is sound : *Carry a pole mast, and do not bother too much about hoisting your topsail.*

A topsail is always a business on a small boat, a business to put up and a business to strike. There is many a wind in which it would add half a knot to your speed, but you are not racing, and the half-knot does not matter. The necessary occasions for carrying a topsail are exactly two : One, when the breeze is very light, and it makes all the difference between sailing at a reasonable pace, and merely crawling; and the other, when you are getting into harbour and have wind aloft, but little along the surface, or when you have your mainsail brailed up to see your way, so that only with the topsail can you get a sufficient amount of canvas and a weather helm.

I know that all this rough and ready talk about the topsail will sound like heresy to the men who are sailing their boats in all weathers, and think, as people do, of speed as a special advantage, but I am sure I am right. Plain sail is the rule, and topsail on a little craft is always something of a frill. It is never a necessity, and over and over again you will find it a handicap. What I mean is, do not use it for the sake of using it. Do not be ashamed of

sailing without your topsail when other craft have
got theirs set, if in your case it is a trouble to set it.
Never, never set your topsail when you think she
might be at all over-canvased under it ; your
business is to sail, and neither to show off nor to
make time.

My eighth rule (which, if I were putting them
in order of importance would come very early in
the list) is : *Look to every part of your gear;* not
only when you are starting out upon a cruise, but
all the time. Look minutely to every point where
there may be weakness. See that all is secure, and
that all the running gear runs freely. This means
running your eye and hand over the ropes and
looking closely to the blocks, and to the attach-
ments of hooks and swivels, and to the ties of the
leach upon the rings, and to the parrel line at the
jaws, and, indeed, to all details of which there is a
very long list, when you come to think of it, even in
the simplest rig. Take nothing for granted, test
everything. When you find anything doubtful—
a cleat that shakes a little, or a run that jams for a
second, or whatever it may be—put it right at once.
The whole thing may be somewhat of a business,
but in this, as in most things on board a boat, work
all the time.

But who am I that I should write thus ? Was
it not also I who, in May-month of the year
1901, ran from France to the English island most
abominably over-canvased, not being able to take
in a reef because my throat halyard had jammed ?
I noticed a jerk in it, even as I left the shores of
the Morini, and I neglected to put the block
right because I was eager to be off. I said to
myself "It will work all right when the time comes!"
But it did not, and, therefore, did I run with a most

astonishing speed, and on to the end of the affair, in no small terror, until I saw tall England, looming up above me out of a sort of smoke ; and ever since then I have been most attentive to that one block. And why not to the others ? Because conduct is by mood rather than by reason, and the do-nothing mood is a mastering one; as witness the home dogs of the rich, the cats of the poor, and sundry other beasts, including man.

Now my ninth rule is : *Keep with you all the charts you can.*

You can never have too many for your purpose. Many people are content with general charts, and do not take with them the plans of harbours. It is an error. The plans of harbours are even, in this sort of knocking about the coasts, more useful than the general charts. For a man can always tell where he is (more or less) along the coast, but the working in and out of harbours is the difficulty, and the knowing of where to lie, and what areas dry out, and the rest. But here it is important to warn those who are not used to such plans that to many of our harbours this guide is only approximate because the channel shifts so much. After almost every gale or exceptional tide, you need new local knowledge.

No plan, for instance, will help you much to get into Etaples or St. Valery, in Picardy, or over Shoreham Bar and into its double fairway. You must get in as best you can by your judgment and the lead, or with a local man aboard. And the same is true of the Arun in a lesser degree, and even, once you are well within the bar, of Barnstaple River, and fifty others. Nevertheless, a plan is always invaluable. It gives you the main lines; and in the case of at least half the harbours, and all the larger ones, it gives you all you need.

In this matter of charts, never fail to have aboard you the book called "The Channel Pilot," or "The West Coast Pilot," or, in general, your book of directions for whatever part of the coast you are dealing with. The English charts are not only the best in the world, but one may almost say the only ones in the world. But our sailing direction books are more than that—they are unique ; no other nation has them, at any rate, not of the same quality. They are exact ; they tell one pretty well all one wants to know.

What gives me great pleasure in them is that they are also picturesque. The unknown authors let themselves out now and then, and write down charming little descriptive sentences praising the wooded heights above the sea, or sounding great notes of warning which have in them a reminiscence of the Odyssey.

One paragraph I have put to memory, and often recite to myself with delight. It runs thus (after praising a particularly difficult passage or short cut behind a great reef of our coasts) : " But the mariner will do well to avoid this passage at the approach of the turn of the tide ; or if the wind be rising, or darkness falling upon the sea." I like that ! If I could write Greek I would write hexameters, translating that noble strain into the original of all seafaring language, telling how the Goddess warned him of peril if he should attempt the passage when the stream of Oceanos was turning, and the night was coming forward over the abyss, and the shaker of the earth had let loose the winds.

I would write how she came up out of the deep, under the storm cloud, like a white sea bird and warned him of peril when darkness was falling upon the sea.

Do not, while I am talking of charts and the

official sailing books—"The Channel Pilot," and the rest—be careless about lights. It is the easiest thing in the world to mistake a light. Time the flashes carefully, and compare them with what your chart or your book tells you. But remember that upon coming into harbour there is always confusion (especially nowadays, with electric lights everywhere and a mass of illumination on shore), where there was not twenty years ago. There is great danger to-day, on approaching any shore town, of mistaking the directions given. I have had trouble in two very different places through this. One, Hastings, where there is no true port at all, but only a breakwater, and the other Dartmouth. Not that civilians, or landsmen, or whatever you like to call them, have yet gone so far as to set up red and green lights in their windows, but that in the glare of the lights you may miss the leading marks, and that a white light when you are close in is hardly any use at all unless it flashes regularly. I speak, of course, of small harbour lights alone. Also you must remember that these are not to be seen, as a rule, until one is quite close.

But I suppose, talking of lights, that the most difficult thing for the poor land-living fellow who now and then sails (the most difficult thing for people like you and me, that is) is dealing with the lights of moving craft when one comes up a fairway at night.

For this there are a number of rhyming rules, which we all of us have by heart :

> " When you see two lights ahead,
> Port your helm and show your red."

Or again :

> " Green to green and red to red,
> All right—go ahead."

But these rules, of which there are about a dozen or so, are only for the simplest cases, and my experience is that in any crowded fairway at night you must depend upon judgment, subject only to the first and most elementary rules, such as passing port to port. But even here there are one or two things the man of the small boat should bear in mind, and they are singularly like the things which the poor man must bear in mind in the company of the rich, or the ruler of a weak nation when he is dealing with a strong neighbour.

For instance, rules or no rules, no large craft will ever make room for you ; you must make room for it. That is especially true of mechanical craft.

I remember lying off the Dorset coast in a dead calm with no steerage way at all, and a huge great tramp going westward, full of some abominable cargo or other, and bound to some fever-stricken swamp beyond the ocean, lumping down upon me like a blind rhinoceros.

It was impossible for my little craft to avoid her. If it had been quite dark, I have no doubt she would have run me down with all the good nature in the world, but as it was still possible to follow from the shore what was happening, she did at the last moment give her helm just the slightest touch, and missed me by a nothing ; so that I had the pleasure of half-shaking my spars out in the tumble of her greasy wake. When, therefore, you are in a crowded fairway at night, always give way ; it is the only rule. And have the sense to behave as the lawyers do : forget that there is such a thing as justice, let alone honour or pride.

Then there is another rule to be remembered, which is serviceable enough, and that is, when you have plenty of room and the larger thing coming at you is still at some distance, keep your course for some little time, in order to give your enemy (as I will call him) the chance to do the right thing. There is nothing so baffling as to have to deal with another craft that does not know its own mind. If the hostile fellow sees you on a definite course, he has at least an opportunity for making his calculations and avoiding trouble.

Here is more advice, never get yourself in the wrong by having your own lights dimmed or out of order. Since they must be screened from the after part whence you steer, have some little splash of white or what not, which shows you from the tiller that they are still alight. And as for your riding light, which so often has to do duty when all are asleep aboard, see that it is sound and of capacity and filled. You can hardly have too large a one ; not for the sake of the light, but for the sake of the number of hours it will burn. And this I say, never having possessed one in my whole cruising life which did not leak or blow out in a gale, or come crashing down on deck through insecure fastening, or in one way or another behave in the fashion true and consonant to the "Nona," which is the chief boat of all the boats in the world, and therefore, like the chief men of this world, is in trouble all the time.

Indeed, I think that there stand out among all the boats of history, supreme, singular, incomparable to lesser things, like the two horns of Hattin, or the Twin Stars, two boats—"Noah's Ark" and the "Nona"; and of these two, the "Nona" is the better ship. I judge this by the pictures of the ark I have seen upon match boxes, which I take to be upon the whole our best text, though late and somewhat corrupt. Such a craft could not have been handled with any satisfaction. It has no gear, only a sort of deck house ;

but it is famous, and of such antiquity that it should be revered—from its time onwards there has been nothing but the "Nona." You talk of the *Nina*; of Columbus's other ships—whose names I never knew, nor you either ; of the *Mora*, that brought William of Falaise to Pevensey ; of the *White Ship* and of the *Ark Royal*; of the *Victory* (which is now, they say, to sail upon dry land) ; of the *Great Harry*, of the *Vengeur*, of the *Hood*, and of the two beautiful enamelled motor boats which are (I hope) to be purchased out of our pockets for the Salaried League of Nations at Geneva, and there moored along the wharf of its private garden, well called Tom Tiddler's Ground. But none of all these ships is to be mentioned in the same breath as the "Nona."

. . . . .

The wind dropped quite suddenly while it was yet dark before we had passed Fairlight, that is, within an hour's running. It left, though it had been an off-shore wind, something of a lump behind it, as nearly always does such a sudden cessation of strong weather. I have often noticed this ; it is as though the wind blew the sea flat, and then, when the pressure of it was relieved, the water would move up again to show its freedom.

It not only dropped; it also, after half an hour's calm, began to run right round ahead to the west, and even to the south of west, so that we had to put out far into the sea upon the starboard tack, and then beat back again towards the shore to make our course. In this way, the holy light of day had already begun to grow by the time we were opposite Hastings and the odd broken breakwater of the place ; whereby they have attempted to restore, but failed to restore, something of the old harbour. That harbour of Hastings has to-day quite disappeared, its defences worn down by the sea, but the Castle still stands there to show how important a haven it was ; one of the great ports of mediæval England. What I have read upon the matter has not left me much clearer as to the exact lie of the sheltered water, but my interest in the place (apart from this, that certain of my forbears are buried there) stands in that odd disappearance of a great political function. Hastings was a port, and it is a port no more. Yet the town has survived, and even its use of the sea has survived ; though now they must draw up their boats upon the shore.

I hope that Hastings has reasserted its right to christen the great battle. When I was at Oxford it was a favourite piece of humbug among the academic to call the Battle of Hastings "Senlac."

This queer Gascon name they got out of a footnote of Lingard's. Now it happens to be a sacred rule at Oxford never to admit any obligation to Lingard. Lingard is the creator of documented, exact English history. Three-quarters of the things you hear put forward as modern conclusions upon the English past come first from that great and unique historian. He invented the science. Before his time no one had written a history from original texts ; nor had any one taken a general survey.

Since his time he has become a quarry for all those who can, or pretend to, teach and write history. But it is an unbroken rule at the Universities of Oxford and Cambridge to boycott his name.

Lingard made that one bad error. He called the battle of Hastings, Senlac. Like schoolboys who give themselves away copying, Freeman and his gang, following Lingard's one mistake, worked the thing to death. They seem to have thought in their

ignorance that Senlac was an Anglo-Saxon term !
And then, it was so grand to give a shock to general
usage, and to introduce that note of the unusual
which is the mark of the charlatan. Round
demolished them.

How often have I not studied that famous field.
It was but this year that I went all over it with a
clinometer, taking contours, with two friends to help
me, so that I might re-establish the battle.

I know not what that fascination is which attaches
to seeing, touching, standing on the very site of some
great business of the past. I cannot analyse its
nature, but I feel the strength of it profoundly, and
I would I could recover the hours I have wasted all
my life long in exactly establishing this, that, and the
other topographical point of the past. What rever-
ence do I not feel, and how justly for such work as
Rice Holmes, in which every movement of Cæsar's,
in those fateful August days of the first Invasion, is
clinched down with iron proof, exact, converging.

There is nothing more delightful in the ocean of
modern historical work, the moving empty sea of
guess and unproved affirmation, than these few solid
rocks of industry and common sense. The people
who get the thing settled once for all are as different
from the question-mongers and theory-spinners as
is a vigorous air from confused harmonies ; or
better, as is the grasp of a living hand from the
ghostly touches of the spooks.

What could be more masterly than Holmes'
establishment of the landing place upon Deal beach,
the calculation of the march to the Stour, the crossing place, the storming of the camp on Bigberry Hill.
It is like the fitting in of a jig-saw puzzle, everything
made complete, certain, absolute, where before all
had been chaos. Over and over again have I

climbed that hill and sat me down on the rampart, in
order to look below towards the ford of the river
where the seventh legion crossed, and over and
over again, sailing in the narrows of the channel, I
have called up that great armament on its summer's
day, the galleys rowing with the tide round the
South Foreland and the heavier transports far away
towards the French shore.

It is, I fear, an evil pleasure of the mind, but it is
a very real pleasure, none the less, which a man takes
in that which should, if he were honest and charitable,
provoke him rather to indignation, and the abnomin-
able follies of the academic fool do give me that
pleasure which I suppose I ought to fly. When a
Don shows his great learning by spelling Clovis
"Hchlodhovech," I feel not pain, as I should,
but pleasure : it makes me think of "Clodhopper."
When the official historian, hall-marked and log-
rolled, assures me that the great officials of fifth-
century Rome knew no Greek, or when his fellow,
similarly hall-marked and log-rolled, assures me that
Homer's poems were composed by a committee,
I, who ought to be pained, laugh. So I do when they
tell me as one Professor solemnly told the world in
the pages of, I think, the *Spectator* (but possibly it
was another learned organ) that the French for " very
beautiful " was " *beaucoup belle*," or that the phrase
" *La volonté generale est toujours droite*," means " The
general will is always right."

There is another trick of theirs which gives me
infinite delight, and that is the solemn perversion of
authority, of which the pleasant name is " Mumbo
Jumbo."

The power to affirm anything at will to an audience
of young and quite unread undergraduates, without
fear of contradiction or examination, produces an

impotent sort of pride in which the very nature of authority is forgotten.

A great scholar steeped in Greek literature says : " The style of this passage is the style of the third century." That is the voice of authority. A man thoroughly familiar with the language can say a thing like that, and men not familiar with the language must accept it, unless they find it challenged by any authority at least equal. If they all find similar scholars making a similar affirmation, humility and common sense demand that the affirmation should be taken as true.

But when the affirmer goes on to say that, because the style of a passage is that of the third century, therefore it cannot possibly have been written a hundred years later, he is talking nonsense so appalling that it makes one catch one's breath.

A man steeped in English can say with authority to a foreigner, " This letter is in the style of Dr. Johnson, and of the eighteenth century ; it cannot possibly have been written in the seventeenth." But of what value would his statement be if he added, " Nor could it possibly have been written in the nineteenth " ? Scholarship has authority when it possesses data which those who accept that authority have not had the leisure or the industry, or perhaps the power, to examine. It possesses no authority whatever against the common sense of the most ignorant man. I come across a document in which there is used strong language against Richard III. The manuscript which denounces him as the murderer of his nephews qualifies the advent of the Tudor, and draws up arguments in favour of his claim. A competent expert who can say to me, " By the nature of the handwriting, I, who am most learned in such documents, can tell you certainly

that this was not written shortly after Bosworth, but
a hundred years later," must be believed.

The statement has authority. He can judge the
date of the handwriting, and I cannot. But if he goes
on to say, " Therefore the statement is not contemporary," he is talking the wildest nonsense, because
our common experience is sufficient to tell us that
men do, and may, take manuscript copies of things
written before their time. If a man steeped in all
the details of Elizabeth's reign, says of a particular
MSS. it is spurious because, " At such a date in the
late sixteenth century, a document of this particular
kind would be found reduced to print and not
re-copied in manuscript," I should answer, by the
use of my common sense, " Why not ? How do you
know what motive the man may have had who copied
it ? How do you know whether it has not been
reduced to print in some form which we have lost ?
How do you know that it may not be some family
possession which the owner did not want spread
broadcast, or which he only had the curiosity to copy
out himself ? "

It is the nature of human pride to assume powers
beyond those really possessed ; but new forms of
such assumption go for a long time unrecognised.
The abuse of religious authority is a commonplace.
Men are only beginning to wake up to the modern
abuse of academic authority. Heaven knows how
much we have heard of priestcraft, and it is true
that men holding only spiritual authority have not
infrequently pretended to an authority in other fields
beyond their lawful scope. But such extravagance is
far more forgivable than the academic assumption of
false authority based upon supposed or affirmed
proof when proof there is none. For the former is a
mere exaggeration, but the latter implies a false-

hood. If a man really possessed of second sight, and having given evidence of enjoying that strange faculty, goes on to pretend a knowledge of things of which he is in fact ignorant, then he is a charlatan presuming upon his merited reputation to acquire a greater and unmerited one. But it is a worse offence when a man pretends to repose his statements on common reason and actual experience in matters where these were absent.

There is one type of this false academic authority which has spread over historical work like a fungus, and particularly over the discussion of the early Church. It is the paying of deference to a man's authority in things which have nothing whatever to do with his scholarship, and which are mere creatures of his imagination, of as much and as little value as similar creatures raised by any wholly illiterate layman. It is in the matter of the Gospel of St. John that this rubbish has accumulated its most monstrous heap. A great scholar like Wernle (I suppose he was a great scholar; I am no judge, but I am assured by other scholars that he was so, and I must take it to be true) has authority when he says, " This or that passage is of the style and manner of this or that period." Even so, his authority is limited by the authority of other scholars, and even so, it is as well that he should put forward, even for the uninstructed reader, some grounds for his judgment. But when he ventured to affirm that the exaltation of spirit shining through the fourth gospel cannot be that of an eye witness, his judgment is worth no more than that of a cook boy's apprentice, or of a street scavenger. A man's power of judging the psychology of his fellow-men varies with capacities quite disconnected from scholarship in letters. My power to decide whether Boswell really knew Johnson (sup-

posing there were no evidence besides the book itself)
is based upon my knowledge of how men feel and
act, and the difference between the way in which
they talk when they are making things up, and
the way in which they talk when they are bearing
witness and recording a real experience. I may be
right, or I may be wrong, in my conclusion : but
my powers of arriving at it have nothing to do with
my powers of judging a text. Yet Wernle's empty
guesswork, even when it is manifestly absurd, is
treated with respect, and, what is exasperating,
with special respect by the orthodox. The
orthodox seem to feel, in approaching the sceptics,
that they are dealing with superiors. It ought
to be just the other way. The people who are
in the tradition of Europe who have behind
them the whole momentum of civilisation, who
have humour and common sense as the products
of Faith, ought to approach their contradictors as
inferiors.

It is certainly so in the case of this Gospel of St.
John. A man, who denies its apostolic authority,
and who comes forward with a disconnected mass
of guesswork, scrappy particularisms and odd con-
jectures, should be regarded as the incongruous
disturber of a judgment upon which millions of men
through centuries had preserved a firm conclusion.
It is true that even the widest tradition, the largest
body of mature judgment, must listen to any objection and weigh it. To refuse that is to deny the
rights of human reason. But it is monstrous that
the sound, admitted, fixed, concluded thing, the
heritage of the human race, should be put on its
defence, and that any assault on it should be supported by a predisposition to accept any conclusion
so long as it be novel.

We are accused of a bias in favour of accepted truth. We should reply that our opponents have a much worse bias against. They say we begin by desiring to find witnesses to Jesus Christ. It is true. But they begin with a fierce desire to destroy the evidence to Jesus Christ. Make them come out with their proofs : accuse them roundly of humbug. Laugh at their provincial rejection of the marvellous. Unmercifully ridicule their lack of proportion; their ignorance of the human mind ; their failure to taste tradition. Rattle them. Believe me, in battle you must be fierce. The louder the victim's cries the nearer you are to victory.

. . . . . .

All that suggested by the mere name "Hastings" and the charlatanry of "Senlac"; but really such a name might suggest whole cartloads of books.

Go to Battle and see the place where Harold fell. You can mark it to a yard. Look at the little tomb in which they say Odo lay ; see the Malfosse still clearly there just westward of the tennis courts in the gardens of the Abbey ; a trap for cavalry. Note how the Normans, Bretons, and all the rest of the foreigners could not deploy until they were at the very foot of the hill, and how they were handicapped by its steepness without the momentum of a gallop down hill to begin with ; it was that which nearly lost them the battle. Mark the length of the ridge, and ask yourself how it could have been held against heavily armed horse with less than thirty or forty thousand men packed in a dense formation, for it is nearly a mile from flank to flank, and would need two thousand locked shields to cover it.

There never was, I suppose, one day spent in
this island with greater consequence to Christendom.

. . . . .

It was but a drift past the Martello Towers during
that morning, and I slept through it, having been
at the helm all through the long night, till my companion relieved me. When I woke we were opposite
that entry to Pevensey which is an entry no more,
but which still holds, strongly challenging the sea,
the Roman walls of the Andred Fort.

The place was a narrows, like those which give
entry to the wide expanse of Portsmouth Harbour ;
and, as in that gully between Portsmouth and
Gosport to-day, there must then have raced through
the gully of Pevensey the gallop of the flood and of
the ebb tides. Within was a vast expanse of level
water that could hold as many score or hundred of
ships as any captain might lead. To-day you can
follow clearly enough the old level of the salt—but
that great haven is now all dry land.

It is full of memories. The ditches in the marsh
still bear the name of such poor branches and inlets
of the once spacious harbour as struggled to live on
into a later time. But no man will sail into Pevensey
again. Thither the *Mora* sailed with William of
Normandy aboard, ahead of his forest of a fleet,
and at its bow a little cupid all in gold, and on its
decks a great cask of wine broached for glory. He
had made his land-fall by the white gleam of Beachy
near at hand. He had outrun all his transports,
and he lay there off this coast awaiting them, until
a man sent up the mast cried that he saw the fleet
approaching " like a wood." It was St. Michael's
Day.

The place is full of memories. The people who
wrote down the legends of England under Alfred

preserved after four hundred years a dreadful memory of some pirate raid, in which all the garrison of Pevensey perished, on some day between the end of the Imperial rule and the landing of St. Augustine.

Strangely enough, we have no record of the process whereby that vast and secure harbour lifted above the level of the sea and lost its usage. Hastings has lived on, but Pevensey died in some darkness, and has disappeared. There still stands the wall of the Roman fort, with its courses of small Roman tile-brick remaining to stamp its origin. The great town that must have stood outside has dwindled to a hamlet, and the vast stretch of flat, beyond which was once what Portsmouth is, lies utterly alone with the sea birds complaining over it.

Beyond Pevensey walls the wind rose somewhat and gave us a fair course round Beachy, coming further round, so that we could carry on without handling the headsail sheets. We ran on a wind all the miles into the Sussex bay. I stood in close to the lighthouse (for the shore is fairly steep there), not a quarter of a mile off shore. It was unwise, for I had experience, as you know, of the way the wind will spill over that height. But I wished to save mileage ; I had sailed the seas enough, and was for home.

The wind from that quarter brings usually a clear air, but in the calm weather of those last few days it had blown from anywhere, for the summer's end had upon it an anti-cyclone, which is a mumbo-jumbo for fine weather. In such weather winds behave unnaturally, the south-west brings no gale or rain, nor is the easterly wind dry, nor the northerly cold, nor the southerly warm ; and this, I suppose,

is because the winds of an anti-cyclone are but
youngling winds ; not great steady ancestored
winds from far away with a weight behind them.

I did wish as I was rounding Beachy that day that
I could see a sea serpent, which, many years ago (I
had read it in print in an old magazine book which
lay about in the parlour of a harbour inn), showed
itself, for the conversion of the unbelieving, in these
very seas.

It reared a great neck and shot at a prodigious
pace through the salt with the movements of its
long body, and having been seen by a whole crew
thereto adjacent, sneered contemptuously at the puny
race of men, and disappeared.

I thought to myself : " How should I behave if
I were to see some such Horrendum, and had to bear
witness to it before my fellow-men ? " I concluded
that I would mix the truth with falsehood, like my
good ancestor, the wise Ulysses, and so shoe-horn
a knowledge of reality into scornful men. For
I have a rule in such matters given me long ago and
since then by me always to be observed. I got it
thus :

When I was a boy an older friend of mine said to
me a thing that then seemed to me extravagant, but
which I now see to have been very sound. It was,
that if you wanted to be believed in any matter
worth believing, you had to bring an admixture
of falsity into your statement. And the reason for
this is plain enough. Either a truth is something
that everybody knows about, and which, therefore,
is not worth telling, or else it is something unusual,
and therefore improbable, and likely to be dis-
believed. It is the latter kind of truth which people
ordinarily tell when they desire to interest their
fellow-beings. But if they put that kind of truth

straightforwardly, they are naturally taken for liars.

For instance, if you were to burst into a man's room, and say, " Only last week I took the train in Paris after breakfast, and I was in London for dinner ! " he would believe you right enough, though he would not stand much of that sort of thing. But if you say, " Only last week I was in Paris for breakfast, and in Rome for dinner," he will think you are not telling the truth, although it can just be done by aeroplane ; and if you say, " I was in London for breakfast, and in Calcutta for dinner " (which may be perfectly true, supposing that the dinner and the breakfast were not on the same day), he will certainly set you down for a liar. Supposing, therefore, that you have really flown in an aeroplane from Paris to Rome, so that you left Paris comfortably after breakfast and got into Rome in plenty of time for dinner, you had far better put it differently, and say that the aeroplane has made a great difference, considering that you yourself had managed, by getting up at dawn on a summer's day, to be in Rome just as it was falling dark, with only two slight mishaps on the way and a relay at Lyons. Then you will possibly be believed.

So do I advise those to speak who desire their fellow-beings to be converted in the matter of the Great Sea Serpent.

Personally I believe in the Great Sea Serpent, and I believe in it for the best of all reasons, to wit, that the proof is sufficient. A sufficient number of people have seen monsters of various kinds rising from the deep, usually monsters with great long necks, or, at any rate, a serpentine appearance. They have seen them, many men at a time, and under ordinary conditions of vision. To deny such

evidence merely because it is unusual is something
stupid. It is a piece of popular doubt, just as stupid
as is the corresponding popular credulity.

The next time the Great Sea Serpent comes within
two cables of one of His Majesty's ships, and is
familiarly seen by scores of men, I strongly advise
the leader and more educated of them, whoever he
may be, not to say that he and his men did, under
such and such circumstances, clearly see the Great
Sea Serpent. For if they do that, they are done.
He had far better say that the weather being thick,
and under conditions when they may have easily
been deceived, he and one companion thought that
they saw something like such and such an apparition;
and he would do well to sketch it in a brumous
fashion. Let him make it as like as possible to
things with which his readers are familiar; then
many idiots will write to the paper saying that it
was sea weed, or a flight of birds, or what not, but
a few will believe. If he tells the plumb truth, no
one will believe. For, just as it is important to mix
truth with falsity, if falsity is to be accepted, so it is
important to mix falsity with truth, if truth is to be
accepted. All lawyers know this. Indeed, it may
be called one of our Rules of Law.

But the lawyers can say this for themselves, at
least, that their trade is advocacy, and that they do
not so much as pretend to truth. There is no
concealment. We are not deceived.

But the practice of advocacy in all those parts of
the nation's life where we used to have information
and direct statement, is a very dangerous as well as
an exasperating ill.

It was an evil growing before the war, but the war
has increased it hugely; men have fallen into a
habit of what was called during the war propaganda.

They both give it and receive it. Upon every side
what you hear (or what is concealed from you) is
put forward or concealed with an object of advocacy,
and, therefore, of distortion. It was, perhaps,
during the war necessary ; or, at least, necessary
in those societies, such as our own, which had
no national tradition of such a conflict. Men
were made to swallow the most enormous camels.
The unfortunate flabby German with his silly
dream of universal superiority became a horrid
fiend quite out of nature, and even those foreigners
who are most hated instinctively and traditionally
by the mass of the populace became gallant
allies.

The most comic part of the affair was the attitude
towards America. We dared not insult America,
for we were naturally as keen on getting American
help as is a drowning man on catching a deck chair
(and, by the way, if by any chance you of the rich
want to save a drowning man from shipboard, don't
throw a life buoy, throw a deck chair ; it is always
loose and always handy, and very apparent, and if it
hits it stuns). In their ignorance many people came
to believe that it was the duty of the Americans to
come over and help, and what was more astonishing
still, it was represented to them as a matter of life
and death, not to us but to themselves. The
Americans were told (heaven knows whether any of
them believed it !) that if the Germans, Austrians,
Bohemians, Slovenes, Croats, Bulgarians, Turks,
etc., won in their push against the English, French,
and Italians, that if the half-baked won against the
baked, the next thing would be a sailing of the
conquerors over the sea for the rude domination of
Scranton, Pa. Fiddlesticks ends !

But people did really talk like that. They shook

their fingers at the United States, and said : " It
will be your turn next ! "

Now at sea there is no advocacy. We are free from
that most noisome form of falsehood, which corrupts
the very inward of the soul. Truth is one of the great
gifts of the sea. You cannot persuade yourself nor
listen to the persuasion of another that the wind is
not blowing when it is, or that a cabin with half a
foot of water in it is dry, or that a dragging anchor
holds. Everywhere the sea is a teacher of truth.
I am not sure that the best thing I find in sailing is
not this salt of reality.

Turning to the statement of any reality after a
dose of advocacy is like getting out into the fresh
air from an intolerable froust.

It would be a boon beyond expression to all of us
if some rich man would found a little weekly newspaper (he would have to be prepared to lose three
thousand a year), in which sheet the reader should be
told things that had happened in Europe and at
home, instead of being given a version designed to
provoke from him a verdict, or to throw him into
a particular mood desired by the writer's master.

The most dangerous form of this advocacy to-day
in England—and it is universal—the most dangerous
gaps in the field of statement, are the advocacy
put forward for a capitalist control of our lives
and the suppression of facts inimical to that
control. They are dangerous because they provoke
passions which lead to social decline, and add
enormously to the sense of injustice under which the
proletariat of the modern capitalist State increasingly
suffers.

I cannot call to mind a single strike or lock-out
during the last twenty years, of all those strikes and
lock-outs which have become for us in England a

sort of daily food—a permanent disturbance of the
English world, and a threat to the English future—
I cannot recollect one, I say, in which our millionaire-
newspaper owners did so much as state the plain
facts of the case in time ; let alone present the
elements on either side dispassionately and as news.
I went in great detail into the conditions of one of
the worst of our railway strikes some years ago. I
discovered that the points of contention had been
under debate for months. I further discovered
that the definite conclusion not to accept such and
such terms, but to stand out for such and such other
terms under threat of a universal stoppage of the
railways, had been made weeks before the catastrophe
fell. The public had had no inkling of this. When
the allotted term expired, and what all those rich
men knew was bound to be the result of the quarrel
came about, the public was at once deluged with
advocacy which still concealed the elements of the
debate, and which calmly took it for granted that
the men possessed of the instruments of production
had a natural right to the labour of the men not
possessed of them. Every conceivable piece of
pleading was put forward, even such as would appeal
to intelligent men, let alone the flood of stuff designed
for their more numerous inferiors. We were told,
for instance, that the number of holders of railway
stock was greater than the number of workers upon
the railway, which was perfectly true, but had about
as much to do with the issue as the great love song
of Mozart. We were *not* told in what proportions
the stock was held.

We were told, all of us until we were tired, that
the men, by refusing their labour, had thrown out
a great public service, which was perfectly true.
What was omitted was the counterpart of the same

truth ; that the owners of capital, by refusing to pay the sum demanded by those with whom they had to enter into contract, were equally throwing out a great public service.

What advantage it would be to the Commonwealth if some one paper would simply state, not only the obvious broad lines of the quarrel between concentrated capitalism and the proletarian majority to-day, but give us rapidly, in detail, and with the facts, the elements in each case. I myself know very well how it should be done, for I have presented it over and over again, and never been able to get these rich men to put it into print. For instance, in the case of a particular dispute one might say truthfully this : " It must be clearly understood that the inconvenience we are suffering from the stoppage of work in the air supply to the underground flats of which a modern city is composed, is a a lock-out and not a strike. The chief shareholders in the Imperial Air Company, whose names are such and such, whose holdings are of such and such an extent, and of whom the directing spirit is So and-so, propose to cut down the men's wages by a tenth. The men refuse to sell their labour for less than the old price. The better paid grades, who receive such and such an average wage, are contented with the terms of the new proposed contract, but they are acting in support of the lower paid grades, whose duties are such and such, and whose average pay is so much. The plea of the directors is that unless the wages are cut, their dividend, which is at present of such and such a value, will have to be lowered to such and such. It must be remembered that the stock is heavily watered. The real capital is only such and such a fraction of the nominal. The men object to negotiations with the

permanent officials of the National Union, because
the general secretary is well known to have betrayed
the cause of his class for money on a previous occasion, and is generally mistrusted; but, as is common
in the caucus of a large Trades Union, it is impossible to dislodge him."

Such a statement as that cannot be printed, though
every word be true and valuable for public information. Such things valuable to the public cannot be printed, partly because the machinery of
printing is in the hands of our highly centralised
capitalist controls, and partly because the Courts of
Justice, which are also nowadays virtually under
capitalist control, would heavily punish not only
the writer, but the printer and publisher of the
truth.

It is a consolation to remember that corruption
pushed beyond a certain point provides its own
remedy, and that this sort of thing cannot indefinitely continue ; but it is less consoling to remember
another truth, to wit, that the correction of political
and social evil may come in the form of irremediable
catastrophe, and that the innocent, who are the
greater number, would then suffer most. It is still
less consoling to remember the universal human
experience that when evil is redressed by the only
partly conscious force of reaction, it is not succeeded by a corresponding good, but by some other
new and unexpected evil.

This subservience to concentrated wealth, which
is appearing in the Courts of Justice, and is universal
in the writers of our day, is like the accumulation of
debt, the process cannot continue for ever ; it is
building up a higher and higher, and more and
more unstable, tower of resentment and secret
protest. The chances are that when the evil has

wrought its own elimination by excess, it will be followed, not by the publication of the truth we need, still less by the enfranchisement of the proletariat, but rather by the publication of a new set of falsehoods under new controls.

. . . .

And so much for that. We sailed along that well-known coast, which is turning into a sort of town ; we aimed to get into the home water of Shoreham, just on the last quarter of the flood before dark. We were disappointed. The wind fell with the approaching evening, and though a westerly stream was with us so late in the inshore tide, by the time we were outside the well-known twin piers, the wooden stanchions of the " Nona's " home, the ebb was rushing out of that river, and there was no making port, though we were just outside.

There were others in the same plight under the warm summer sky of that evening : a London barge, a Norwegian ship with timber, and a little snorting steamer, which let go her anchor with a rush somewhat further out just at the moment when we also dropped anchor in that very shallow water, in not five fathoms deep. A great full moon rose up out of the east, out of the seas of England, and the night was warm. There was a sort of holiness about the air. I was even glad that we had thus to lie outside under such a calm and softly radiant sky, with its few stars paling before their queen.

We slept under such benedictions, and in the morning woke to find a little air coming up from the south like a gift, an introduction to the last harbour. We gave the flood full time (for they do not open the gates, and cannot, till high water) ; then, setting only mainsail and jib, we heaved our anchor up for

the last time, and moved at our pleasure majestically
between the piers, and turned the loyal and wearied
"Nona" towards the place of her repose.

> "And now good-bye to thee,
> Thou well-beloved sea."

as John Phillimore very excellently translates the
Greek of other landed sailors dead.

. . . . .

The sea is the consolation of this our day, as it
has been the consolation of the centuries. It is the
companion and the receiver of men. It has moods
for them to fill the storehouse of the mind, perils for
trial, or even for an ending, and calms for the good
emblem of death. There, on the sea, is a man
nearest to his own making, and in communion with
that from which he came, and to which he shall
return. For the wise men of very long ago have
said, and it is true, that out of the salt water all things
came. The sea is the matrix of creation, and we have
the memory of it in our blood.

But far more than this is there in the sea. It
presents, upon the greatest scale we mortals can bear,
those not mortal powers which brought us into
being. It is not only the symbol or the mirror, but
especially is it the messenger of the Divine.

There, sailing the sea, we play every part of life :
control, direction, effort, fate ; and there can we
test ourselves and know our state. All that which
concerns the sea is profound and final. The sea
provides visions, darknesses, revelations. The sea
puts ever before us those twin faces of reality :
greatness and certitude ; greatness stretched almost
to the edge of infinity (greatness in extent, greatness in changes not to be numbered), and the certitude

of a level remaining for ever and standing upon the
deeps. The sea has taken me to itself whenever
I sought it and has given me relief from men. It has
rendered remote the cares and the wastes of the land ;
for of all creatures that move and breathe upon the
earth we of mankind are the fullest of sorrow. But
the sea shall comfort us, and perpetually show us
new things and assure us. It is the common sacra-
ment of this world. May it be to others what it has
been to me.